D0065643

DATE DUE

PEACE &

GRAND RAPIDS, MICHIGAN

REVOLUTION

THE
MORAL CRISIS
OF
AMERICAN PACIFISM

GUENTER LEWY

WILLIAM B. EERDMANS PUBLISHING COMPANY

Library of Congress Cataloging-in-Publication Data:

Lewy, Guenter, 1923-
    Peace and Revolution: The moral crisis of American pacifism / by
Guenter Lewy.
    p. cm.
Bibliography: p. 273
Includes index.
ISBN 0-8028-3640-2
1. Pacifism — History. 2. Peace — Societies, etc. — History.
3. Pacifists — United States — History.   I. Title.
JX1952.L546 1988
327.1'72'09 — dc19
                                                    88-1374
                                                        CIP

CONTENTS

PREFACE

Over the past twenty years American pacifism has undergone a remarkable transformation. While at one time pacifists were single-mindedly devoted to the principles of nonviolence and reconciliation, today most pacifist groups defend the moral legitimacy of armed struggle and guerilla warfare, and they praise and support the communist regimes emerging from such conflicts. This crucial change in outlook began during the American involvement in Vietnam when the leading pacifist organizations not only opposed the U.S. role but gradually became ardent supporters of the National Liberation Front. This friendly disposition toward so-called national liberation movements has continued — although, significantly, it does not include movements battling communist domination. Few pacifists show any sympathy for the Afghan *mujaheddin* fighting the Russian occupation of their country, for Angola's Unita struggling against Cuban-aided communist rule, or for the various groups opposing the Sandinista regime of Nicaragua.

As a result of this compromising of pacifist principles, the prestige accorded American pacifism has suffered. Until the 1960s, it should be pointed out, American pacifism enjoyed a generally undisputed reputation of moral rectitude. There was criticism, here and there, of the pacifists' alleged lack of political realism and of what some saw as their utopian faith in the peaceful resolution of all international conflicts, but the moral integrity of the movement's leading personalities was never in doubt. Individuals like Rufus Jones, John Haynes Holmes, Nevin Sayre, and Norman Thomas were highly respected figures on the American intellectual scene, and their political influence extended well beyond the circle of their pacifist followers. In 1931 Jane Addams, founder of the Women's International League for Peace and Freedom, received the Nobel peace prize; in 1946, the same distinction was bestowed on Emily Greene Balch, another leader of the same organization. A year later, in 1947, the Nobel peace prize went to the American Friends Service Committee. During the last twenty years, however, searching questions have been raised — from inside as well as outside the peace movement — about the intellectual honesty and probity of the major pacifist organizations and about their political alignments.

Whereas in the 1930s and 1940s most American pacifists showed a healthy skepticism about the sincerity of Communist-led peace movements and the political utility of collaborating with them, in recent years pacifist organizations have increasingly abandoned their earlier opposition to a united front with communist groups and their front organizations. This trend began during the 1960s, when the antiwar movement, including its pacifist component, quite deliberately accepted the principle of nonexclusion, which has continued to the present day. Thus a recent protest demonstration against American intervention in Central America, for example, held in Washington on 25 April 1987 saw the major pacifist organizations marching side by side with the American Communist party, the U.S. Peace Council (its front), and the Trotskyite Socialist Workers party. Such political coalitions lead to the downplaying of criticism of Marxist-Leninist regimes, whether in Eastern Europe or in the Third World, since such criticism could jeopardize the carefully constructed united front against "U.S. imperialism" and, as pacifists argue, could inflame the cold war. The Communists in turn gain legitimacy and respectability through this association, a political windfall that, in view of their tactics of deceit and deeply flawed political values, they surely do not deserve.

This book analyzes the intellectual development of American pacifism since 1965, the beginning of the American war in Vietnam and an important political watershed. It concentrates on the recent history of the four major pacifist organizations: the American Friends Service Committee (AFSC), the Fellowship of Reconciliation (FOR), the War Resisters League (WRL), and the Women's International League for Peace and Freedom (WILPF). The latter organization has never required adherence to pacifism as a requisite of membership, but until the 1960s the American branch of the WILPF in fact embraced the pacifist tenets of opposition to all wars and a commitment to nonviolence. These groups have considerable overlap in members as well as in leadership, yet each of them also has its distinct profile. In order to do justice to both differences and similarities, I treat the organizations separately during the Vietnam war years, when far-reaching changes first began, and I switch to a topical analysis for the years from 1975 to 1985, by which time all four groups had arrived at a similar ideological stance.

The pacifist movement in America as such has never been very large, yet its political influence has often been extensive and has always reached well beyond the relatively small number of the movement's active members. Today American pacifists are a crucial core of the larger peace movement in this country, and they supply much of its organizational talent. The AFSC, for example, with its large headquarters in Philadelphia, aided by ninety full-time staff members in thirty-three regional offices nationwide, was the driving force behind the movement for a nuclear freeze that for a time appeared to sweep the nation. Together with its allies in the churches and numerous church-related social action groups, American pacifists today constitute a potent grass-roots network that can mobilize substantial voter sentiment and at times have considerable impact on Congress.

This political influence is at its strongest when it coincides with and can build on widespread existing political attitudes such as the American public's growing disenchantment with the war in Vietnam in the late 1960s and early 1970s. At the same time, one should not underestimate the peace movement's political clout and its ability to shape the larger worldview of a substantial part of the American intellectual elite, traits that have persisted despite many defeats and setbacks on particular issues like the nuclear freeze. The recent repudiation of the doctrine of nuclear deterrence — the cornerstone of the West's defense posture for four decades — by the unanimous vote of the United Methodist Council of Bishops reveals the inroads that pacifist thinking has made in the religious community. A better understanding of who these groups and their leaders are and what constitutes their political ideology is therefore of more than academic and historical interest.

Many of the findings of this study will surprise readers. Organizations like the AFSC have established an admirable record of ministering to the needs of the destitute and unfortunate of this world; others have earned their reputation of moral integrity by years of uncompromising witness for peace. The assertion that such organizations now have become apologists for violence and repression and have developed friendly ties to movements and regimes that are anything but humanitarian will be met with disbelief unless fully documented. Therefore, I felt compelled to include many lengthy quotations in this book. I hope that they, together with the sources listed in the notes, will convince any skeptics that the developments and trends I have described are things I have neither invented nor exaggerated.

In addition to making use of published writings, I have relied extensively on the internal records of the previously named orga-

ix

nizations and on the personal correspondence of their leading personalities. I have consulted the papers of the FOR, the WRL, and the WILPF and of many of their leaders at the Swarthmore College Peace Collection, which functions as their official repository; and I have examined the records of the AFSC through 1978 at its national office in Philadelphia. I should like to thank the archivists of both of these collections for their cooperation and assistance. I have also talked with many individuals in the pacifist community, a necessary complement to the printed and written record.

Thanks are also due to several of my friends who have given me the benefit of their criticism, and, last but not least, to my truly outstanding editor at William B. Eerdmans, Mary Hietbrink. As is customary, I should add that the opinions and conclusions reached in this book remain, for better or for worse, my own responsibility.

G.L.
Washington, D.C.
December 1987

PART I

Origins

CHAPTER 1

Early Years: When Pacifists Were Pacifist

The term "pacifism" characterizes the doctrine of those who are morally opposed to bearing arms and who refuse to sanction war for any purpose, defensive or otherwise. In this sense, pacifism has a long history. Pacifist ideas can be found in many of the major religions of the world, both East and West. While the major Christian denominations today do not on principle oppose the state's employment of force for purposes of national defense, minorities within the Christian community like the Mennonites, the Brethren, and the Quakers continue to espouse a pacifist creed.

The theory and practice of pacifism must be distinguished from the views and efforts of those who are engaged in organized endeavors to prevent war. Many leaders as well as members of the peace societies that sprang up in the United States in the first half of the nineteenth century were inspired by religious convictions and held all wars to be unchristian. Others were more pragmatically oriented and concentrated on promoting the peaceful settlement of international disputes. Pacifist ideas as such, it would appear, did not find a very congenial environment in America. The rugged life of the Western frontier encouraged martial rather than pacific virtues, and the rising tide of nationalism during the latter half of the nineteenth century further hampered the spread of pacifist convictions.[1]

Currents of pacifism began to gather strength following the war with Spain and especially in the aftermath of World War I. Writings portraying the brutality and carnage of that conflict found a wide readership; the rise of fascism in Europe contributed to a wave of disillusionment with a war that, contrary to Wilsonian rhetoric, had failed to end the threat of armed conflict between nations or make the world safe for democracy. Pacifist sentiments now were encouraged not only by humanitarian opposition to the horrors of modern war but also by the spread of socialist ideas, especially the arguments that wars are based upon the economic rivalries of imperialistic nations and are encouraged by the traffic in armaments carried on by profit-hungry capitalists. The pacifist organizations that were founded during and after World War I included a strong core of socialists, and all pacifists stressed the importance of opposing the imperialism of the capitalist order, of ending the arms race and achieving economic and social justice in order to remove what they considered to be the ultimate causes of war.[2] We find here the roots of a conflict of loyalties between the pacifists' ideals of nonviolence and their aspiration to liberate the exploited and oppressed. This conflict of moral principles afflicted to varying degrees all of the pacifist groups from the very beginning, until, in the 1960s and 1970s, it finally changed the very nature of contemporary American pacifism.

The Debate over Violence in the Class Conflict

The Fellowship of Reconciliation (FOR) was founded in England in 1914 as an international Christian fellowship committed to a religiously based pacifism. Its American branch, established in 1915, from early on had among its leaders many prominent socialists. *The World Tomorrow*, its unofficial organ launched in 1918, counted among its editors well-known socialists like Kirby Page; Devere Allen, candidate of the Socialist party for the U.S. Senate from Connecticut; and Norman Thomas, the Socialist party's presidential standard bearer. Indeed, during the late twenties and early thirties, pacifism and socialism increasingly overlapped, and for socialistically inclined Christian pacifists and antimilitaristic socialists, the FOR became the organizational tool with the help of which they hoped to defeat both capitalism and war. The question of whether the struggle for the peaceful and classless society could be waged with the weapon of nonviolence alone now became a highly contentious issue for the organization.[3]

One of the first to explore the relationship between violence and an unjust domestic social order was A. J. Muste, a Protestant minister who was a longtime labor organizer and the national chairman of the FOR between 1926 and 1929. In an article entitled "Pacifism and Class War," published in *The World Tomorrow* in 1928, Muste argued that it was wrong to consider only the violence of the rebels who strove to usher in a new social condition. The present system

4

itself, he maintained, was based on violence; revolutionary action to force the present rulers to give up their privileges could not in principle exclude violence. "In a world built on violence," Muste concluded, "one must be a revolutionary before one can be a pacifist."[4]

For a time Muste attempted to remain both a pacifist and a revolutionary. Then, from 1934 to 1936, he repudiated pacifism altogether and affiliated himself with the Trotskyite American Workers party. When, after a conversion experience, Muste returned to being a Christian pacifist, he resumed his active role in the FOR, serving as its executive secretary from 1940 to 1953. Yet, while he had abandoned the Trotskyite variant of communism, Muste remained committed to radical direct action, and, as we shall see later, during the 1960s he became one of the key figures responsible for the growing politicization of American pacifism.

During the early 1930s Muste was by no means the only FOR leader to accept the moral legitimacy of using violence in the struggle for a new and better society. Under the impact of the misery and despair of the Great Depression, a growing number of FOR figures now began to qualify their pacifist beliefs. In April 1931 the Christian socialist Reinhold Niebuhr noted that American society still maintained important ethical values "which the naive simplicities of communism would ruthlessly destroy and which only a primitive world can regard as dispensable."[5] At the same time, Niebuhr warned against preferring peace to justice, thus supporting an unjust status quo, and he contended that religious radicals might have to abandon their "pure pacifism" and accept coercion and resistance as necessary to the social struggle.[6]

During the year 1933 the dispute within the FOR over the role of violence in the class conflict turned into open dissension and schism because of the views and activities of J. B. Matthews, a Protestant minister who was one of the organization's secretaries. Matthews' strong anticapitalism was shared by practically all of the leadership of the FOR, but his colleagues were uneasy over his belief that coercive rather than persuasive techniques were necessary to bring about social change, and that in the overturn of existing social controls, constitutional and legal processes could be relied upon only slightly. Matthews argued that capitalism used the educational system to prevent the spread of radical ideas. In these circumstances, pacifists, while refusing all participation in international wars, had to accept "varying degrees of coercion as regrettable necessities" in the class struggle for the abolition of capitalism. Pacifists, Matthews insisted, should "support an advancing proletariat by more than well-wishing."[7]

Matthews' view that pacifists had a duty actively to support revolutionary change led him into active cooperation with the American Communist party, and this position, too, was criticized by most of the FOR leadership. On 5 April 1933 Matthews spoke at a large, Communist-sponsored anti-fascist rally at Madison Square Garden in New York and told the cheering twenty-two thousand listeners that "the dictatorship of the proletariat is the only answer to Fascism."[8] A little later he agreed to chair the organizing committee charged with planning the First United States Congress Against War. When that congress convened in New York in late September 1933, Matthews was elected national chairman of the newly formed American League Against War and Fascism. The dominant role of the Communists both in the organizing committee and at the congress itself was obvious to most observers at the time. Devere Allen, who had attended the congress, resigned from the League a few months later because the Communists used the organization not only as a training and recruiting ground for the party but also as a means of disrupting and attacking the various groups that had agreed to participate in the work of the League, especially the Socialists.[9] Matthews' willingness to serve as the head of the League, which quickly revealed itself to be a highly successful front organization for the Communist party, was another issue that troubled the majority of the FOR leadership.

The annual conference of the FOR, which was held at Swarthmore College in October 1933, took up the growing dispute. John Haynes Holmes warned that pacifism was crumbling in the face of the class war. "The end does not justify the means. The capture of power by the use of mass force is the new transfer of power. It really cannot solve the industrial problem." Professor Arthur L. Swift of Union Theological Seminary maintained that a true pacifist rejects "the familiar platitudes which attempted to justify the world war and rejects a 'holy war' in behalf of the poor and downtrodden and for the creation of a classless society. That would be the same old cry for 'a war to end war.' A civil war is the most uncivil of all wars." Reinhold Niebuhr, on the other hand, called himself a pacifist with qualifications: "I am opposed to continuing to be true to certain principles rather than to achieve social justice. No means or ends are absolute. . . . There is no choice except between more violence and less violence." Roger Baldwin went even further. "The ethics of Jesus," he insisted, "are identical with those of communism. We are confronted today with the choice between communism and fascism, ... between a proletarian or a military dictatorship. There can be no neutrality in this struggle."[10]

Unable to resolve the controversy, the FOR national council decided to conduct a poll of the membership. A questionnaire was sent out which posed several questions, all related to the acceptance or rejection of violence in the struggle for a just social order.[11] The results of this poll were reported to the council meeting on 16 December. To the key question — "Should the F.O.R. hold on to non-violence in the class war as well as in international war?" — 877 respondents answered yes, 97 no.

With this decisive mandate in hand, the council determined that only resolute pacifists should be employed as secretaries, and by a vote of eighteen to twelve they decided not to re-engage J. B. Matthews, whose contract expired on 1 February 1934. Following this action, several distinguished members resigned from the FOR. In an article published in the *Christian Century* entitled "Why I Leave the F.O.R.," Reinhold Niebuhr acknowledged that he was a pacifist only with regard to international armed conflicts. Calling himself a Marxian and a Christian, he explained that he had left the Fellowship because of his conviction that economic justice could not be achieved "without a destruction of the present disproportion of power" and without a struggle from which violence could not be excluded.[12]

The Fellowship of Reconciliation
Rejects the United Front

The FOR's rejection of the use of violence in the class war was followed by a rejection of political cooperation with the Communists. An editorial in *The World Tomorrow* in March 1934 pointed out that the American League Against War and Fascism was primarily a supporter of Russian foreign policy. Any group working with the League, therefore, was open to the suspicion that it was simply an agent of the Soviet Union, and this would necessarily destroy the effectiveness of any of its work for peace. Two weeks earlier the Communists had systematically disrupted a mass meeting called by the Socialist party in Madison Square Garden to protest the suppression of Austrian workers by the Dollfuss government. The conduct of the Communists, the editors pointed out, further confirmed the impossibility of any united front with the Communists. Cooperation, the editorial declared, "depends upon fair play and ordinary honesty in dealing with fellow-workers. The Communists regard these virtues as bourgeois prejudices."[13]

In February 1935 Kirby Page, vice chairman of the FOR, wrote that the united front with Communists was logical for those convinced that a revolution could not be carried out without the armed seizure of power. But pacifist radicals would only weaken their efforts for peace and a nonviolent revolution in America by joining forces with the Communists. "Communists have nothing but contempt for religion and for pacifism," Page declared. "They use the united front as a means of boring from within."[14] Consequently, the FOR decided against affiliating itself with the American League Against War and Fascism, and in February 1935 it went on record as opposing affiliation with "communistic, fascist and other organizations sanctioning the use of armed violence in international, racial and class war."[15]

A firm opposition to violence in the service of any cause and the rejection of political cooperation with the Communist party and its various front organizations continued to be FOR policy until the 1960s. This policy was reaffirmed in a statement adopted by the FOR executive committee early in 1940. The FOR pointed out that the Hitler-Stalin Pact, signed in the fall of 1939, had led overnight to the Communists' complete about-face with regard to the party's position on war and to American foreign policy generally. Following the line laid down by the foreign ministry of the Soviet dictatorship, the party had abandoned the principle of collective security and now regarded the conflict between the democracies and Nazi Germany as one between rival imperialist powers. The Communists' failure to pursue a consistent policy meant that any effort put into antiwar organizations dominated by the party was therefore to a large extent wasted. The recent collapse of the League for Peace and Democracy (the organization that succeeded the American League Against War and Fascism) demonstrated the precarious existence of Communist-led antiwar groups.

Moreover, the FOR statement declared, "the Communist Party rejects pacifism in principle, its basic literature is full of bitter attacks on pacifism. For the F.O.R. to be associated with the C.P. in 'anti-war activities' could therefore only confuse multitudes of people as to our aim and function and thus stultify our efforts." The statement affirmed the FOR's strong support for the civil liberties of all Americans, including the Communists, but concluded that "consistency and honesty forbid our participation in anti-war activities with Communists and Communist organizations." Despite the fact that the FOR, too, sought to keep America out of the European war, the Fellowship concluded that it was sound policy "not to engage in united front activities with organizations which welcome Communists and avowed 'fellow-travellers' on their governing boards and among their officers."[16]

The FOR maintained its firm rejection of a united front with the Communists during the later years of World War II, when the American alliance with the Soviet Union against Nazi Germany encouraged a large number of such cooperative ventures, and during the heady days of optimism about constructive cooperation with Russia that followed the conclusion of the war. A statement issued by the FOR executive committee in March 1946 once again warned against Communist united-front tactics that the party used in order to infiltrate and take over other organizations. According to the statement, the Communist party shifted its positions overnight in accordance with the policies of another government, and this represented a "serious obstacle to the working out of friendship and frank relationships." Religious pacifists, the statement affirmed, "maintain faith in and desire fellowship with all men whatever their allegiances and beliefs, but true fellowship must be built on straightforwardness and truth. We deem it confusing, unwise and harmful to our cause to engage in organizational collaboration with movements which one day oppose American participation in war and the next day favor it."[17]

It should be noted that this and other similar policy statements rejecting collaboration with the Communist party predated the 1950s and its anti-Communist fervor. The FOR adopted its opposition to a united front with the Communists not because it had succumbed to cold-war thinking or anti-Communist hysteria — a mind-set quite foreign to the intellectual climate of the 1930s and early 1940s — but because it had experienced the fruits and dire consequences of such collaboration. When the rest of the country caught up with this insight in the later 1940s, as is so often the case with sudden changes of political mood in a democratic society, America veered sharply to the opposite extreme. Political intolerance and attacks upon the political rights of Communists or suspected Communists became the order of the day. The FOR responded to this outburst of anti-Communist zeal, later known as the age of McCarthyism, by reaffirming both its traditional defense of civil liberties and academic freedom and its refusal to collaborate with the Communist party and its front organizations.[18]

In 1948 many liberals and pacifists reacted to the outbreak of the cold war and the growing fear of an armed collision with the Soviet Union by joining Henry Wallace's Progressive party. The FOR's official organ, *Fellowship,* now published an article entitled "Beware the Common Front!" by Morris Milgram, the veteran Socialist and longtime executive secretary of the Workers Defense League. During the past fifteen years, Milgram pointed out, members of the American peace movement had "found themselves the object of the most cajoling blandishments from Communists and fellow-travellers anxious to embrace them whenever the foreign policy of the Soviet Union would be aided by antiwar sentiments in this country." Many American pacifists—himself included, Milgram admitted—at one time or another had sought to oppose war preparations through the medium of organizations that included Communists.

What they discovered was that almost invariably such organizations (the American League Against War and Fascism, the American Student Union and the American Youth Congress, for instance) were captured by the Communists and their positions changed to suit the Communist Party line. Later, when it had become clear that they were so widely known as Communist-controlled that they were no longer effective for recruiting innocents, they were disbanded. New fronts sprang up to take their place, such as the American Peace Mobilization—which later became the pro-war American People's Mobilization when Russia was being attacked by the very Nazis with whom she had divided Poland!

The well-meaning Henry Wallace now had begun another effort to work with the Communists in the Progressive party. Judging from past experience, Milgram argued, the result was easily predictable:

The machinery of the new party, already largely under Communist control, will become increasingly so, until virtually all the key non-Communists leave the organization. Wallace prefers to say what his Stalinist-engineered audiences wish to hear, as when he deleted sections of his speech slightly critical of Russia at a Madison Square Garden rally because his audience booed one such reference. Today Wallace is silent when asked his position on slave labor in the Soviet Union, and has no criticism of the USSR for its totalitarian coup in Czechoslovakia.

Those who participate in the Wallace Party will find themselves considered by many to be dupes of the Communists, will find their community leadership sharply weakened, and will find the Wallace party reduced to nothing when the USSR finds a change of line requires its dissolution.

Milgram concluded that the test of a bona fide antiwar individual was whether he opposed militarism and imperialism by *all* nations. "Anyone who welcomed Hitler backers into FOR groups during World War II would have weakened the FOR. Similarly, anyone who welcomes Stalinists into the peace movement, or who works with them, weakens his cause." The editors of *Fellowship* ran Milgram's article accompanied by an editorial statement headlined "Red-Baiting?": "*Fellowship* believes in free speech, for Communists as for anyone else. It deplores the present anti-Communist hysteria and in no way condones attempts to persecute and harass people for their political beliefs. All of that does not change the facts of life as they relate to Communist political action."[19]

There were those in the FOR who disagreed with this stand. The writer of a letter to the editors, which *Fellowship* published in February 1949, argued that anything said against communism *now*, true or untrue, added to the flames of hate, fanaticism, and "our crazy witch hunt" that afflicted the country and ruined the careers of both Communists and their innocent associates. Communists were idealists, in their own way seeking to make the world a better place. The letter-writer suggested "that we turn on Communists and Russians a constant stream of good will. . . . If God could only bring it about so that we might work with them! Let the Fellowship of Reconciliation publish all those facts and arguments that will reconcile — only them, and lots of them."

The editor of *Fellowship* in 1949 was Alfred Hassler, a future executive secretary of the FOR, who in the quite different political climate of the early 1970s was to lose his leadership role in the FOR because he opposed the kind of thinking exemplified in this letter. An editorial statement, unmistakably reflecting Hassler's views, responded to the letter by pointing out that neither *Fellowship* nor the staff of the FOR had any wish to add in any way to the prevailing hysteria about Communists and suspected Communists. However, "one is not necessarily a saint because one is persecuted." The common fronts sponsored by the Communists, the editors maintained, frequently have actual purposes vastly different from their professed ends; sincere liberals and pacifists often are misled by statements of noble aims and by a reaction against red-baiting to participate in such Communist-inspired and Communist-controlled groups. "No FOR member, however deep his concern to avoid war, would have suggested in the prewar years participation by the Fellowship of Reconciliation in anti-war activities of the German-American Bund. For exactly the same reasons, the FOR cannot cooperate with the far more skillfully devious Communist and Communist inspired efforts of the present, no matter how noble-sounding their stated purposes may be."[20]

Acting in the same spirit, the FOR shunned participation in Soviet-sponsored peace activities, which it saw as serving the interests of the Soviet Union rather than the cause of peace. A statement issued in May 1951 suggested that "the best way to test any 'peace' project or joint effort which is proposed" is to discover whether its promoters clearly stated "that it is opposed to militarism and war preparations *both* in Russia and in the United States, that it is critical of the foreign policy of both countries, and opposed to all forms of totalitarianism, including the Communist."[21]

In July 1962 the World Peace Council, an organization that since its founding in 1950 has consistently and faithfully promoted the foreign policy of the Soviet Union, convened a congress on peace and disarmament in Moscow. Because of the history of previous such "peace conferences," most major American peace organizations, including the FOR, declined to send representatives or even observers. Disturbed by this snub, Professor J. D. Bernal of Great Britain, president of the presidium of the World Peace Council, promised a group of people active in the American peace movement that they would be given an opportunity to present a statement before a plenary session of the congress. Anxious to improve communication and understanding between the peace movements of East and West, the American peace groups drafted such a declaration, which was read to the congress by Erich Fromm, psychoanalyst and writer, and Homer A. Jack, national director of the Committee for a Sane Nuclear Policy (SANE) and a prominent FOR member. Fromm and Jack explained that they had come to Moscow as individuals and not as delegates or representatives of American peace organizations because of the difference that they and the other signers of the declaration saw between the American peace movement and the organizations associated with the World Peace Council:

> We of the U.S.A. peace organizations openly criticize and oppose policies of our own government with which we do not agree. We

maintain our independence and our opposition. When government policies emphasize military measures, we oppose them. When government policies represent a turn toward peace, we praise and support them. We try to use the same criteria and principles in judging all governments. We do not believe in having one standard for judging ourselves and another standard for judging others. Everything must be examined in terms of a single standard of loyalty to the principle that above all nations is humanity. . . . We do not look for the approval of our government first and only then come out for peace. We do not say this to praise ourselves nor to condemn others. At the same time we cannot ignore the difference between being independent and not being independent. We feel that the first job of the peace movement is to challenge governments to put peace as the first item on the agenda. We do not believe that we can challenge other governments effectively until we have first spoken clearly to our own government. We believe that this is the basic difference between the communist peace movement and our U.S.A. peace movement. The peace movement in the United States speaks *to* its government; the World Council of Peace speaks *for* government. We consider this to be a decisive difference. When everything is boiled down, the peace organizations of the Soviet bloc espouse the policies of their governments, whether those policies happen to be developing greater bombs or calling for disarmament. It is this difference between the peace organizations in your part of the world and ours which makes it difficult for us to enter with you into any joint effort.[22]

Alfred Hassler, executive secretary of the FOR, defended the same position at the first meeting of a new international peace organization, the International Confederation for Disarmament and Peace (ICDP), which convened in Oxford, England, in January 1963 and was attended by forty-four peace organizations from eighteen countries. At a meeting called to discuss the question of admitting ten observers from the World Peace Council, Hassler took issue with the tendency of many Americans, revolted by the excesses of McCarthyism, to reject automatically anything that sounded as though the State Department might agree with it. "Confronted by an official America that argues that nothing the Communists say can be believed, the peacemaker is tempted to act as though nothing the Communists say may be disbelieved. . . . Official America seeks to exclude Communists from everything; therefore, a 'sincere' peace movement may exclude them from nothing."

This reaction, Hassler stated, was understandable but not defensible. "We who work for peace must seek every possible way of identifying ourselves with those of all nations who also work for peace, but we do not resolve differences by pretending that they do not exist, nor do we build peace by allowing ourselves to be used to advance one side of the cold war against the other." Hassler argued that the minimum standard of conduct which the new Confederation had to insist on as a requirement for membership was a "clear opposition to war and preparations for war on the part of any government, including one's own."[23] Despite opposition from some of the American delegates, Hassler's views opposing the anti – anti-communism growing in the ranks of the American peace movement prevailed, and the ICDP declined to seat the observers from the World Peace Council.

Social Justice and the Women's International League for Peace and Freedom

During the years prior to 1965, other American pacifist groups experienced the same ideological divisions and controversies that afflicted the FOR, and by and large they, too, resolved them by rejecting any compromise with the principle of nonviolence. Most forthright in seeking the social and economic transformation of society in the direction of greater social justice and yet refusing to enter into a united front with the Communists was the American section of the Women's International League for Peace and Freedom (WILPF).

The WILPF developed out of the International Congress of Women meeting in 1915 at the Hague in Holland in order "to protest against the war, to stop the slaughter if possible, and to take counsel together on ways of preventing future wars." After the end of World War I, many of the League's leading members, who were trade unionists and socialists, expressed strong support for the radical movements spreading in Europe and the United States in the aftermath of the war. The International Congress of Women that met in Zurich, Switzerland, in May 1919 adopted the name WILPF and voted on a resolution that took note of the widespread revolutionary changes facing the world at a time when a world war had fostered a habit of violence. Indicative of the strength of the French and German delegations, who wanted active cooperation with revolutionary mass movements, this resolution, rejecting violence in the struggle for social justice, passed by only one vote: "The International Congress of Women recognizes that there is a fundamentally just demand underlying most of these revolutionary movements and declares its sympathy with the purpose of the workers who are rising everywhere to make an end to exploitation and to claim their world. Nevertheless the women of the Congress reassert their faith in methods of peace and believe it is their special part in this revolutionary age to counsel against violence from any side."[24]

Divisions within the WILPF over the use of violence by the oppressed continued into the 1930s. At the 1934 congress, again meeting in Zurich, the French and German sections succeeded in passing a statement that made it the "first duty" of the League "to facilitate and hasten the social transformation" which would inaugurate a new system of social, economic, and political equality. However, the Franco-German statement did not receive the two-thirds majority necessary to effect a change in the constitution, and after protracted and often stormy discussions, a compromise statement of aims was finally adopted, which remained official WILPF policy until 1959:

> The Women's International League for Peace and Freedom aims at bringing together women of different political and philosophical tendencies united in their determination to study, make known, and abolish the political, social, economic and psychological causes of war, and to work for a constructive peace.
>
> The primary objects of the Women's International League for Peace and Freedom remain: Total and universal disarmament, the abolition of violent means of coercion for the settlement of all conflicts, the substitution in every case of some form of peaceful settlement, and the development of a world organization for the political, social and economic co-operation of peoples.
>
> Conscious that these aims cannot be attained and that a real and lasting peace and true freedom cannot exist under the present system of exploitation, privilege and profit they consider that their duty is to facilitate and hasten by non-violent methods the social transformation which would permit the inauguration of a new system under which would be realized social, economic and political equality for all without distinction of sex, race or opinion.[25]

From its beginnings the American section of the WILPF tended toward an absolute pacifism, though adherence to pacifism was not a requisite for membership. Many of the group's early members were Quakers who were able to exert a decisive influence upon the organization. Among them was the suffragist and peace activist Mildred Scott Olmsted, who joined the staff of the U.S. section in

1922 and played a prominent role in the development of the WILPF for more than forty years. Another strong voice for nonviolence was the social worker and feminist Jane Addams, the first president of WILPF and a future Nobel laureate. Writing in 1922, Addams stressed that social advance depends as much upon the process through which it is secured as upon the result itself. "[We] believe that we are not obliged to choose between violence and passive acceptance of unjust conditions for ourselves and for others; [we] believe, on the contrary, that courage, determination, moral power, generous indignation, active good will, can achieve their ends without violence."[26]

The depression of the early 1930s strengthened the conviction of the WILPF that a real and lasting peace could not be achieved under the existing capitalist system and led to its sympathetic involvement with various radical causes. After some initial hesitation, the national board of the WILPF authorized its executive secretary, Dorothy Detzer, to participate in the newly organized American League Against War and Fascism, but Detzer soon developed serious concerns about the Communists' mode of operation within the organization. In her memoirs she recalls that it was disconcerting to discover that "Communists imagined that if five of them yelled louder than twenty other members of a subcommittee, the noise they made constituted an affirmative vote on a given question. Or that it was perfectly ethical to postpone a vote on a motion until most of the non-communist members present had to leave to catch trains." Finally, in 1937, the WILPF withdrew from the League. Experience had shown, Detzer concluded, "that there is no basis for co-operative ventures where there is no basis of moral integrity. The clash of ideas, the conflict of thought can be healthy adjuncts to human effort, but only, I am now convinced, when they are secured by the veracity of the pledged word. Trust and good faith are the necessary underpinnings of co-operation."[27]

During the 1950s, when the WILPF opposed NATO and the Korean War, the League came under attack for its alleged softness on communism, and there were charges of Communist infiltration. Nevertheless, a statement called "WILPF and the Cold War" adopted in August 1960 reaffirmed the League's policy of open membership. "We use acceptance of WILPF's principles, policies and methods as the sole criterion for membership. We put new members in policy-making or program-making positions only after they have given ample evidence that they sincerely support all our principles and policies and the non-violent, democratic methods of promoting them which we advocate." This policy, the statement maintained, provided adequate protection against subversion.

At the same time, the League reiterated its long-standing opposition to totalitarianism of any kind. Because the WILPF insisted on the right to criticize government policy, it had no sections in countries where this freedom did not exist. "And WILPF does not collaborate with organizations such as the World Peace Council and the Women's International Democratic Federation, even though they support some of the same specific proposals for peace that we have always favored." In order to build contacts across ideological lines, the WILPF sometimes sent nonparticipating observers to Soviet-sponsored international conferences, but, the statement continued, "WILPF does not cosponsor conferences in which Communist organizations take the initiative, like the Youth Congresses in Moscow and Vienna, nor participate by sending delegates to such conferences."[28]

In 1961 the WILPF began a program of meetings between small groups of American and Soviet women. Most of the leaders of the League had no illusions about the kinds of women who participated in these meetings from the Soviet side. They knew that these women had been carefully picked by the Soviet government for their political reliability and could be counted on to defend official Soviet positions. Dorothy Hutchinson, president of the WILPF from 1961 to 1965, recalled years later that the Soviet women assumed as a matter of course that all concessions on disarmament had to be made by the United States because the USSR, being a "peace loving" nation, had already adopted an entirely correct position on disarmament. American women, they believed, should cooperate with their Soviet sisters by working for changes only in American foreign policy. "I was reminded," Hutchinson wrote, "of the joke about an American and a Russian arguing about the relative status of civil liberties in their respective countries. The American says, 'I can frankly tell President Kennedy at any time that I don't like what he's doing.' The Russian enthusiastically replies, "It's exactly the same with us! I can tell Mr. Khrushchev frankly that I don't like what President Kennedy is doing.' "[29]

The Question of Cooperation with Communists

During the years prior to 1965, similar views about Soviet foreign policy and the sincerity of the Communist party's concern for peace existed within the American Friends Service Committee (AFSC).

Founded during World War I (in 1917) as a Quaker organization to give conscientious objectors an alternative to military service by allowing them to aid civilians, the AFSC quickly developed into a large organization carrying out a wide variety of far-flung relief, service, and educational programs. The growing involvement with political, economic, and social issues, which emerged as part of the AFSC's concern about eliminating the deeper causes of war, often drew the criticism of more conservative Friends, and even within the AFSC, divisions emerged over tactical questions.

When the peace section of the AFSC held a retreat in October 1933, one of the main issues discussed was, Can and should Friends cooperate with groups like the Communists, who advocate the forceful overthrow of the capitalist system in order to do away with the causes of war? Devere Allen, who a month earlier had attended the First United States Congress Against War and Fascism and who was still optimistic about the future of the League, felt that if enough pacifists would stay in such organizations they could outvote the Communists and thus create a useful public platform for pacifist ideas. Moreover, he argued, "all the violence that Communism in this country advocates and desires is as a drop in the creek as compared with the violence which we live under in the present economic system." Pacifists did cooperate with those who maintained the status quo; why not cooperate, he asked, with those who sought to change the capitalist system?

The opposing view was defended by Vincent D. Nicholson, chairman of the AFSC peace section. Nicholson maintained that in view of the Communists' methods of operation, to work with them was "destructive of the whole principle of life for which the best people of the Society of Friends have stood." Friends would not cooperate with bootleggers who favored prohibition because they made money out of it. Similarly, Friends should not cooperate with the Communists because they were "bootleggers in the cause of peace." More important than achieving immediate political gains was "the slower but much more important and fundamental task to change people's basic attitudes."[30]

Nicholson's rejection of a united front with the Communists continued to be AFSC policy for the next thirty years. At a meeting of the AFSC board of directors held on 7 May 1941, a motion was adopted that laid down a case-by-case approach to possible coalitions but also insisted that cooperation was possible only with "organizations whose fundamental purposes and methods of work are in accord with our ideals." No member of the executive staff was to allow his name to be used by the governing board of another organization without approval by the AFSC board of directors or the consultative committee.[31] On another occasion in 1951, when a leftist group had misused a prayer for peace by Clarence Pickett, the executive secretary of the AFSC, Pickett stated AFSC policy on cooperation in these words: "The use of other people's names as fronts or the active participation with groups whose ultimate objectives are short of the universal and religious ones which are ours cannot be permitted. Our own concern for peace stems out of our deepest religious convictions and our 300 year testimony along this line, and has no temporal relationship to the political platform of any one country or party which currently happens to use the same words."[32] Acting in the same spirit, Stewart Meacham, head of the peace education division of the AFSC, was one of the signers of the declaration read at the congress of the World Peace Council held in Moscow in July 1962, a declaration that dissociated the American peace movement from government-sponsored peace groups in Eastern Europe.

During the early 1960s two pacifist organizations began to assume somewhat different positions. They were the Committee for Nonviolent Action (CNVA), organized in 1959, and the War Resisters League (WRL) — the U.S. branch of the War Resisters International, established in 1923 as a secular pacifist group opposed to any kind of war, international or civil. After the end of World War II, the WRL had experienced a large influx of young conscientious objectors, radicalized by their experiences in civilian public-service camps and prisons, and the organization increasingly came to favor a program of sweeping political, economic, and social transformation, albeit by nonviolent means. The WRL and the CNVA cooperated closely and finally merged in 1968. Playing an important role in changing the political outlook of both groups was A. J. Muste, a member of the executive committee of the WRL and the national chairman of the CNVA.

Back in 1949 Muste had insisted that pacifists had to "condemn Russian militarism and Communist violence as unconditionally as any other" and should not collaborate with the Communists.[33] Members of the Communist party, he argued, "use deceit and violence at the behest of the Party; they do conceal and lie about membership in the Party; they do penetrate organizations of all kinds for ulterior purposes and without hesitating to resort to the most egregious chicanery."[34] In 1956 Muste had declared that Communists are human beings whom Christians have to love like other children of God. But, he went on, "I do not take this to mean that we have to work with them politically or be sentimental and naive about certain aspects of their behavior and strategy."[35] Yet only one year later, in 1957, Muste organized the American Forum for Socialist Education, which brought together Communists and non-Communists in a series of conferences and debates held in various cities.

For this move Muste was criticized by many members of the democratic Left. Norman Thomas argued that the Forum would help the Communist party, severely weakened after the Russian suppression of the Hungarian revolt of 1956, to revive itself and confuse people politically. "The Forum gave some of those Communists the false impression that they could remain in the party and still be accepted in the community. The Communists don't belong in jail, but they also don't belong in any party with which I want to be connected."[36]

Another rejection of collaboration with the Communists came from Roy Finch, a leading figure in the WRL. Finch had attended the 1957 convention of the Communist party as an observer, and he reported in *Liberation,* a magazine operated with the financial support of the WRL, that the Communists were anxious to overcome their isolation from American life. "Non-Communists and anti-Communists will rightly be sceptical of such professions. . . . Labor and liberal organizations have been inoculated against popular fronts. That tactic will not work again."[37] Finch resigned from the editorial board of *Liberation* in 1961 because he objected to the magazine's favorable attitude toward Castro's Cuba; this indulgent position toward Castro was shared by Muste. Other WRL leaders joined in the criticism of Muste's new views. Tracy Mygatt, a founding member of the WRL, wrote Muste in 1961 after reading several of his articles in *Liberation:* "The curious thing to me is that it was in part some of your very own words . . . some years ago that have made me anxious to keep myself from any cooperation with communists."[38]

Pacifists Abide by the Democratic Process

Another striking difference between American pacifism before and after 1965 involved the question about what position pacifists should assume after a war had actually broken out. Unlike the war in Vietnam in the 1960s, World War II did not give rise to an organized antiwar movement, but even had there been one it is doubtful that many pacifists would have joined it. The idea that pacifists should not merely refuse to fight in war but actively try to stop it had not yet taken hold.

During the years prior to the outbreak of World War II, American pacifists actively sought to keep the United States out of the threatening European conflagration. In 1936 the AFSC served as a kind of sponsor of the Emergency Peace Campaign, an effort to pull together in a broad coalition many antiwar groups and individuals in order to oppose increased military appropriations and to promote a nationwide propaganda campaign against the idea of collective security. Even after Hitler had demonstrated his aggressive designs in Europe by swallowing Austria and Czechoslovakia and attacking Poland in 1939, pacifists continued to make common cause with isolationists and argued against American involvement on the side of England and France.

In a book entitled *How to Keep America Out of War,* published cooperatively in 1939 by the AFSC, the FOR, the WRL, the WILPF, and other antiwar organizations, Kirby Page contended that Hitlerism could not be stopped by war and that, on the contrary, a long war would lead to the entrenchment of wartime dictatorships and spread totalitarianism over the entire globe. The war in Europe was "not a war between democracy and totalitarianism, but a death grapple between rival imperialisms, with aggressors arrayed against oppressors." Britain and France were fighting for empire and continued domination far more than for liberty. The most pressing task, Page maintained, was to remove the causes of international hostility, to build a new economic order and a true democracy free from the stranglehold of financial oligarchies.[39] For A. J. Muste, similarly, the war was not a struggle between aggressors and lovers of peace but a conflict between satiated powers determined to hang on to their privileges and another set of powers equally determined to change the imperialist status quo. It therefore made no difference which side won.[40]

Yet, while American pacifists thus denied the moral legitimacy of the war against Hitler and, for the most part, maintained a personal pacifist position by refusing to bear arms, they did not publicly demand an end to the war, and still less did they engage in activities to cause their country's defeat. To some extent, this stance was dictated by prudential considerations, especially the fear of a violent backlash. Many pacifists also gradually came to realize that in fighting the Nazis the United States was fighting an evil without precedent. But there was also the feeling on the part of most pacifists that it was undemocratic to obstruct the nation's war effort and to prevent their fellow citizens from fulfilling their patriotic duty. "We seek to wean our fellows from the desire to make war," wrote Muste in 1941, "not to interfere from without with their war efforts or to destroy their property. Our non-cooperation with the war effort of the nation, if enough were moved to participate in it, might of course at some stage have a decisive effect upon that war effort; but this would not be the result of a position and deliberate destructive act on our part but simply the result of our inability to cooperate with what seems to us an evil and ruinous course."[41]

Pacifists became even more determined not to engage in direct opposition to the war activities of the nation after the Japanese attack upon Pearl Harbor and America's formal entry into the war. On 9 December 1941 the FOR went on record disclaiming "any purpose to sabotage or obstruct the war measures of our government or any officials, soldiers or citizens in the performance of what they regard as their patriotic duty."[42] "The people of our country—through their elected representatives—had spoken by a declaration of war," recalled Dorothy Detzer in her memoirs. "Therefore, in this terrible ordeal for our nation, we would do nothing which would circumvent the will of the people."[43]

A few Quakers were concerned that the Society of Friends had merely protested against the war in general terms and advised its members to refuse to fight but otherwise had made no attempt to end the war. In 1943 Dorothy Hutchinson, a member of the Society of Friends and later a prominent leader of the WILPF, urged her fellow Quakers to work for a prompt negotiated peace with the Axis powers. But even as Hutchinson argued that Quakers should go beyond a mere personal peace testimony, she insisted that they "work in a spirit of love and with the purpose of converting rather than coercing other men."

> In working for a prompt peace-by-consultation we must, of course, avoid active obstructionism of the war effort. We must work in the spirit which has always restrained us from sabotage and rioting in war-time as well as in peace-time but which has prompted us to withhold our cooperation from wars and to declare our reasons for doing so in order that all who share our convictions may follow our example. Our present program for ending the war is simply a positive corollary to our traditional negative testimony. Until such time as our fellow Americans are converted to our program, we must accept the continuance of the war. But we must strive to change the will of

the American people so that they may express their will within the democratic framework by peaceful methods.[44]

Harbingers of the New Left

The commitment to the democratic process, no matter what its results, and an unequivocal anti-communism that had characterized American pacifism for several decades began to be called into question in the late 1950s and early 1960s. Once again, as in the 1930s, some pacifists started to deride America's pseudo-democracy. Pacifist journals began to run articles by men like C. Wright Mills and Sidney Lens, progenitors of what soon became known as the New Left, who called the United States a status quo power that ignored the new revolutionary forces of anticolonialism and national liberation in the Third World.

The Soviet Union and Communist China were still occasionally criticized as totalitarian powers who had betrayed the humanistic essence of socialism, but writers like Lens assigned responsibility for this development not to Leninist theory and practice or to Stalin and Mao but to the Western democracies. "The West likes to shrill about Soviet and Chinese terror," wrote Lens in *Fellowship,* the official organ of the FOR, in 1959. "But it does not concede its own role in this terror. If it were not for the anti-revolutionary activity of the West for more than a century, and now the policy of military encirclement, the East might have been won over to a democratic course. Britain, France, the United States and others have never accepted their share of guilt for the crimes of Stalin; nor their role as accessories to the Chinese totalitarianism."[45] Cuba, Lens conceded in 1961, had become part of the Soviet bloc, but the "basic humanism of Castro's revolution . . . remains predominant." It was America's "vulgar and sterile anti-communism" that threatened to consolidate Communist rule in Cuba.[46] In May 1962 *Fellowship* announced that Lens had become a member of the FOR.

During the early 1960s views such as those held by Sid Lens, blaming the United States for most of the world's problems and casting an admiring look at Third World revolutions, gradually spread into the larger pacifist community. This development was encouraged by the Soviet "thaw" following the death of Stalin in 1953, which weakened the old anti-communism and undermined what came to be called deprecatingly the "cold war mentality." There was also the impact of the civil rights movement in the South, which exposed the injustice of racial segregation and encouraged a more critical attitude toward American institutions generally. The fear of nuclear war and concern about nuclear fallout from the testing of nuclear weapons contributed to the spread of "nuclear pacifism" and to the growing tendency to hold both Russia and the U.S. equally responsible for world tensions and the arms race.

It was in this political climate that many pacifists, left-of-center liberals, and the emerging New Left increasingly embraced the same political agenda. Mass organizations like the Committee for a Sane Nuclear Policy, founded in 1957, enabled pacifists to break out of their political isolation and gain a wider, sympathetic audience for their demand for disarmament. Radical pacifists like A. J. Muste and Dave Dellinger developed a following among young people who had not experienced the politics of the 1930s and who did not share the pronounced anti-communism of the older generation of pacifists. Indeed, for many of these young people the excesses of "McCarthyism" in the 1950s had discredited the very idea of anti-communism, and they quite deliberately embraced the doctrine of anti – anti-communism.

When in 1965 America became involved in armed conflict in a faraway land in Southeast Asia, and large numbers of students faced the prospect of fighting and dying in a war with an ambiguous rationale, the stage was set for a mass movement of political protest that eventually was to create a symbiotic relationship of pacifism and New Left politics. By the time "the Movement," as it became known, had run its course some ten years later, American pacifism had assumed a new political identity.

PART II

The Impact of the Vietnam War

CHAPTER 2

The American Friends Service Committee Joins the New Left

The American involvement in Vietnam developed gradually and at first without attracting much attention or opposition. President John F. Kennedy considered the defense of South Vietnam against subversion and aggression from Communist North Vietnam a test of American responsibility and determination in Asia, and this view was widely shared by Congress, the media, and the articulate public. By the end of 1963, the U.S. had over 16,000 military personnel in Vietnam who provided the South Vietnamese with advice and support. Still, Vietcong strength was growing rather than declining. Following the overthrow of Ngo Dinh Diem in November 1963, political instability in South Vietnam increased, and North Vietnam stepped up its assistance to the guerillas. In February 1965 President Lyndon Johnson, faced with the spectre of a communist takeover, authorized a series of bombing attacks against North Vietnam that soon became a sustained air offensive. In early March the first American ground combat units entered Vietnam, and by late June, American forces had gone on their first search-and-destroy operations. In July 1965 the U.S. had 75,000 armed men in Vietnam, and a steady buildup of additional forces was under way.

A Policy Takes Shape

The opposition of the American Friends Service Committee to American policy in Vietnam developed slowly and cautiously. A proposal to mount an emergency effort against the growing American involvement was brought to the national board of directors in

September 1965 but failed to gain approval. On 4 October the board issued a statement on Vietnam, "An Appeal for the People of Vietnam," which called for a cease-fire, negotiations to settle the conflict peacefully, and the withdrawal of all armed forces, but it did not attack the U.S. position in any direct way.

Pressures for a more forthright stand came from the peace education committee of the New England regional office, headed by Russell Johnson. Before taking this post, Johnson (born in 1918) had been minister of a Universalist church in Massachusetts. A coworker has called his belief system a mixture of Christianity and socialism.[1] In an article published in the November 1965 issue of *Liberation,* Johnson raised the question of how a pacifist should relate to revolutionary violence against imperialism and injustice. Pacifists, he argued, should encourage nonviolent solutions, but "equal to if not more significant than the violence of revolutionaries in Asia and elsewhere (which we condemn correctly but all too easily) is the seldom discussed 'violence of the status quo.' Degradation, poverty, exploitation, famine, death of the innocent, etc., are caused by existing political, economic and social conditions"; therefore, pacifists had a duty to condemn this violence of the status quo as well. Johnson saw "an absolute qualitative difference between ... the calculated political assassinations by the National Liberation Front in Vietnam and the indiscriminate violence of saturation bombing by the American Air Force. In this confrontation, I know within myself which side I am on, but I remain largely immobilized, haunted by Aldous Huxley's persuasive arguments about "ends and means.' "[2]

Johnson discussed the same dilemma in a memo, "Revolutionary Movements and War," addressed to the annual meeting ("Roundup") of AFSC peace education secretaries held in January 1966. In this memo he took issue with the national board's "plague on both your houses" position—the equal condemnation of the violence of the National Liberation Front (NLF) and Hanoi and that of the Saigon and U.S. governments. "I identify with and approve of the objectives of the revolutionary groups" in the developing world that seek "self-determination and economic justice," Johnson declared. How then could a pacifist, opposed to the use of evil means for good ends, show his support for the revolutionary endeavor? "What about efforts to assist the revolutionary groups, i.e., the N.L.F. in Vietnam, short of military combat?" Johnson asked. Should civil disobedience and other nonviolent obstruction be employed to try to prevent the American counter-revolutionary role? Could the AFSC work in a united front actively supporting social revolution with Communists and others who accept violence? If the U.S. policy suppressing revolutionary change is "a result of political control exercised in the U.S. by certain special interests, what moral obligation do pacifists have to work for changes in the political/economic structure of the U.S. which will ensure basic change in foreign policy?"[3]

A very similar position was taken by Stewart Meacham, a one-time Presbyterian minister who had joined the AFSC staff in the 1950s and eventually had become head of its peace education division. Pacifists condemn all resort to violence, Meacham declared in an article published in *Liberation* in March 1967, but this did not mean that they "should be aloof and unconcerned with judgments regarding the justice or the injustice of one side against the other." The American intervention in Vietnam was an affront to common decency, a denial of justice, and it had to be condemned. It was counterproductive, Meacham declared, for pacifists to join in public or private expressions of solidarity with Vietnam; it might also prolong the war by stiffening resistance. However, those pacifists who believed that they had to give such positive support to the NLF and North Vietnam challenged the rest of the pacifist community to respond to the situation in different ways. "Thus far we have not done that. We have not yet established the relevance of nonviolence to revolutionary struggle." Pacifists had to find answers to such questions as how to "relate constructively" to revolutionary struggle, how to respond when the U.S. attempted "by violence to suppress a revolutionary struggle," and whether nonviolent resistance might be relevant to these tasks.[4]

The questions raised by Johnson and Meacham soon received an answer. It did not take long for the AFSC to discover a formula that enabled pacifists to assist the revolutionary cause in Vietnam without themselves engaging in overt violence, to wit: working for the withdrawal of American troops from Vietnam. Given the fragility of the Saigon government and the poor performance of its troops in the field, who were faced by a resolute opponent supplied and steadily reinforced by Hanoi, such a withdrawal, as everyone was fully aware of, was a sure recipe for an NLF victory. For a short while, concern was expressed about the possibility that the victorious NLF might engage in violent retribution against its defeated enemies, but assurances from Hanoi and the NLF that they sought reconciliation rather than revenge soon put these concerns to rest. The AFSC and other pacifist groups adopting the position of withdrawal now had the perfect political line: they could affirm their commitment to peace and nonviolence and at the same time help their revolutionary friends in Vietnam by pressuring the United States to get out of the conflict. Many rank-and-file members probably were not aware of the strategic meaning of this demand. However, the fact that the AFSC sought as its primary objective not a cease-fire to end the killing in Southeast Asia but the speedy removal of U.S. forces from the area revealed the real priorities of concern and who was in control.

The AFSC adopted this position largely as a result of prodding by several of its regional offices as well as the peace education staff in the national office in Philadelphia. Like all large organizations, the AFSC for the most part is run by its bureaucracy. Formal policy decisions and official statements are made by the board of directors, but the board and its executive committee act on information supplied by and within the framework of an agenda prepared by the organization's staff, which usually gets its way, sometimes after some delay. Moreover, while the members of the national board must be Friends, for most years of the AFSC's existence less than one-third of the staff have been Quakers, and in recent years the number of Friends has slipped to below 20 percent. In the 1960s many of these staffers were relatively young people, radicalized by the civil rights and disarmament movements of the 1950s. As the debate over the war in Vietnam heated up, views such as those held by Russell Johnson, who was openly supportive of the NLF, became more and more acceptable until they finally became AFSC orthodoxy.

A lengthy analysis of the Vietnam situation sponsored by the AFSC and published in January 1966 still lagged behind the thinking of many of the organization's staff, although it shared some of the same basic assumptions. The book-length study was prepared with the help of academic Asia specialists like Professor George McT. Kahin of Cornell University, known for his view that the NLF was a broad-based, indigenous South Vietnamese organization. Another academic author was Professor W. Allyn Rickett from the University of Pennsylvania, who, after many years in a Chinese prison, returned to the U.S. in 1957 full of praise for Communist correctional practice and the new Chinese man. Entitled *Peace in Vietnam: A New Approach*, the AFSC report called for a negotiated settlement and the withdrawal of all outside forces, both North Vietnamese and American, under the surveillance of an international force. The AFSC insisted that the United States had to accept the inevitability of revolutionary change in the developing world;

these revolutionary forces could not be met by a "dogmatic anti-Communism." Revolutionary social change so far had always exacted a cost in terms of human lives and misery, but this cost had to "be seen in relation to the alternative of extending the hunger, disease, ignorance, and chronic violence of the past into an overpopulated and overarmed world of the future."[5]

Becoming Part of the Antiwar Movement

As the American involvement in Vietnam deepened and the chances of a negotiated settlement became more remote, the AFSC gradually abandoned the qualifications it had placed on the American withdrawal, and its demand for a phased disengagement of outside forces under international supervision became a call for an unconditional American withdrawal. This change in AFSC policy came first in the regional offices, which have always been allowed considerable autonomy; it was facilitated by the active involvement of many AFSC staffers in the more radical antiwar movement. At first they operated there as individuals rather than as representatives of the AFSC. Gradually the permission for individual participation turned into an organizational and financial commitment of the AFSC to antiwar activities in which distinct pacifist voices were less and less audible.

The steady enmeshment of the AFSC in the antiwar movement and the development of a position clearly sympathetic to the NLF can be traced by following the ideas and actions of Stewart Meacham. In April 1965 Meacham had still expressed concern about the possible consequences of a North Vietnamese Communist victory. "None can view with enthusiasm the prospect of the triumph of repressive communism. Even those who seek victory over repressive poverty and ancient tyranny, and turn to communism, probably will soon find themselves pressing for the right to dissent, as has been the case in Russia."[6] But Meacham soon became convinced that the NLF was a genuinely patriotic organization rather than a front for the Communists and that the North Vietnamese would not impose communism on the South.

Meacham's change in position was in part the result of personal contacts that he had developed with the NLF and North Vietnamese leaders through several face-to-face meetings with them in Europe and in Southeast Asia. These meetings were arranged in order to explore the possibility of AFSC relief activities but also to understand better the character and aims of the NLF and North Vietnam.

Meacham was touched by the high morale of these Asian revolutionaries. After spending three weeks in North Vietnam in July 1968, Meacham returned convinced "that the government of North Vietnam is in fact a decent government." He reported to an audience in Houston, Texas, that he was impressed when Prime Minister Pham Van Dong told him, "We fight well because we believe in the decency and the humanity of all people."[7] In Hanoi, unlike in Saigon, there existed an obvious rapport between the people and their leaders. The reunification of the country, Meacham was sure, would proceed gradually, and South Vietnam would retain its own social and political system with "a mixed economy, focused on the needs of the people."[8] Once the U.S. was out of Vietnam, Meacham wrote a correspondent in May 1969, the Vietnamese would concentrate on restoring and rebuilding their own country. "I would doubt very much if the North Vietnamese or the South Vietnamese will be interested in military adventures in the neighboring countries."[9]

The influence of Stewart Meacham can also be seen in the policy decisions that eventually caused the AFSC to become an integral part of the antiwar movement. During World War II, pacifists had urged their followers to refuse to bear arms but to respect the democratic process that had led America into the war. This time most pacifists rather quickly determined to try to stop the war itself. Unable to convince a majority of the American people or a majority of Congress to end the American involvement, the antiwar movement, its pacifist component included, took to the streets, venting its political frustration by shrill attacks upon America's conduct of the war and the legitimacy of its institutions generally. Seeking to find allies wherever they could, pacifist groups now abandoned their former rejection of cooperation with the Communists and other organizations accepting revolutionary violence, and they went along with the New Left's principle of nonexclusion.

In July 1966 the AFSC participated in a meeting of antiwar activists in Cleveland, called by a faculty group at Western Reserve University in order to explore plans for a nationwide antiwar mobilization before the November 1966 elections. Out of the July meeting came a decision to have a second gathering in September to be based on the principle of nonexclusion. About 150 people attended the September meeting, representing about fifty different organizations, including the American Communist party, one of the most loyal, pro-Soviet Communist parties in the world. Also present were members of the Trotskyite Socialist Workers party (SWP) as well as their respective youth affiliates, the W.E.B. DuBois Clubs and the Young Socialist Alliance. The AFSC delegation consisted of four people, including Stewart Meacham.

In a report on the meeting and its aftermath, Meacham expressed concern about the length to which the principle of nonexclusion had been taken. Plans had been laid to have as a member of a steering committee "a person chosen because of his leading role in the Communist Party. I find myself perplexed at this point. On the one hand I would not want to get involved in a coordinating effort that set up some sort of machinery for loyalty investigations, etc. On the other hand I think it is both inconsistent and unwise to include as a matter of policy anyone committed to disciplines that would require him to give partisan support to the military efforts of one side or another in the conflict." For this reason, Meacham concluded, he was against the AFSC being represented even informally and indirectly on the steering committee.[10]

Opposition to Coalition Politics

Some in the AFSC questioned the very principle of participation in such coalition efforts. Ben Seaver, peace secretary of the San Francisco regional office, conveyed to Meacham the uneasiness of his group "over the possibility that in the attempt to include all who oppose the Vietnamese war, for whatever reason, we would blur irretrievably the basic message of our opposition. We see no good purpose being served by the AFSC co-sponsoring a demonstration in which some of the groups march with Vietcong flags and cheer the downing of U.S. planes and the killing of U.S. soldiers. Moreover, in the Bay area at least, demonstrations which have included the DuBois Clubs and other such groups have been characterized by a violence of feeling and attitude, if not action, with which we do not want to be associated."[11]

Not surprisingly, instances of verbal and actual violence continued to multiply. Once the principle of nonexclusion had been accepted, it proved virtually impossible to control the conduct of the many diverse groups and individuals who were attracted to the growing antiwar demonstrations. The mobilizations against the war held in the spring and the fall of 1967 were both accompanied by violent outbursts such as flag-burning and attacks upon law enforcement officers that were followed by mass arrests. The mood of both leaders and many of the demonstrators was getting uglier;

the distinction between nonviolent civil disobedience and active resistance to state authority began to be ignored. By now many in the movement had convinced themselves that the war in Vietnam was no accidental occurrence, the result of mistakes in policy, but rather the necessary consequence of a corrupt system that had to be destroyed.

The participation of the AFSC in this amorphous and increasingly militant antiwar movement drew the criticism of Dan Seeger, executive secretary of the AFSC's regional office in New York City. A lengthy memorandum dated 22 December 1967 that Seeger addressed to his executive committee remains to this day one of the most incisive analyses and critiques of the protest movement of the 1960s. Seeger took note of the loss of faith in the democratic process that had occurred in the antiwar movement. There had emerged "a trend toward hateful and vengeful behavior." In some circles, he said, "there is an impatience with representative democracy and parliamentarianism, and a considerable interest in Fidel Castro's ineluctable ability to sense the needs of the people without resorting to the troublesome electoral process. Within the Movement there is an increasing tendency, particularly in coalition situations, to make decisions in largish and open meetings run on an anyone-who-wants-to-come basis with a kind of consensus process blurring imperceptibly into decision making by self-appointed or 'natural' leaders."

In addition, Seeger pointed out, there was a loss of faith in nonviolence that reached deep into the pacifist component of the antiwar movement. Calls for the assassination of the president made by extremists "produce[d] only silence or mild apologies." Indeed, pacifists had "lost all effective influence in the peace movement. Some were seduced by the sudden potentiality of impact through numbers to blur their principles in the interest of being 'relevant.' " Seeger argued that the continuing horror of the Vietnam war had reduced the reasoned objections of many of those who opposed the conflict to mere fury. Public discussion was being debased and rage substituted for reason. "The mindlessness of the government tends to be matched with a mindlessness in the peace movement.... Genuine radical peace activity has been superseded by tendencies toward spurious and emotional catharsis." In these trying circumstances, Seeger said, Friends should stay actively involved but remain "clear and direct with everyone regarding our commitments. We cannot really gain respect, popularity or effectiveness for our cause by

34

jumping on everyone's bandwagon and entering false collaborations."[12]

Seeger continued his criticism of the antiwar movement and the AFSC's role in it in another memo issued on 26 February 1968. The United States was experiencing a serious moral and political crisis, Seeger pointed out, but some militants in the antiwar movement did their best to exacerbate it. "The oversimplification and emotionalization of issues, the exchange of invectives, the general degradation of debate, the howling down of people with whom one disagrees, the undercurrent of hints and threats of violence, contempt for rational political discussion and contempt for civil liberties are all ways in which some of the very people who see the danger of fascism are collaborating in bringing it about." In dealings with such people in a political coalition, the cards were often stacked against pacifists. "Meetings lasting until the small hours of the morning are frequently called on short notice or with no notice at all," Seeger explained. "This immediately loads the dice in favor of people with no other responsibilities." The consensus process, too, produced odd distortions:

> The impossibility of achieving any kind of true consensus among persons or organizations gathered on a non-exclusive basis, which often means they have practically nothing in common, means that decision-making is actually done behind the scenes after the melee of consensus gathering has proven impossible, or else that there is simply a consensus to decide upon nothing. Since there can be no consensus on discipline, there will be no discipline; if there can be no consensus on placards or slogans, any placard or slogan will be welcomed; if there can be no consensus for the procedure of the demonstration, everyone will come and do their own thing. What you end up having in such a demonstration is a mixed bag of practically everything under the sun. Often it isn't even an anti-war demonstration, since some participants approve of wars of liberation. About the only thing missing in some of these situations is something which an ordinary American can reasonably be expected to identify with.

The fact that a coalition with such elements and the participation in massive, emotion-laden demonstrations without any inner coherence were attractive to AFSC staff and committee members, Seeger argued, was "in itself a mark of our bankruptcy." In addition

35

to insisting on democratic and regularized procedures — adequate notice of meetings, a prepared agenda, orderly meetings — the AFSC should establish three "minimum requirements" for participation in antiwar coalitions. First, activities should have an explicitly stated, nonviolent discipline publicized well in advance. Second, activities should take place in the context of some reasonable rationale for effecting social change rather than being geared to ventilating the emotions of the participants. They should promote an understanding of war/peace issues rather than reinforce anti-democratic and anti-civil libertarian trends. Third, the activity should address the problems created by resort to violent techniques on all sides — the shortcomings of American society as well as those provoked by the armaments and violent policies of communist states and other such groups. The policy of nonexclusion should be viewed with skepticism, Seeger maintained. "Rather than pretend that a project is truly non-exclusive, it is more sensible to establish a coherent basis and rationale for having the activity and letting those draw around the concept who feel they can identify with it. Other persons would exclude themselves and form activities of their own."

Holding on to some basic principles of nonviolence and democratic procedure, Seeger urged, "is simply a matter of being true to our own convictions with humility and not being bought off by the prospect of a quickly developed mass following. . . . Through nonviolent, open civil disobedience unjust laws can be confronted and disobeyed without undercutting the principle of a society organized lawfully. . . . The revolution is still a long way off, but if it were not, we know that good ends do not justify any means whatsoever. A politics of outrage will only lead to yet another outrageous society."[13]

Then, as later, Daniel Seeger and his New York colleagues found themselves in the minority, and the AFSC continued on its path of collaboration with "the Movement." Indeed, as the war continued without any sign of coming to an early conclusion, the AFSC's involvement with the more militant elements of the antiwar movement deepened. The Tet offensive of January-February 1968 had raised American casualties to new highs, yet public opinion was slow in reacting to the intensified warfare. For a time, opponents of the war took comfort from the challenge to President Johnson's policies presented by the campaigns of Eugene McCarthy and Robert F. Kennedy. But the assassination of Kennedy in June by a disgruntled Palestinian ended any hope of uniting the Democratic party behind an antiwar candidate. The killing of Martin Luther King, Jr., in April of the same year contributed to the atmosphere of violence in the country.

Doubts about Nonviolence

In early October 1968 the AFSC participated in a gathering of activists at the Quaker center Pendle Hill, a meeting called to assess the "direction and relevance of the nonviolent movement." The participants in the meeting agreed at the start that the normal decision-making processes and resources of American society were losing their capacity to respond constructively to public opinion and the growing discontent. Police and federal authorities used violence and repression against peaceful and orderly demonstrators. The peace movement, therefore, had to consider whether its traditional non-violent philosophy and tactics were still adequate and how the non-violent movement should relate to the non-nonviolent resistance groups.

The majority of those attending agreed with Sid Lens, who argued that the pacifist movement should stop seeking to pacify the middle class and instead should talk about revolution. To talk about nonviolence without talking about revolution was a mistake. Organizations like the AFSC, the FOR, and the WRL "should be out in the streets with the Yippies, the Black Panthers etc. Channels of democracy are virtually closed." Revolution would come in "spurts and spasms, [through the] progressive destruction of existing institutions." Pacifists had to take the lead. "We want a world in which the individual has full control with a planned economy, participatory democracy. There must be more militancy, sacrifice, etc., and we must learn to think [of] ourselves as part of a revolution." At the suggestion of Lens a steering committee was appointed to plan nonviolent actions and to make suggestions concerning the kind of relationship that should be developed with organizations oriented toward non-nonviolence. The larger group was then to act on these proposals. Stewart Meacham was asked to be the convenor of the steering committee.[14]

When the full group, now calling itself the National Action Group, reconvened on 22 October 1968, a lengthy but inconclusive discussion ensued over the question of "the rightness and usefulness of a project centered on the destruction of property." During the preceding months several such destructive incidents had taken place. One of the most publicized incidents had occurred on 17 May 1968:

two Catholic priests, the brothers Daniel and Philip Berrigan, joined by seven other Catholics, had entered a draft board office in Catonsville, Maryland, and had set fire to about six hundred draft cards with homemade napalm. On 16 October, a few days before the meeting of the National Action Group, the "Catonsville Nine," as they were known, had been found guilty of conspiracy and destruction of government property.

Against this background, Alan Brick, the peace education secretary of the AFSC's Baltimore regional office, took the position that since to a considerable degree democracy had disappeared, the destruction of property was necessary to restore real democracy. Others raised the question of the "appropriateness and usefulness of projects which lead to the prolonged jailing of people who possibly could be more useful on the outside." Such actions, it was argued, might also lead to "stricter police and record controls, and rightist-directed action against pacifists." The group did agree that it would support the "Catonsville Nine" and the "Milwaukee Ten" by arranging speaking tours for those involved in these actions, attending the trial still to be held, and engaging in an educational campaign.[15]

The year 1969 saw a further escalation of AFSC protest activities and rhetoric. Linda Quint, a community organizer in the AFSC Chicago regional office, was one of a group of people (the "Chicago Fifteen") who on 25 May 1969 entered a draft board office on Chicago's South Side and burned the draft records. At a meeting of the national peace education committee, there was a discussion about how the AFSC should interpret this event. Quint, who attended the meeting, argued that "the line between violence and nonviolence is becoming blurred today." A member of the committee, however, spoke of this act as "being in a very risky and dangerous area." Unlike the action of an individual who burned his own draft card, this was an "action 'dismissing the government.' It is disregarding the state by not allowing it to continue existing (since it can't exist without its files), and threatening the state by trying to change it and obstruct its laws." Another member argued that "the law is on the side of violence in our society today and anything we can do to oppose this is commendable." He was glad that at least one AFSC member had had the courage and the fortitude to undertake such an action. Finally the following minute was adopted:

> The Peace Education Division Committee has heard our colleague,
> Linda Quint, describe the action of the Chicago 15 in destroying

draft board records, and we have discussed with her the motivations and the moral religious imperatives of the group. Within the context of the war in Vietnam — a context of crimes against humanity, crimes against the peace, and crimes as defined by the rules of war — those laws which force young Americans to go to Vietnam and kill Vietnamese are laws which violate the principles of legality and thereby undermine the legitimacy of the basic social authority itself. To accept and obey meekly such laws, or to stand aside while they operate, is to sanction violence, murder, and wholesale destruction of property and thereby debase the very concept of legitimacy. When this occurs the basis for order and justice in society is destroyed; law and order becomes a slogan of suppression and an instrument of human degradation. In this grave circumstance hope for change and deliverance rests with those brave and steadfast souls who, unmindful of their personal fortunes and willing to risk everything in a spirit of nonviolence, and accepting the harshest social penalties, engage in direct acts to disrupt the violence of illegitimate authority and to release from bondage and death those who are held by the state for purposes of atrocious, illegal and unjust war.[16]

Bronson Clark, executive secretary of the AFSC, was unhappy with this statement. In a letter to Stewart Meacham, head of the peace education division, Clark expressed the fear that such an act could be counterproductive and increase the polarization already present in the country. Moreover, burning records was "a game that can be played by the right and [they can] probably [play it] more effectively than we can. I would object to AFSC records being burned and would regard it as an act of violence, although not an act of violence against persons." The AFSC, Clark argued, was committed to the basic approach of reconciliation and communication.

While we do believe in speaking truth to power and confronting authority, these confrontations come out of a long history of program experience and usually are confrontations in which we do not inflict suffering or damage on others but are prepared to take it on ourselves. I am afraid that the AFSC general consensus which keeps corporation lawyers, members of the resistance, social workers, and others within a broad area of agreement with respect to AFSC programs would be shattered if it was somehow indicated that AFSC support of an individual act of conscience extended to approval of that act.[17]

Despite this slight slap on the wrist, Stewart Meacham and the peace education division continued to advocate challenging the state and resisting what they called "the illegitimate exercise of authority." The orderly process of change available to the people by which inhumane policies and laws can be reversed and removed simply no longer exists, Meacham declared in a speech at the Seabeck Summer Institute in the summer of 1969. The young people of the nation who resisted the instruments of violence, wielded by a state that had lost its basic legitimacy, had now become the "VC" and "niggers" of America. "There is a growing revolution in our society," said Meacham. "Many of us have at times engaged in the rhetoric of revolution. Today we are living in the midst of the reality of it. And let none of us think we can turn it back or make it different by piecemeal reforms."[18] When the peace education division committee met on 24 September 1969 to discuss a special Washington lobbying project, "several persons questioned the very validity of trying to do anything at this point to legitimately work through our 'corrupt' government, saying that we should instead be going beyond in terms of illegal action and massive demonstrations."[19]

Participation in the New Mobe

During the year 1969 Stewart Meacham became a key figure in the antiwar movement, and he put aside his earlier hesitations about sharing a leadership role with members of the Communist party and others "non-nonviolently oriented." The National Antiwar Conference was held in Cleveland on 4-5 July, and Meacham was a member of the steering committee, together with Arnold Johnson of the CPUSA and Fred Halstead of the SWP. The AFSC provided financial support for the New Mobilization to End the War (New Mobe), which was founded at that conference and of which Meacham became one of the co-chairmen. Students for a Democratic Society (SDS), which by then had moved toward an open endorsement of violent revolution, withdrew from the New Mobe. Nevertheless, as Meacham informed the peace education secretaries in September 1969, "We are not engaging in criticism or making any attacks on SDS even by negatively attempting to advertise our disassociation from it." The *New Mobilizer* from time to time would announce SDS activities.[20]

Not surprisingly, some members of the Society of Friends became uneasy about the AFSC's close association with the New Mobe. In October 1969, two members of the Friends' Meeting of Washington and former financial supporters of the New Mobe wrote Meacham to express their disapproval of the New Mobe's "increasingly sloganeering" literature. For people who believed that the Vietnam war was only an incidental aspect of the "military-industrial complex," they conceded, it was probably appropriate to use the protest against the war as a means of encouraging radical action against the entire American system. However, that was not the Quaker way. "We are aware of the concentrations of economic power in the United States, but there is no conspiracy of the right or the left. The Vietnam war is a tragic mistake of American pride for which we all share responsibility. It is not a calculated drive of American imperialists to gain economic domination of Asian resources and markets. This kind of dogmatic analysis omits to notice that [the] Wall Street stock market rises with hopes of peace and falls with spurts of war." The two Friends ended their letter by suggesting that Quakers withdraw from the New Mobe and instead concentrate on pressuring Congress to end the war. "It is in the ending of this war and the resultant release of creative energies and the money to translate them into social change that our hopes lie, not in the political dogmas of the New Left."[21]

In January 1970 the AFSC's board of directors took up the issue of participation in the New Mobe. It had before it a memo by Sam Levering, a member of the North Carolina Yearly Meeting as well as of the AFSC Corporation, the AFSC's legal entity composed of between 120 and 180 Friends appointed by Friends' yearly meetings and the AFSC nominating committee. Levering expressed his sympathy for the motives that had brought the AFSC into the New Mobe to protest and work against the immoral American war in Vietnam. "The Mobilization gave expression to a deep, sincerely held feeling in many Americans. Coming together brought a real sense of participation in a great cause, and genuine spiritual uplift." The New Mobe's policy of nonexclusion, too, was understandable. "We wish to include all persons in our love and fellowship. We do not wish to exclude anyone." Nevertheless, Levering argued, he had come to the conclusion that the AFSC's participation was undesirable and unfortunate. "Joint participation was morally ambiguous, at best. It appeared to give approval to violent rhetoric and action." Some officially sponsored speeches at the fall 1969 demonstrations had threatened and actually advocated violence against policemen, property, and so on, and had resulted in just such acts.

In addition to these moral problems, Levering noted, prudential considerations led to the same conclusion. He pointed out that the

American public had reacted negatively to the fall mobilization, as was to be expected; the Gallup poll of 23 November 1969 had shown a five-point rise in support of President Nixon's Vietnam policy. The majority of clerks, executive secretaries, and peace committee chairmen of yearly meetings whom he had polled had expressed the view that the total effect of the New Mobilization events of 13-15 November 1969 had made their work for peace more difficult. Most Americans are fearful of mass demonstrations, Levering noted. They feel, with Aristotle, "that masses of people in the streets is the chief way democracies are destroyed. I tend to agree, having seen first the Communists, and then the Nazis control the streets on the way to the destruction of the German Weimar Republic." When such demonstrations are accompanied by violence, people become doubly fearful. If the choice becomes "between a violent radical left and violent radical right, most Americans will choose the radical right."

Participation in the New Mobe was also damaging the relations between the AFSC and the Society of Friends, Levering argued. "This issue was a factor in [the] severance, by [the] California Yearly Meeting, of relations with the AFSC. It is a growing factor in the same type of feelings in Iowa, Indiana, North Carolina, and other Yearly Meetings. If all the facts were known about the Mobilization and AFSC participation, the situation would be much worse." Levering proposed that the AFSC board adopt a clear policy for the future which would make it clear "that we are committed to major change in the United States, by non-violent means, and that we support and wish to improve the democratic process. However, the AFSC should also make the following clear:

A. The AFSC will not participate in projects aimed to influence United States public opinion or policies jointly with groups that:
   1. Would use violence to destroy the democratic process in the United States.
   2. Would use violence to prevent the democratic process from making necessary changes in the United States. In the case of the Vietnam war, this means that we would not take part in such projects jointly with groups who seek military victory for either side.
B. Those holding responsible positions in AFSC would refrain from participation in joint projects with such groups. Such participation would be interpreted as AFSC participation. All of us in responsible positions must similarly restrict our actions.

Levering concluded his oral presentation to the board by noting that so far he had kept this issue within the AFSC family. However, if present policies continued, the matter would have to be discussed at yearly meetings and publicly at the corporation meeting. If this happened, injury was certain, both to Friends and to the AFSC.[22]

Despite Levering's strong plea for the AFSC's disassociation from the New Mobe, the board of directors could agree only on initiating a study of the problem. Meanwhile, Meacham and his staff continued their active role in the various and frequently changing groups making up "the Movement." In the spring of 1970, the New Mobe had broken up when its strong Trotskyite component had pulled out, insisting that the antiwar coalition be a single-issue movement and not link antiwar activities to other social and political problems. In September 1970 those in favor of making the antiwar movement a multi-issue effort organized the National Coalition Against War, Racism and Repression, which in January 1971 changed its name to the People's Coalition for Peace and Justice (PCPJ). One of several organizations that joined this new umbrella group was the Communist party; it was represented on the coordinating committee by Sylvia Kushner of the Chicago Peace Council and on the steering committee by Gil Green. As Sid Lens recalls in his memoirs, it was easier to work with the Communists tied to the Soviet Union than with the more rigid Trotskyites. Meacham, who had become a member of the coordinating committee of the PCPJ, was hopeful that the antiwar movement would really turn the country around. After one large antiwar demonstration he told Sid Lens, "For the first time in decades I think we can build a big socialist force again."[23]

On 3 March 1971 the executive committee of the AFSC national board decided against the formal affiliation of the AFSC with the PCPJ but instead determined to "allow, encourage and give support to staff to participate." The executive committee expressed the hope that peace education staffers "will have the skill to provide an influence and a point of view which will help strengthen actions along lines we could support and that staff will have the judgment and the clarity to step out when this is not possible." The committee also voted $3,500 in support of these staff activities, with $1,500 specifically earmarked for training in nonviolence.[24]

But it was easier to express the hope that the pacifist caucus in the new coalition would succeed in keeping activities nonviolent than actually to achieve such an influence. The PCPJ included among its diverse constituents Rennie Davis's May Day Tribe, who had decided that if the government would not stop the war, they would stop the government from operating. The PCPJ at first was reluctant

43

to endorse this plan but finally went along with it. As was to be expected, the three-day attempt in May 1971 to "bring everything to a halt" in Washington by blocking traffic, harassing government employees, and invading the meeting rooms of congressional committees led to mass arrests of participants — twelve thousand by the end of the action. Many of those arrested had had no share in the more violent antics of the May Day Tribe, but clearly the concept of nonviolence had been stretched considerably by these direct-action tactics aimed at preventing the functioning of a democratically elected government.[25]

Lining Up behind the Provisional Revolutionary Government

One of the slogans of the May demonstration had been the demand that Congress adopt the People's Peace Treaty. Brought back from Hanoi in December 1970, this document incorporated the insistence of the Provisional Revolutionary Government (PRG) on an immediate and total withdrawal of American troops from Vietnam but otherwise made no provision for a general cease-fire. In February 1971 the People's Peace Treaty had been signed by the National Action Group that included Stewart Meacham, but several AFSC regional offices declined to endorse it. The New York metropolitan office argued that the AFSC "should support proposals to bring an immediate end to the violence in Vietnam and not support efforts for peace that allow the violence to continue until after certain conditions are fulfilled." The Chicago and San Francisco staff took a similar position.[26]

After the AFSC board at its June meeting had similarly refused to ratify the treaty but allowed individual members of the AFSC to endorse it, Charles Bloomstein, executive vice president of the New York Friends Group though not personally a Quaker, expressed an even stronger criticism to Bronson Clark, the AFSC's executive secretary. It was clear, wrote Bloomstein to Clark, that Stewart Meacham was "convinced that the NLF and Hanoi have justice on their side and therefore 'deserve' to win." The People's Peace Treaty reflected this position, and Meacham supported it for this reason. However, Bloomstein insisted, a pacifist should not rank justice over peace.

Nothing, but nothing, comes before peace. Otherwise we certainly should have supported the Loyalists in Spain, the Allies over Hitler, and today the violent revolutionaries in South Africa. Unpopular though that position may be today, it is an inescapable obligation of a pacifist to insist on peace first, and to seek justice under that aegis. We are convinced that justice cannot be achieved through violence, that to use that means results in neither justice nor peace. Our task is to stop all the killing, and to stop it as soon as possible. It is not our task to sift the various claims of the competing parties.[27]

The ability of Meacham and his peace education staff to have their way and gradually move official AFSC policy toward demanding an end to "U.S. military intervention" is reflected in the AFSC white papers issued during the course of the war. Until 1969 the AFSC supported a phased withdrawal, but by 1970 the organization had accepted the demand of Meacham and the radical antiwar movement for a "complete and unconditional withdrawal of American troops from Vietnam." America, declared the AFSC white paper *Indochina 1971,* was guilty of waging an undeclared war in which war crimes were "a considered aspect of U.S. policy in Vietnam." The government manipulated false charges of cruel treatment of U.S. military captives in Vietnam and the fear of a bloodbath following a defeat of Saigon in order to prolong the war. Such fears, the white paper argued, were unwarranted. The PRG had indicated that elements of a just and lasting peace such as a coalition government and fair elections in the South could be negotiated among the Vietnamese once the U.S. had withdrawn. The early and total withdrawal of U.S. troops "is the best way to promote the survival and welfare of the Indochinese people."[28]

The extent to which, by the early 1970s, the AFSC had positioned itself on the side of the PRG and North Vietnam was brought out by the AFSC's reaction to the North Vietnamese Easter offensive in 1972. In response to this full-scale invasion of South Vietnam by heavily armed North Vietnamese divisions, President Nixon on 6 April had ordered the resumption of the bombing of North Vietnam, suspended since 1968, as well as air strikes and naval gunfire support for the beleaguered South Vietnamese. On 3 May the AFSC held a vigil in front of the White House, and a statement, drafted by the board of directors, was delivered to the president. The statement made no mention of the North Vietnamese invasion, which had prompted the new American involvement, but instead denounced Nixon for calling off the Paris peace talks and for ordering the resumption of the bombing of Hanoi and Haiphong. "We cannot stand idly by while a President who promised peace ravages the cities and villages of a people who have already suffered from a lifetime of war." The AFSC therefore demanded "an immediate end to the American bombing as well as withdrawal of all troops and military aid from all of Southeast Asia. . . . This holocaust must end."[29]

The one-sided nature of the AFSC position did not pass unnoticed. The Philadelphia Yearly Meeting of the Society of Friends agreed, after lengthy discussion, to endorse the vigil in Washington but noted the "concern deeply felt and expressed by several friends, that our endorsement *not* be interpreted as a support for any one side in the Vietnam struggle, but that it express our opposition to all war as a means of settling disputes, and that it be seen as a method toward reconciliation. To this end the suggestion was accepted that those who feel so motivated should stand in worship before the Russian Embassy."[30] A stronger criticism came from Ed Doty of the AFSC New York metropolitan regional office. In a memo circulated to all peace education secretaries and the national executive officers in Philadelphia, Doty agreed that President Nixon should be condemned for escalating the war. However, he went on, "we must also condemn the North Vietnamese for launching their most recent offensive. . . . While I do not mean to suggest that all the combatants are equally guilty in the destruction and killing they are causing, I do feel we should not and cannot condone the use of organized mass violence, war, for any cause."[31]

Doty's insistence that the AFSC condemn the use of violence by all sides drew a sharp rejoinder from Bronson Clark, the AFSC's executive secretary. Clark's letter provides a good summary statement of the position regarding revolutionary violence which the AFSC had developed by that time and to which it has adhered ever since:

> I think it is a clear AFSC position that we reject the employment of violence as a tool for social change which we would not ourselves employ. This does not mean that others who do not hold our nonviolent position are to be condemned because they have not reached the same conclusions about nonviolence that we have. In the presence of great social injustice there is the violence of the status quo. There may be further violence to change a situation of injustice. We may wish that more of our fellowmen and women accepted the theory that in the presence of injustice methods of nonviolent social change should be employed. However the NLF and the North Vietnamese and the Saigon government have never accepted this concept of non-

violence. In the case of the Vietnamese who are resisting American aggression on their country they have never proclaimed that they shall resist us nonviolently. As long as they believe in violence they certainly have every right to attempt to alter the injustice which we are inflicting on them by the means that they believe in. This is not the means of AFSC but they are certainly justified in using military tactics to drive out what they regard as [an] aggressor from their land. . . .

As American citizens we have a particular responsibility to get our own government off the backs of the Vietnamese and to bring a halt to the gross criminality of our attacks on their peoples and cities. Once we have removed the Americans in this way there might be some better climate for exchange of views on the power of love and nonviolence but it is improper and perhaps even immoral to condemn them for not using nonviolence when 1) they don't believe in it as a tactic and 2) the moral lesson would be coming from citizens whose country is the major perpetrator of their difficulties. . . . If men are to be reconciled to one another there must be social justice and it seems to me that on the one hand we can maintain our individual and group position against the employment of violence but at the same time we should be understanding of those who are suffering social injustice who choose to employ violence in an effort to relieve their condition.[32]

The May 1972 statement of the AFSC board of directors, it will be recalled, had demanded not only the withdrawal of all American forces from Southeast Asia but also the cessation of military aid to the governments of the region. Bronson Clark referred to these demands as designed "to get our own government off the backs of the Vietnamese." The underlying assumptions of this AFSC position were spelled out more fully in a 1972 pamphlet authored by James E. Bristol, a former Lutheran pastor and later the director of the AFSC's program on nonviolence. Entitled *Nonviolence not First for Export,* the pamphlet not only provided a theoretical justification for the AFSC's support of the Vietnamese revolution in 1972 but also served as a programmatic statement of things to come. Not only would the AFSC not condemn revolutionary violence but it would also seek to prevent governments faced with such violence from successfully fighting the revolutionaries by cutting off American aid and supplies. In line with this strategy, all during the year 1972 and especially after the Paris Peace Agreement of 27 January 1973 had formally concluded the military involvement of the United States in the Vietnam conflict, the AFSC now focused its activities on ending American aid to the government of South Vietnam. Since the AFSC made no effort to promote a similar cutoff of military aid to the PRG, and since the Paris Peace Agreement contained no effective machinery to prevent North Vietnam from reinforcing its forces in South Vietnam, a unilateral halt in military aid to South Vietnam was of course bound to lead, sooner or later, to a defeat of the Saigon regime. Thus, once again the AFSC had found a way of continuing to affirm its opposition to the use of violence but at the same time aiding a revolutionary movement that the AFSC wanted to win.

Bristol began his essay by deploring the exploitation of the Third World by the West, which had made millions of oppressed people despair of achieving a peaceful liberation from the thralldom under which they suffered. "To them violence, and violence alone, would appear to work effectively and to be capable of toppling the tyranny which oppresses them." And yet, violence brutalizes those who resort to it. "All too frequently, in human experience, wars of liberation have been fought with lofty courage and high idealism only to result tragically and ironically in the rebirth of tyranny with new tyrants in charge." A new just society could not be reached by way of revolutionary violence; however, Bristol claimed, it was not up to Americans to prescribe for people in a totally different situation. "The necessity to be nonviolent must be urged with passion, and persuasion, *not* upon the oppressed revolutionaries, but upon those who oppress them, and upon the accomplices of the oppressors." Many of the regimes rebelled against were the incarnation of a greater violence and terrorism than any used in the struggle against them. "While two wrongs never make a right, before we deplore terrorism it is essential for us to recognize fully and clearly whose 'terrorism' came first, so that we can assess what is cause and what is effect."

Americans, and pacifists in particular, Bristol urged, must attack the violence of the status quo in the Third World—the suffering created by the lack of a decent standard of living and the brutal practices of the police and penal system. The thrust of their effort should be the removal of injustice, not the urging of nonviolence. "To put it simply: We believe in nonviolence and in revolution and therefore in the possibility of nonviolent revolution. We understand that the oppressed do not share our faith in nonviolence. We have given them little reason to. Still we identify with the justice of their cause and we urge all who are able in good conscience to do so to

48

unite with them and support them in their revolution." How could people committed to nonviolence aid the violent revolution of the oppressed? "It will make it easier for the disadvantaged to succeed in their revolutionary struggle if we remove both direct American domination and/or American support for their oppressors, and this, in turn, will serve to minimize the violence which they feel compelled to use to reach their goal." Thus, for example, instead of urging nonviolence upon the Guatemalan guerillas, "we should endeavor to keep the U.S. Marines at home, and U.S. military and economic support from being sent to buttress and undergird the repressive Guatemalan government. This would allow the Guatemalan revolutionaries to use nonviolent methods." Bristol concluded with a plea for radical and far-reaching changes in U.S. foreign policy in order to achieve the better and more just world for which the oppressed were striving.[33]

The full application to Central America of the strategy Bristol sketched out in 1972 was still years away. Meanwhile, the AFSC used it first in Southeast Asia, though not all went according to script. To be sure, the North Vietnamese were helped to victory by the sharp reductions in U.S. aid to the Saigon government, for which the AFSC labored tenaciously and successfully. As General Van Tien Dung, the North Vietnamese chief of staff, put it in 1976, these cuts forced President Thieu "to fight a poor man's war,"[34] suffering from serious shortages in spare parts, ammunition, and fuel. Yet since Saigon refused to surrender without putting up a fight, the North Vietnamese, to use Bristol's language, were unable "to minimize the violence which they [felt] compelled to use to reach their goal," and the war continued for another two years before the outgunned South Vietnamese finally threw in their cards. Bristol could, of course, argue that AFSC policy was not to blame for this prolongation of the war. Had the AFSC's demands been fully accepted by the American Congress and had South Vietnam been prevented from getting any military aid at all, the North Vietnamese undoubtedly would have been able to seize South Vietnam without another round of bloody fighting — they could have triumphed over their adversaries nonviolently. After all, why would even dedicated revolutionaries use force if they could have the fruits of battle without actually engaging in battle? But we are getting ahead of our story.

On 8 May 1972 President Nixon ordered the mining of Haiphong harbor and other North Vietnamese ports. Even though this blockade had no immediate effect on the fighting in the South, it buoyed the spirits of the South Vietnamese and by the end of June

49

enabled them to begin a counteroffensive. The AFSC responded to Nixon's actions by escalating its own activities against the war. On 10 June the board of directors authorized a program called "Nonviolent Direct Action to Blockade American Arms to Indochina." National and regional staff members were encouraged to plan and organize actions such as blockading sea terminals, air bases, and munition factories and depots, blocking rail lines that transported ammunition, and using small boats to harass warships bound for Vietnam. The AFSC publications issued during the summer of 1972 charged that the U.S. was systematically bombing dikes and dams in North Vietnam. The major obstacle to a peaceful settlement of the conflict was said to be American unwillingness to accept a coalition government in Saigon. A high North Vietnamese official, authorized to speak for his government, was said to have stated that, "contrary to the claims of the Nixon Administration, the North Vietnamese are not demanding control over South Vietnam." The United States was urged immediately to "end all its military activities and aid in Southeast Asia and begin at once the complete withdrawal of its naval, air and land forces, advisers and material."[35]

The Campaign against Aid to Saigon

By 1972 the antiwar movement had become a sideshow in some ways. The negotiations with the North Vietnamese in Paris conducted by Henry Kissinger were inching forward, and, after several false starts and another round of heavy bombing of Hanoi and Haiphong in December 1972, a peace agreement was formally signed on 27 January 1973. A news release issued by the AFSC welcomed the end of the American involvement, but warned that this was not yet the end of the war. "The continuation of aid to the regime of President Thieu may contribute to the collapse of ceasefire hopes and the resumption of warfare."[36] The focus of AFSC activity now became the stopping of any further aid to the Saigon regime.

Some of those engaged in getting the U.S. government "off the backs of the Vietnamese" may have sincerely believed that by weakening the ability of the South Vietnamese to fight, they helped to shorten the war. For others, both inside and outside the AFSC, the new campaign to curtail and end the American aid to Saigon was clearly a vehicle for helping the North Vietnamese achieve their longtime aim of taking over the South. Public AFSC statements still spoke of helping to implement the Paris accords and creating a coalition government for South Vietnam, but the AFSC staff involved in the campaign to end aid to the Thieu regime already had their eye on another goal. John McAuliff, the director of the new Indochina program within the peace education division, put it this way in a memo to Stephen (Steve) G. Cary, associate secretary: while heretofore the "AFSC has defined its role in respect to its opposition to the military aspects of the war, . . . now it needs to examine its continuing role and responsibility regarding the political aspects, that is the anticipated consolidation of anti-Thieu forces in the context of aspirations for ending neo-colonial intervention and achieving reunification."[37]

In February 1973 the AFSC announced the launching of a million-dollar campaign, the North/South Vietnam Fund for War Relief and Peace Action. Sixty percent of the funds raised were to be spent for relief, 30 percent were to support peace action, and 10 percent were to defray the administration costs of the campaign. By July 1973 fundraisers in the national office had become concerned about some of the activities supported through the peace action portion of the fund—a working party on industrial militarism, a conference on social change, exploration of a campaign against the B-1 bomber, support for regional G.I. organizing. We know, one of the fundraisers argued, "that in a real sense the present situation is related to fundamental deficiencies in American society and consequently anything which offers the possibility of altering American values and institutions to correct these evils is relevant to the N/S [North/South] Fund. However, this is hardly a conclusion we could expect the typical donor to the Fund to draw."[38] This minor administrative flop was soon corrected, and funds thereafter were limited to programs with an obvious and direct relationship to the situation in Indochina.

From 26 October to 28 October 1973, about two hundred longtime antiwar activists met in Germantown, Ohio, to plan the next phase of the campaign to halt American aid to Saigon. The cooperating organizations included SANE, Women Strike for Peace, the FOR, the WRL, the WILPF, and the AFSC. The outgrowth of this conference was the Coalition to Stop Funding the War, which set itself the goal of ending all U.S. military and paramilitary aid to Vietnam, Cambodia, and Laos. As the focal point of its campaign, the Coalition chose "the plight of Saigon's 200,000 political prisoners" incarcerated in "tiger cages" and similar inhuman places of detention. A nationwide outpouring of books, pamphlets, films, and speakers now sought to drive home the message that a regime guilty of such massive political repression was obviously not worthy of

American support. The church and civic groups, bombarded with these tales of horror, had no way of knowing certain facts: that the charge that there were 200,000 political prisoners in Saigon had first appeared in Hanoi's *Vietnam Courier* in January 1971; that the man who had repeated the allegation in Saigon in June 1973, the Redemptorist priest Father Chan Tin, was, after the fall of Saigon, revealed to have been part of the Vietcong underground in Saigon; and that the figure of 200,000 political prisoners exceeded by far the total prison and detention population in South Vietnam, which two exhaustive investigations by American embassy officials had put at around 35,000. The latter figure included all common criminals as well as those detained on account of "political activities" such as planting bombs under civilian buses and assassinating hamlet chiefs. The accuracy of the embassy figures was confirmed after the collapse of South Vietnam.[39]

Serving the campaign against American aid for Saigon in an advisory capacity were the Indochina Resource Center, with offices in Washington and Berkeley, California, and the Vietnam Resource Center in Cambridge, Massachusetts. On account of their faithful service to North Vietnam, both centers had developed the reputation of being propaganda agencies operated by Americans for the Hanoi government. The AFSC's project NARMIC (National Action Research on the Military-Industrial Complex), which previously had sought to expose American atrocities in Vietnam, now cooperated with the Vietnam Resource Center in publicizing the story of Thieu's "tiger cages" and his political prisoners. In a publication entitled "Questions on U.S. Military Aid to South Vietnam," issued in May 1974, NARMIC stated that Saigon troops had launched the majority of the military operations in violation of the Paris ceasefire provisions, that the PRG and North Vietnam received only about one-tenth of the foreign aid that South Vietnam received from the United States, and that any additional military aid would "only encourage Saigon to initiate offensive operations against the PRG." The AFSC publication argued that charges of a "bloodbath" during North Vietnam's land reform in the 1950s were a CIA fabrication; allegations of "Hue massacres" supposed to have taken place during the 1968 Tet offensive were similarly false. By stopping military aid to South Vietnam, the U.S. would not be turning South Vietnam over to the Communists. Because of the Paris Peace Agreement and the political framework established by it, "a 'communist takeover' can only come about if it is the wish of the South Vietnamese people."[40]

Despite these efforts to allay concern about the likelihood and consequences of a Communist victory in Vietnam, a May 1974 progress report by the AFSC Indochina program on the campaign to halt aid to Indochina noted that many Americans were still worried about what might happen in Southeast Asia once all American aid was cut off. "The strategy adopted tentatively in the confusing days after the Peace Agreement was signed, then clarified and strengthened at the Germantown united campaign conference, has been remarkably effective." In response to thousands of letters, phone calls, and telegrams from constituents, many prompted by local peace education efforts, Congress had voted to stop the bombing of Cambodia and had sharply reduced military and economic aid to Indochina. In order to capitalize on the momentum created and to end the American intervention once and for all, it merely remained to counter American fears of a Hanoi victory. This could be accomplished by putting more emphasis on the process of reconciliation created by the Paris Peace Agreement and especially by stressing the role of the "Third Force" in Vietnam. To some extent, the report acknowledged, this was "a tricky proposition" because this new emphasis had to be achieved "without utilizing and validating still widespread anti-communist prejudices." The AFSC therefore had to avoid counterposing the Third Force against those identified with the PRG, and more education was needed "about the PRG and DRV [Democratic Republic of Vietnam] which overcomes hostility inducing propaganda about the 'enemy.' "[41]

Interest in the Third Force, including its Buddhist component, was new for the AFSC. Until 1974 the AFSC had been critical of the sympathy shown to the Buddhists by other pacifist groups, in particular the FOR. In 1971 a former AFSC volunteer worker in Vietnam had expressed her concern about the AFSC's obvious bias in favor of the NLF and its complete neglect of the Buddhists, who were avowed pacifists. Not only did the AFSC exclude the Buddhists from its medical aid program and limit this aid to the NLF and North Vietnam, but she had not even been permitted to use AFSC facilities in order to duplicate and mail to the U.S. a newsletter of the Unified Buddhist Church.[42] However, in 1974, when the AFSC wanted to show the existence of widespread political opposition to the Saigon government and calm the fear that an abandonment of Thieu meant the victory of the PRG and North Vietnam, the AFSC played up the Third Force and especially those groups within it that were close to the PRG.

On a visit to Saigon in August 1974, AFSC staffer Ronald (Ron) J.

Young interviewed Madame Ngo Ba Thanh, a lawyer and a leader in the Movement of Vietnamese Women for the Right to Live. Madame Thanh affirmed her belief in neutralism and national reconciliation. The Third Force, she said, supported neither the Communists nor the Americans; it merely sought to achieve Vietnam's neutrality and independence. Despite Thieu's "policy of repression which is carried on in a Fascist way," the Third Force was getting stronger. If the Americans would refrain from aiding Thieu, she claimed, the Third Force would be able to operate more freely and achieve peace through the full implementation of the Paris Peace Agreement.[43] After the fall of Saigon, the Movement of Vietnamese Women for the Right to Live was revealed to have been one of several political fronts for the PRG; Madame Thanh was rewarded for her skillful performance by being made vice president of the Vietnamese Women's Union, a mass organization under the control of the ruling Communist party.[44] The usefulness of the Third Force and the PRG having come to an end, the victorious North Vietnamese washed their hands of both of these groups, and all important posts in the new administration of South Vietnam were given to North Vietnamese cadres. At that point, the AFSC's short-lived interest in the Third Force also disappeared.

In the autumn of 1974 the AFSC redoubled its efforts to mobilize public support for a complete halt in U.S. aid to Saigon. After an AFSC group had met with the PRG delegation in Paris, Ron Young wrote the head of the delegation to thank him for the help received. "Our discussion with you gave us important new information and inspiration for the continuing peace struggle here in the United States. As we said to you, we are optimistic about this year 1975, but we also are very much aware that the struggle to cut off military and paramilitary aid to the Saigon regime will be a difficult one. As we get closer to having a decisive effect on the situation in South Vietnam we recognize that the struggle will probably get more difficult. We believe, however, that we can succeed."[45]

Young's hope proved to be correct. A war-weary Congress refused President Ford's requests for supplementary appropriations of aid. Hanoi, convinced that the U.S. would no longer intervene in Vietnam, now opened a concerted series of attacks in the Central Highlands that the beleaguered South Vietnamese forces were unable to stop. By 18 March 1975 Pleiku and Kontum had fallen; Da Nang was lost on 30 March. A statement issued by the AFSC board on 15 April called for a "political settlement and establishment of the National Council of National Reconciliation mandated by the Paris

Accords," but the North Vietnamese had no intention of sharing power with anyone and refused all pleas for negotiations and a cease-fire. On 30 April North Vietnamese tanks entered Saigon, thus consummating the final defeat of South Vietnam.

The ideological assumptions that led to the AFSC's close enmeshment in the radical antiwar movement and to the support of revolutionary violence have continued to govern AFSC thinking. This worldview, like that of the New Left in the 1960s, continues to see America as the root of most of the world's problems. American foreign policy is said to be based on an irrational anti-communism, on the "myth of the Soviet threat," the defense of right-wing dictatorships, and the hunger for profit on the part of multinational corporations. The estrangement from American society, allegedly dominated by the military-industrial complex, leads to the idealization of revolution and revolutionary regimes in the Third World — as long as these movements and regimes claim to be committed to some kind of socialism and are opposed to America. The unsavory record of many of these regimes with regard to political freedoms and human rights generally is denied or, if that is not possible, defended as temporary and the result of American hostility. Not surprisingly, the stands and policies of the AFSC since 1975, derived from these ideological premises, have led to some of the same moral paradoxes that afflicted the organization during the Vietnam war period.

CHAPTER 3

Alfred Hassler: The Pacifist Conscience of the Fellowship of Reconciliation

The Fellowship of Reconciliation (FOR) entered the Vietnam era under the firm leadership of Alfred Hassler. As a long-time editor of *Fellowship* and, after 1960, as executive secretary of the FOR, Hassler had proven himself a man not only of solid pacifist convictions but also of political and moral integrity. During the 1950s and early 1960s, as we have seen in our introductory chapter, Hassler had successfully argued that pacifists must condemn the militarism of all countries, and he had opposed cooperation with the Communists and their various front organizations. In April 1964 the national council of the FOR adopted a statement on Vietnam that reflected Hassler's nuanced political views. The council declared that the United States should never have become involved in the Vietnam conflict. However, after the U.S. presence had become a fact, the new equation of interests and power made the idea of an immediate and unilateral American withdrawal politically unacceptable. Moreover, such a withdrawal, "while it would bring a stop to the killing of some people, . . . would certainly create the conditions for the retaliatory slaughter of a lot of others, hardly an unequivocally attractive solution for pacifists." Of the practicable possibilities, therefore, only negotiations leading to the neutralization of Indochina offered hope, and that not much.[1]

Divisions over Collaboration with the New Left

In April 1965 Students for a Democratic Society (SDS) organized the first mass demonstration in Washington against American involvement in the expanding war in Vietnam. The SDS had begun in 1960 as the student wing of the League for Industrial Democracy, an educational organization close to Norman Thomas's Socialist party that sought the extension of democracy into all areas of social and economic life. At its 1962 convention in Port Huron, Michigan, the SDS had gone on record against an "unreasoning anti-communism." By 1965 the organization had outgrown its social-democratic origins and had emerged as the leading edge of the New Left. For young radicals like Tom Hayden and Todd Gitlin, who had not experienced the manipulative activities of the Communist party in the 1930s and 1940s, anti-communism was synonymous with McCarthyism; it was an excuse used by reactionaries to mask their own viciousness and intolerance of all social change. SDS leaders therefore rejected out of hand the argument of anti-Stalinist socialists like Michael Harrington that the struggle against reactionary anti-communism required, in the name of democratic values, an equal struggle against Communist totalitarianism. Consistent with the SDS philosophy of anti – anti-communism, the organizers of the March on Washington refused the demand of Harrington and other veteran socialists that the march be clearly opposed both to reactionary militarism in Saigon and to any support of the Vietnamese Communists. In this way, Harrington maintained, if a few of the demonstrators were to wave a Vietcong flag, it would be possible to dissociate the majority of the marchers from the small minority who were not so much advocates of peace in Vietnam as partisans of the Vietcong.[2]

The conviction of Harrington and Norman Thomas that American peace activists could not fly the flag of an organization engaged in battle with American soldiers was shared by Hassler. Thus, on the eve of the April 17 demonstration, Hassler joined with A. J. Muste, Charles Bloomstein, and several other pacifists in issuing a statement that welcomed the students' concern about the war in Vietnam but also asked that they not become pro-Communist out of an overreaction to American policy. "We welcome the cooperation of all those groups and individuals," the signers of the statement declared, "who, like ourselves, believe in the need for an independent peace movement, not committed to any form of totalitarianism nor drawing inspiration or direction from the foreign policy of any government."[3]

Hassler's critical attitude toward the New Left was not supported by all of the FOR leadership. In early 1966 two younger members in particular began to express ideas that in due course were to bring them into sharp conflict with Hassler. They were Ronald J. Young, director of FOR youth work, and Allan Brick, peace education secretary of the AFSC's Baltimore regional office and chairman of the FOR executive committee. At their urging, a substantial part of the annual meeting of the FOR national council held in late April 1966 was devoted to a discussion of the New Left.

In a memorandum distributed to the members of the council prior to the meeting, Young outlined the reasons why he regarded this discussion as very important. Most members of the New Left, Young acknowledged, were not pacifists. "And yet, most of the strongest commitments of the new left tend toward pacifist conclusions. Are the new radicals not asking in quite an effective way just what we mean when we call ourselves pacifist?" Young pointed out that the New Left had been criticized for its silence on Vietcong terror, but pacifists who took the "plague on both your houses" position avoided the hard questions posed by the political realities of the world in which they lived. "We must be clearer in defining what we mean by violence, and must in addition be able to distinguish differences in violence," Young noted. The new radicals, following the teaching of Herbert Marcuse, drew attention to the fact that modern industrial society was "more dangerously manipulative than a society like the present one in Cuba." The current situation, Young concluded, demanded that the FOR devote its attention "to new questions, new patterns of thought, and new forms of action; it is doubtful whether new resolutions are of much value."[4]

By the spring of 1967, the FOR national council had become sharply divided over the issues of principle and tactics raised by the burgeoning antiwar movement. A discussion on Vietnam held at the April council meeting was lengthy, but no agreement could be reached on a resolution. In his remarks to the council, Hassler agreed that the U.S. was more of an aggressor than anyone else in the Vietnam situation and that America was doing obscenely indecent things in Vietnam. All this had to be said. However, Hassler insisted, "this does not mean that we go from there to the condoning of violence by the other side. There is some very ugly violence inflicted by the Vietcong and the North Vietnamese on individual victims who suffer just as much, just as tragically as any other victims." Disagreement also developed over the role of pacifists in antiwar coalitions. Council member Robert Gilmore opposed participation in the Spring Mobilization to End the War in Vietnam, "because while we have a responsibility to oppose American policy in Vietnam, we must do so within the context of pacifist insights, remembering that the other side also has a responsibility for peace."

Gilmore's view was opposed by W. H. Ferry, who argued that "anti-communism is this century's 'biggest hoax.' " He did "not want to be known as a 'good American' in 1967 any more than he would wish to have been known as a 'good German' in 1941/42."[5]

During the course of the year 1967, tensions continued to build up within the FOR staff. Some of the problems were organizational and involved lack of coordination between the paid staff, the elected national council that met once a year, and the executive committee charged with making interim decisions on policy and programs. More basically, however, the FOR was being challenged and divided by the same ideological questions that separated the different elements in the larger antiwar movement. These issues were the subject of a lengthy and incisive paper that Hassler distributed in March 1968 to the members of the national council prior to their meeting in April of that year.

The antiwar movement, Hassler maintained, consisted of two loosely defined groupings. There were, first, the "apocalyptics," a coalition of the New Left, the Old Left, and militant pacifists. For these elements the war in Vietnam was a direct expression of an aggressive American military-industrial complex acting against the forces of social revolution in Southeast Asia and represented a fundamentally imperialist and neo-colonialist policy. The American political system was said to be unequipped to deal with these problems, and therefore, instead of relying on electoral politics, the apocalyptics called for resistance to a state that had become illegitimate. This segment of the antiwar movement was anti – anti-Communist and sought the victory of the NLF and North Vietnam. Hassler referred to the second grouping as the "evolutionists" or "antiwar liberals." They saw the Vietnam war as a mistake rather than as the natural product of an evil American society. These elements favored tactics of persuasion and the use of instrumentalities provided by a democratic system, including the courts and action at the polls, in order to change the policy of the Johnson administration. The evolutionists supported programs of social justice but were anti-Communist.

The division over anti-communism, Hassler argued, was fundamental to an understanding of what was happening. The apocalyptics flatly rejected any form of anti-communism; they reflected the swing of the pendulum from an obsession with communism as totally bad to a preoccupation with American society as totally bad. For the young activists of the New Left, who dominated the apocalyptic camp, anti-communism had few roots in reality and was identified with the primitivism of Senator Joseph McCarthy. It was worth remembering their age, Hassler noted:

> The twenty year old of 1968 was eight at the time of Hungary, the East German workers revolt and the Twentieth Congress of the Soviet Communist Party that heard Khrushchev's de-Stalinization speech, and not so much as a gleam in their daddies' eyes when the Stalinist purges were going on in Russia. Within the experience of the contemporary student generation, and even some of their older mentors, "communism" has been identified primarily with such phenomena as the Castro revolution in Cuba and the courageous resistance of the Vietnamese National Liberation Front against the overwhelming power of the United States. Conversely, the reality of the brutal American campaign in Vietnam measured against the pretensions of American society has induced a feeling of deep disillusionment and growing cynicism.

The tactics of the apocalyptics, Hassler pointed out, reflected their bitterness and frustration. They had moved "from dissent to resistance." Unlike earlier conscientious objectors who had recognized the right of society to make decisions on war and peace but had claimed for themselves the right to refuse to abide by the command to bear arms, the new "resisters" engaged in acts of obstruction and even sabotage of the war effort. There was little concern with the question of whether a minority had a right to attempt to impose its will on the majority. According to Hassler, "Either it is assumed that this aspect of democracy has been totally vitiated and that the moral indignation that the protesters feel is sufficient justification for their act, or that in fact the majority is really on the side of the protesters but has been silenced or rendered impotent by the machinery of a corrupt government." Many of the apocalyptics held to the desirability of nonviolence, but on a tactical rather than a moral level — violence alienated the people they were trying to win over to their side. The apocalyptics, including many pacifists among them, also refused to equate the violence of the NLF and North Vietnam with that of the United States. They charged other pacifists and liberals with falsely concentrating on the overt violence of the war and with overlooking or muting the violence of the system that had produced the war.

Hassler reminded the members of the council that many of these issues were not really new. "The cast of characters is different, but the question of support of wars of national liberation and revolution is the same argument as the proposal in the thirties that the FOR drop its objection to class wars, and not very different from the just war concept of traditional Christianity." Many pacifists had once again convinced themselves that all wars were to be opposed except the current one, "with the piquant addition that in the immediate situation those whom we support are the enemies of our country." Hassler maintained that pacifists who insisted on remaining consistent in their denial of the legitimacy of all resort to violence and who opposed supporting the NLF were not insensitive to the claims of justice. They refused, however, to sanction the murder of human beings for whatever admirable reasons. The "killing of peasants or village officials by terror in order to make an example of them to other villagers is not sanctified by the fact that the murderers are trying to achieve national independence." Moreover, what had started out preeminently as a striving for national liberation had now become part of a far more complex pattern. While virtually all South Vietnamese wanted the war to end, millions of them were opposed to a victory by the NLF and to Communist domination. Finally, Hassler noted, the "war does take place within the context of a struggle between communism and the West, and neither side has been blameless in this struggle."

Hassler pointed out that the National Mobilization to End the War in Vietnam had succeeded in drawing together a wide spectrum of people — from pro-Vietcong Maoist Communists to respectable moderates. Yet the Mobilization had no recognized leadership, its attitude toward violence was not clearly defined, and the coalition was easily manipulated by parasitic ideological groups. While individual FOR members would undoubtedly continue to participate in the Mobilization, Hassler proposed that the FOR, as an organization, not be heavily involved. Similarly, he suggested that the FOR not engage organizationally in civil disobedience. Whereas, in the past, civil disobedience had been invoked as a last resort, it now was often practiced in order to indicate a rejection of "the system" and to show contempt for its laws. Such actions alienated many people who opposed the war, and even many FOR members seriously objected to these tactics. The Fellowship, Hassler cautioned, should not try to force on any of its members practices or tactics with which they were in fundamental disagreement. Instead, the FOR should express the pacifist witness and insight and fulfill the role of the peacemaker. It should continue to mobilize religious leaders of all faiths in opposition to American policy in Vietnam and engage in medical and other humanitarian aid. It was not necessary for FOR to be in on everything that happened.[6]

When the national council convened on 16 April 1968 for its three-day meeting, debate was keen and was marked by some sharp exchanges. David McReynolds of the War Resisters League agreed with Hassler that the FOR should not become an adjunct of the New Left, but at the same time he argued for a much more active role in the leadership of the Mobilization and for a "much closer identification with the Resistance, which is the most hopeful, courageous, basically pacifist phenomenon we have had since the Freedom Rides." To block induction centers physically and use other means of nonviolent resistance, he held, was perfectly in line with FOR traditions and purposes. "Non-violence may even in certain circumstances seek to polarize conflict in order to identify it and deal with it." McReynolds was supported by Allan Brick, who argued for "listening to new thinking, [to] young theologians, and examining the pacifist stance from such new perspectives."

Staff member Ron Young gave an account of his trip to the University of Wisconsin at Madison, where a group of students had prevented access to Dow Chemical recruiters. He felt this was "a legitimate and commendable use of non-violence." On the other hand, veteran civil rights leader Bayard Rustin of the A. Philip Randolph Institute took strong exception to such tactics, which he branded "anti-civil libertarian." "If you do not permit General Hershey to speak," he declared, "you are destroying the very fabric of society in which your own values have developed." Rustin insisted that Young, a member of the Mobilization leadership and an active participant in the October 1967 rally in Washington, had the duty to resist "putschism" and elitism. "Who gave two hundred people the right to march on Congress and try to close it down?" To prevent people from doing what they sincerely believed in was violence, said Rustin, and contradicted pacifist principles. Hassler questioned whether the staff should be free to operate in any way they wanted. The key question was whether the FOR was going to be "a healing and reconciling group even within the terms of this society or whether we are a group engaged in confrontation."

When the time came to adopt resolutions, Hassler won some and lost some. The resolution on coalitions to some extent followed Hassler's recommendations. Staff members were to maintain communication with coalition movements and could participate as individuals, but no major part of staff time was to be devoted to such efforts, and the FOR itself was not to be an official part of these coalitions. Exceptions to this rule could be approved by the national council or the executive committee. Clearly running counter to Hassler's thinking, however, was a lengthy and detailed resolution on resistance — authored by McReynolds, Young, and several other council members — which made draft resistance a major concern of the FOR program and staff. An amendment by Rustin that the FOR put equal time into communicating to youth "the mood of reconciliation and love in a program of analysis, education and action" failed to win approval. One council member declared that "he was appalled by the resolution and had never seen a similar attempt by a Board to try to spell out details of program for its Executive Secretary." In another defeat for Hassler, a group of members succeeded in getting the council to adopt a resolution that mandated the executive committee to prepare a public statement on Vietnam calling for the immediate unilateral and unconditional withdrawal of American troops.[7]

The Issue of Withdrawal from Vietnam

The executive committee met on 12 June. Hassler had prepared a statement, "On Vietnam and the Peace Talks," which embodied his own thinking far more than the mandate of the council. As he told the committee, he could not write a statement with which he did not agree. Hassler's draft demanded an immediate end to the bombing of North Vietnam and the right of the NLF to participate both in peace talks and in the formation of a new South Vietnamese government. Instead of calling for an immediate and unconditional withdrawal of American troops, however, Hassler's formulation called for an "explicit, unambiguous commitment to complete American military withdrawal from Vietnam, regardless of the form of government that emerges in that country," and for a standstill cease-fire while the peace talks go on "so that thousands may be kept alive who will otherwise die." Several committee members noted correctly that Hassler's draft statement did not conform to the council mandate, and they succeeded in attaching several amendments to it. One amendment stated that "America's greatness would best be demonstrated by the unilateral and unconditional withdrawal of our forces"; another called for a definite timetable for such a withdrawal and for initiating the removal of the first American units in this timetable.[8]

Hassler himself had acknowledged in his draft statement that some of his proposals were unpolitical and unrealistic, and the same could be said for certain other views he held on the Vietnam conflict. For example, Hassler repeatedly praised the pacifist ideas of the Unified Buddhist Church of Vietnam, attached great importance to their political role, and shared their illusions about the possibility of organizing a coalition government with the NLF and the North Vietnamese Communists. In 1966 Hassler had been instrumental in arranging a lecture tour in America for Thich Nhat Hanh, a leading Buddhist monk and poet who became a member of the FOR and eventually one of its vice presidents. Nhat Hanh demanded an American withdrawal from Vietnam and talks with the NLF leading to the neutralization and eventual unification of Vietnam. He believed that the non-Communist elements in the NLF would prevent a Communist takeover.[9] Hassler shared Nhat Hanh's optimism about reconciliation as a way of ending Vietnam's civil strife. In an exchange with McReynolds in the summer of 1967, he wrote that Nhat Hanh had said that "since the Vietnamese are not barbarians, we should not worry about blood baths," and added, "and I suspect he knows better than either of us does."[10] In due time, both Nhat Hanh and Hassler were to regret their optimism about the basic decency of the Vietnamese Communists.

There were warning signals that should have alerted the Buddhists and their American friends about what lay ahead. In July 1967 an international conference on Vietnam, sponsored by several independent peace organizations and the World Peace Council (WPC), convened in Stockholm. The conference in the Swedish capital was attended by 452 delegates from sixty-two countries, but the WPC forces dominated the proceedings and turned them into a pep rally for the NLF. At the insistence of the NLF, representatives of the Unified Buddhist Church had been excluded from the conference, and the NLF delegates made it clear that in postwar Vietnam, anyone outside of the Front would be branded a traitor and treated accordingly. They hinted strongly that they had no intention of accepting the Buddhists and other petty bourgeois intellectuals preoccupied with Western liberal ideas into a future government of South Vietnam. Some Buddhists found it odd that while Nhat Hanh expected the NLF to share a government with the neutralists, the NLF would not even share a platform with them in Stockholm. Most Americans, however, failed to understand the significance of these events and persisted in their misconceptions about the indigenous character of the NLF and its benevolent patriotic sentiments.[11] Hassler himself, protesting the exclusion of the Buddhists from the conference, refused to attend, yet he continued to argue that the FOR should support Nhat Hanh's striving for dialogue and reconciliation with the NLF.

Meanwhile, the internal divisions within the FOR continued to fester. In July 1968 Hassler took the unusual step of stating his dissenting views in the pages of *Fellowship,* the official organ of the FOR. He acknowledged that the ideas put forth did not reflect any specific actions by either the national council or the executive committee, but they were important and in the spirit of the Fellowship and therefore had to be communicated to the membership. Many in the peace movement, Hassler declared, had become so horrified by American actions in Vietnam that they had moved to the opposite pole and supported anything the NLF and North Vietnam did in the war. They "justify and defend all the means used by the NLF and, in religious terms, substitute for the theology of the just war a theology of the just revolution. This is not a pacifist position." The NLF used terror, assassinations, and the shelling of noncombatants in its struggle. Pacifists had to insist that murder, even in pursuit of the best objectives, was unacceptable. This principle had to be affirmed also in the context of American society, including the struggle of black Americans for a rightful place in that society. Violence was dehumanizing, and to characterize a man by his color, whether this was done by whites or blacks, was to rob him of the uniqueness of his personality.

Hassler argued that the preoccupation with revolution on the part of some elements of the peace movement was similarly ill-advised and dangerous. The majority of Americans were leagues away from any pre-revolutionary frame of mind, and any attempt at a coercive revolution could only result in a right-wing backlash and more repression. Pacifists who threw themselves into reinforcing the disruptive efforts of student radicals while hoping to keep them nonviolent were making a bad situation worse. The issues before the country such as the danger of nuclear war, the challenge of automation, and the threat of ecological catastrophe required "patient inquiry, debate and professional knowledge. Hot commitment will not take us far."[12]

Hassler still had a public platform and was still executive secretary of the FOR, but day-to-day control of the organization was beginning to slip out of his hands. At the meeting of the executive committee in September 1969, Allan Brick, program director of the FOR since the fall of 1968, announced that Ron Young had been "lent" to the New Mobilization to End the War in Vietnam to serve as co-director of the large demonstration planned for Washington on 15 November. Committee member Ross Flanagan questioned this decision. There were reasons to expect that the demonstration would be marked by the display of Vietcong flags and pigs' heads, and violent disruptions were likely. The American people were disillusioned and brutalized by these mass actions, and Flanagan expressed doubt that pacifists should be part of efforts that they could not hope to control. "The more times we lend our pacifist credibility to mass demonstrations that in fact lead to such brutalizing confrontations ... the more we lose our credibility." The FOR, he charged, had been de-democratized, and the executive committee no longer had full control over policy and staff.

Allan Brick responded that projects such as the New Mobilization had their own unpredictable dynamics, but that pacifists had to give the project the benefit of the doubt and "take risks with their reputations in order to be a part of an important manifestation of antiwar sentiment." Most other committee members agreed with Brick and approved of Young's new role as consistent with the decision of the national council in April 1968 that the FOR be involved with aspects of militant resistance. When Hassler was asked for his own personal views on the matter, he indicated that he had expressed serious doubts about these kinds of coalition efforts at the April 1968 council meeting but that his views had been rejected. The decision to release Young to participate in the New Mobilization, therefore, was consistent with the actions taken by the council at that time.[13]

Pacifism and Violence

As predicted by the critics, the demonstrations organized by the New Mobilization resulted in confrontations, violence, and mass arrests. In his report to the national council, which met in May 1970, Hassler voiced his deep concern about the erosion of the pacifist witness "by the rhetoric of anger, cynicism and violence which passes among pacifists for 'rethinking' their nonviolence and pacifism." However, by then Hassler's influence on the policies and pronouncements of the FOR had become limited. A statement entitled "Violence and the United States," adopted by the council, reflected the bitterness, extremist language, and New Left vocabulary of the radical antiwar movement of which the FOR had become an integral part. The major violence of American society, the statement declared, was that practiced by the government of the United States against the people of Southeast Asia and against poor people the world over. At home, poor people suffered malnutrition and disease, had their life spans cut, and, in effect, were being murdered. Abroad, the American "policy of giving military aid to the power structures and financial interest groups that support our military-industrial complex, results in the continued exploitation of the poor in these countries by our society and their own power elite. Indeed," the statement asserted, "the violence both of the war in Southeast Asia and of the widespread exploitation of the poor has its roots in an economic system that is based on enriching the few at the expense of the many. The private profit system is inconsistent with a world society in which individual freedom and the unity of the human family are more than catchwords."

In this situation of state-sanctioned violence, the statement continued, it was inevitable that people would feel justified in using violence for their own ends. The power structure in the United States was increasingly resorting to oppressive and racist practices. The police killings at several black colleges in the South and the National Guard killings at Kent State University were recent examples. "It is such government-sponsored violence against *people* by which the violence done to *property* by some protesters must be measured, with the former being far greater than any kind of violence that has come from groups and individuals on the Far Left. Santa Barbara students who burned a branch of the Bank of America ... committed a very mild act of violence in comparison with, for example, the dropping of 12,000 tons of bombs on South Vietnam by the American high command." After these words of indulgence for revolutionary violence, it was a somewhat lame afterthought for the council to add, "we deplore any apology for violence used for any ends however good they may be. We plead that all who struggle in behalf of humanity dedicate themselves to serious and therefore nonviolent action against the forces that proceed with the war and with the exploitation of poor people."[14] It made little sense for the FOR to counsel nonviolence at a time when its own vituperative rhetoric stirred up anger and hatred.

At the same May 1970 meeting, the national council adopted a resolution calling for a unilateral American cease-fire, the immediate withdrawal of all American forces from Southeast Asia, and an end to any kind of support for the Saigon government. South Vietnamese who felt themselves in danger from what were euphemistically referred to as "subsequent developments" were to be offered sanctuary in the United States.[15] The activists now almost in full control of the FOR had, of course, no expectation that these proposals handing South Vietnam over to the Communists would be accepted by the Nixon administration. On the contrary, in a memo written in July 1970, Allan Brick argued in rather desperate language that the government was "engaged in an expanding multi-front war throughout Indochina" in which it was probable that even China "will be sucked in and/or will be preemptively struck with atomic weapons by our military." Without adequate ground forces, the American policy to "destroy population will increase to even greater levels." Some decisive escalatory move, Brick predicted, was inevitable, and this military escalation would be accompanied by a "sharp move of repression against dissenters at home," including the imprisonment without trial of people active in the antiwar movement and/or of militant blacks.

If this scenario were to come to pass, Brick announced, the antiwar movement and "related social change forces" had decided on a response called t.d.a. — "the day after" — which would involve actions such as the following: "Mill-in's and sit-in's in city halls, State capitols, federal buildings, for the purpose of stopping the operations of government; sit-in's and corresponding actions to stop traffic at key arteries for the purpose of stopping social and economic life in this country from proceeding as usual; turning on electricity and water and letting them run so as to weaken the main sources and further impede the normal functioning of the society." Other actions were being planned by a working party. The role of pacifists was to be twofold: to train in nonviolent direct action and to provide "support and interpretation of those (probably chiefly students) involved in more militant activities." It was important that teams be ready to cope with the "fear and anger" that such "militant activities" would undoubtedly provoke in the community. These teams should explain the reasons for these actions and, at the very least, "appeal rationally to upset people to show what *really* must be done if they want to restore order."[16]

Hassler took strong exception to this call for sabotage and disruption. In a memo entitled "Pacifism and the Problems of the 70s," distributed to the staff in September, he denied that a revolution in America was a historical probability, and he criticized the concept of "the violence of the status quo" and other "seductive assertions" that he saw having a subversive effect on the nature of pacifism. Those who resorted to violence, no matter what their motives, had to be condemned, and to make adherence to nonviolence dependent on the achievement of results was a betrayal of the pacifist creed.

"The pacifist who deals with his faith as a weapon that must work or be discarded is naive and no pacifist." There were situations, Hassler conceded, in which the heaped-up evil of the past was more than could be dealt with by the amount of love and nonviolence capable of being mobilized. In such circumstances the pacifist had to reconcile himself to the agony of being irrelevant and to stand aside unable to affect the course of events. What he could not do, if he was to remain a pacifist, was to throw in his lot with those engaging in violence.[17]

By now, however, Hassler's exhortations asking the FOR to return to the basic principles of pacifism were a largely wasted effort. In December 1970 the national council, now meeting twice yearly, voted to make the People's Peace Treaty—drawn up in Hanoi and embodying the demand of the Provisional Revolutionary Government (PRG) for an unconditional American withdrawal[18]—a major program priority. In January 1971 the executive committee agreed that Ron Young could accept the position of coordinator for the national coalition that would push the treaty and organize mass demonstrations in Washington for April and May. At this moment in history, Young told the committee, pacifism was "being expressed crucially in terms of coalition activities."[19]

By that time the forces opposed to Hassler had also decided to rid themselves of his irritating presence on the staff. When Hassler returned in February from a meeting in Europe, he realized, as he wrote a fellow FOR member, that there now was "an organized putsch on to push me out as Executive Secretary and put Allan [Brick] in."[20] Both Young and Brick, he explained in another letter, had become deeply involved with various coalitions that had "drifted toward the hard left positions." These coalitions had adopted a tone that "contributes to the polarization of the community rather than to its reconciliation, that depersonalizes human beings both by the contempt with which it dismisses 'liberals' and the 'middle class' and by the romanticism with which it categorizes the poor, the blacks, and other minorities by endowing them *as a group* with special admirable qualities." There prevailed "varying degrees of defense or apology for people or groups whose own perception of the needs of justice is violent and divisive." Brick and Young had come under the strong influence of Stewart Meacham, the AFSC's peace education secretary, and, Hassler noted, "I would venture to guess that more of our national program is formulated in meetings with Stewart and others in the group than in meetings with me."[21]

Executive Secretary Hassler Is Eased Out

The national council, which convened in May 1971, met, at the request of the personnel committee, in executive session with no staff members present. This session, which lasted fifteen hours, resulted in a resolution that was discussed and approved the following day. The resolution took note of the tensions that had developed among the staff of the FOR and proposed a reorganization designed to insure better implementation of council policy decisions, including "matters relating to solutions to the Vietnam war, to all revolutionary action in the present age, [and] to collaboration with other organizations or movements." To this end it was proposed that a new executive secretary (called a co-secretary) be secured within the next six months, and that Hassler be reassigned to the newly created post of co-secretary with primary responsibility for international programs. Since 1969 Hassler had also functioned as general secretary of the International Fellowship of Reconciliation, and some members probably thought that after this demotion Hassler would remove himself entirely to Europe. The new chief executive officer was to be an individual "capable of winning persons to religious pacifism [and] interpreting pacifism in relation to contemporary events," an individual "open to new ideas as well as the spawning of new movements." Until the new secretary assumed office, Hassler, Brick, and Young were to continue their respective work assignments. Important decisions were to be made collectively by the entire staff.

Hassler was the loser also in the discussion on how to end the war in Vietnam. The council adopted a resolution, drafted by McReynolds, which called for an immediate unilateral American cease-fire and a total American withdrawal by 31 December 1971. An amendment to this resolution — one that sought to make clear that the FOR sought a unilateral cease-fire and the withdrawal of American forces not in order to help the NLF and North Vietnamese win a military victory but "out of concern for human life and because we oppose American control of another people" — drew the opposition of Brick, Young, and several council members. Brick argued that the amendment sounded like "an anti-Communist disclaimer" and was not necessary. "If there is a feeling that some staff are pro-NLF politically, it is a horrifying thought, and if that is what the statement is getting at, [it] is even worse." Others, however, felt that it was important to make clear the FOR's motivation, and the amendment was approved.

Nobody, of course, could have any illusions about the effect the resolution would have if implemented—its disclaimer amendment notwithstanding. The intent of the council majority was made clear also by its rejection of an alternative strategy for ending the war proposed by Hassler and Thich Nhat Hanh, which called for a worldwide campaign for a general cease-fire to be followed by free elections. By putting the emphasis on a unilateral American cease-fire and withdrawal, the council in effect made sure that the war would go on until the NLF and the North Vietnamese had achieved their objectives. In Hassler's view, this was a complete denial of what pacifism stood for and a failure to uphold the vitality of nonviolence and reconciliation.[22]

While a majority of the council had agreed to dismiss Hassler, there was no consensus on a replacement. Some members supported the candidacy of Allan Brick and warned that the selection of an outsider as executive secretary would lead to the loss of both Brick and Young. Others were hesitant to entrust the leadership of the organization to this ambitious but relatively young man. When Brick realized that he did not have decisive backing for the post he sought, he resigned, and Young left with him. Three months later, Hassler informed the personnel committee that he planned to retire in June 1974. He was not really a "retiring type," he declared, but the year 1971 had been a traumatic experience, and "right now I don't see much chance of recovering the job-enthusiasm that I've had for most of the thirty years I've been with FOR." The deep schisms that had opened up in the organization had to be healed or bridged if the FOR was to amount to anything, but he was no longer the man who could do this. It was important to realize, Hassler wrote, that these schisms had "grown out of the frustrations of the last few years, and the inability of our best efforts, even while we've worked our balls off, to stop the Vietnam war, and our discouraging but human insistence on blaming each other for our failure." Instead of confronting the basic issues of principle and strategy that divided the FOR—and not only the FOR—the personnel committee and others had sought explanations for the problems that had arisen in terms of a clash of personalities and the alleged "authoritarianism" of the FOR's organizational structure.[23]

Hassler also made it clear that in his view collective leadership was unworkable in a large organization. He told the council in May 1972, "I can't have my title suspended and still take the responsibilities without authority." Others gradually realized that Hassler was right, and a year later the "collegium" arrangement was rescinded. For the most part, however, Hassler's constructive role in the FOR had ended. At its May 1972 meeting, the national council once again went on record as demanding the unilateral ending of all American military operations in Indochina, the immediate and unconditional withdrawal of all U.S. forces and advisors, and an end to all military aid to the governments of South Vietnam and Cambodia. The tone of this pronouncement, approved without dissent, was more shrill than ever before and followed the then-fashionable New Left rhetoric. "Stopping the war in Vietnam is both an end in itself and a means for pointing to new personal and social commitment against the military and corporate structures that threaten people here and in other countries. The Vietnam war exposes the military-industrial complex, the American conglomerate empire and those in power who talk of peace while preparing for and fighting wars."[24]

At that time such language was not unusual in "the Movement," and it may help explain why by 1972 the antiwar coalition, divided into several rival sectarian groupings, was in almost complete disarray. After the Paris Peace Agreement of January 1973 had brought an end to the direct American involvement in Vietnam and while the country was full of righteous indignation over the Watergate scandal, Hassler, in one of his last public pronouncements, asked pacifists "to look with some humility at their own actions." Pacifists, he insisted, are not exempt from the end-means temptation, and in the last few years the movement at times had strayed dangerously close to the edge of the cliff over which the Magruders, Porters, and Liddys had toppled.

A good many people in the movement, seeing the origins of the Indochina war in "the system," and recognizing that the institution of war will not be eliminated until the system is changed, let their logic drift into the untenable conclusion that the killing in Indochina could not be ended until the system, especially in the United States, was changed. Consistently then, they became more assiduous for the victory by the other side, which would be a defeat for the system, than for an end to the killing and a transfer of the conflict, which was not all that simple, to the diplomatic arena.

It is a point we pacifists need to get straight in our thinking. The broadest possible alliances are not constructive if they rest on the abandonment of our central belief. War is our first enemy; when we justify it for any ends (which is different from understanding the reasons people go to war) we have lost.[25]

Jim Forest Fights a Rearguard Action

Hassler formally ended his work for the FOR on 30 June 1974. For a short time the new young editor of *Fellowship,* James (Jim) H. Forest, emerged as a successor to Hassler as the keeper of the pacifist conscience in the FOR. In the summer of 1973, Forest published in *Fellowship* an appeal on behalf of imprisoned Soviet dissidents, an action that critics called a revival of the cold war. The October 1973 issue carried major extracts from a letter by Aleksandr Solzhenitsyn in which the Nobel laureate pleaded for a more forthright condemnation of violence committed by the Communist countries. In a brief essay Forest defended both of these editorial decisions. He indicated that he did not agree with all of Solzhenitsyn's reflections, but the Soviet writer's appeal for greater moral integrity was important, especially since it appeared to be a voice in the wilderness.

> Tragically, compassion for the victims of violence usually seems to be a highly partisan matter, highly dependent on where lines lie on maps. It is dreadful that bad governments kill but just and necessary that good governments kill. It is awful that bad governments torture but understandable that good governments do the same. It is unforgivable that bad governments deny freedom of expression and movement, but it is tragic necessity that compels the good governments to do likewise. This double-vision is otherwise known as hypocrisy. It is pretending to hold certain ethical norms while in fact requiring obedience to them only of one's enemies.

The foremost obligation of Americans was to protest the harassment and imprisonment of those for whom the American government had a special responsibility. As an example, Forest referred to the thousands of Vietnamese he alleged to be tortured and incarcerated by the Saigon government. "But there is a mandate to respond to prisoners of conscience elsewhere as well, including those in the USSR. Our first allegiance is, after all, to the planet, not to any state or political group."[26] During the years of the antiwar agitation, Forest had been among those in the FOR arguing for a militant course of action, and he had spent time in prison for participating in a raid on a draft board in Milwaukee. At the same time, unlike most of his fellow pacifists, Forest had never romanticized the Vietnamese Communists, and therefore he did not hesitate to criticize them when he thought such criticism to be appropriate. In the September 1973 issue of *Fellow-*

ship, Forest published an article by Daniel and Philip Berrigan in which the two Catholic peace activists reported on a correspondence with Pham Van Dong, North Vietnam's prime minister, concerning charges of widespread torture made by the American prisoners returned from captivity in North Vietnam. The Berrigan brothers had written to Pham Van Dong on 10 April 1973, addressing him as "our friend in the struggle for human justice." The letter had expressed their "grief and distress of spirit" caused by the testimony of the released prisoners that they had been extensively tortured. "We have been perplexed by this," the brothers noted. It had been the common assumption of the Movement, in which they had been active, that the Vietnamese people, under the most atrocious air assault in history, had shown magnanimity toward the captured fliers. "We were sure that you would not permit even the destroyers of hospitals, schools, pagodas; the destroyers of the sick, of children and the aged — that you would not permit even such men to be degraded in spirit or wounded in body." The Berrigan brothers assured the prime minister that their letter was motivated by "deep love and admiration for the Vietnamese people. We will do everything possible to refute these charges, once the facts are made known to us."

A reply from Hanoi had been received in mid-June, a response written by Tran Trong Quat of the Vietnam Committee for Solidarity with the American People. The North Vietnamese official flatly denied all charges of mistreatment made by the American captives and called them part of a "campaign of slander" launched by the U.S. administration against the government of North Vietnam. That campaign was designed to justify the long American war against Vietnam and Nixon's "further plot of military involvement in Indochina."

After summarizing the correspondence, the Berrigan brothers went on to explain that, in addition to the reasons stated in their letter, they had decided to write to the prime minister of North Vietnam because of their dissatisfaction with the way their fellow peace activists had responded to the allegations made by the returned prisoners.

The American peace movement had taken a position on the charges of torture which ranged from silence through outraged denial. In any and every case, it was an inadequate response, to say the least. There was, as far as we could learn, no unequivocal condemnation of such charges — if true — as the airmen had made. Most peace people, including pacifists, were seriously embarrassed by the charges; one sensed that an idol had fallen in the night. North Vietnam was the unimpeachable hero, undefeatable, vanguard of the human future, ethically out of sight, an angel of light in comparison with the slouching western beast. Now an IF had raised its ugly head. If true, the charges forced us to face, not the *apogee* of our alienated dream, but a nation beset, morally diverse, potentially violent men and women; a nation that had learned with utmost finesse the art of survival, and then (IF) had applied the art to the shrinking flesh of their tormentors.

It was a sad fact of life, the Berrigans wrote, that the peace movement's admiration for an admirable enemy had gradually turned into idolatry of that enemy. "At the same time, one finds nothing, or very nearly nothing of substance to admire, emulate, build on, hope for, cherish in his own culture — including his own community." There were times when one could do little or nothing to right the most atrocious wrong. At such a time, it was necessary to put something on the record. "A kind of human manifesto: that we would not countenance, or ourselves inflict, physical torture or moral degradation, on any other human. Whatever the provocation, whatever the crime."[27]

The Vietnam war era ended for the FOR with Hassler forced out and Jim Forest trying to fight a rearguard action against the dominance of New Left ideology in the Fellowship. When Forest resigned as editor of *Fellowship* in December 1976, the FOR lost a key figure from among the few remaining members able and willing to articulate a truly humanitarian position. From that point on, the politics of the FOR became virtually indistinguishable from that of the AFSC and the rest of the "peace and justice" force, as it likes to call itself.

CHAPTER 4

The Women's International League for Peace and Freedom Supports the Social Revolution

During the early 1960s, the WILPF was a liberal organization that despite its pacifism was in the mainstream of American politics. It criticized government policies with which it disagreed, and it provided active support for policies of which it approved. As the conflict in Southeast Asia began to receive attention, the WILPF advocated negotiations leading to a cease-fire in Vietnam and the neutralization and demilitarization of all of Southeast Asia.

At the 1965 annual meeting, outgoing president Dorothy Hutchinson stressed that while the WILPF sought an end to the war in Vietnam, it did not favor an immediate, unilateral withdrawal of the United States from South Vietnam. The WILPF did not adhere to "the absolute pacifist position, which says that because all war is wrong the United States should withdraw unconditionally from any war in progress regardless of the results to its friends, its enemies, or the United States itself." There should be negotiations between all the parties leading to a cease-fire, and peace terms that did not amount to unconditional surrender for either side. The WILPF, Hutchinson pointed out, was "an organization with a rather unique combination of the spiritual and the intellectual approach to issues of public policy." The League enjoyed the respect of the government and its fellow citizens even when they did not agree with the organization because of the consistency of the WILPF's witness. "This and our *self*-respect depend on our moral and intellectual integrity," noted Hutchinson. To maintain its independence and integrity was the WILPF's "greatest contribution to the present and our most valuable bequest to the future."[1]

WILPF Principles under Attack

In line with its stress on intellectual independence and integrity, the WILPF for many years had refused to collaborate with Communist-sponsored peace drives and had even been wary of sending observers to such gatherings. A proposal to change this policy was debated on the last day of the annual meeting of 1965. By a close vote and with less than half of the delegates present, a motion was adopted urging that the WILPF be represented at all international peace conferences and that national sections be allowed to send observers to such meetings. Also passed was an amendment that this proposal be circulated to the membership and the final decision be made at the next annual meeting.[2]

Orlie Pell was a member of the national executive committee and a former president of the WILPF. She wrote a letter to Elizabeth Polster, the new president of the organization, expressing her unease about WILPF attendance at Communist-run peace congresses. She pointed out that the issue had been brought up at the end of the very last day of the meeting, when many of the delegates, she included, had already left. The affirmative vote, therefore, represented the opinion of a rather limited segment of the membership.

> I'd like to mention, too, that in section IX A of the Principles and Policies approved by this Annual Meeting, we disapprove of an attitude which "equates liberalism with Communism." It seems to me that we ourselves should always be quite clear about the difference. For example, we would not want to confuse our own position in favor of negotiation in Vietnam with the position of those who want a military victory for one side. Won't it be difficult to keep this distinction clear if we participate as the WILPF in a gathering whose official resolution may "hail the brilliant victories" of one side? . . . I think we should ask ourselves very honestly, do the liberals and the Communists mean the same thing by "peace"?[3]

When this issue was brought back to the 1966 annual meeting for final resolution, Hutchinson, representing the international executive committee, explained the rationale of the policy of nonattendance. The WILPF, she pointed out, had always believed that it should have friendly contacts and discussions on any and all subjects with women of any and all ideological and national backgrounds. It therefore had favored intensive two-way political discussions in small groups such as the Soviet-American Women's Conference, with twelve people on each side. Conferences with Communist women on nonpolitical subjects were also possible. At large international congresses, however, WILPF observers had found that no distinction was made between observers and delegates. "Therefore WILPF's name appeared to be among those agreeing with statements which were partisan and inflammatory. This made difficult the work of national sections in their own countries because their effectiveness depended on their maintaining a policy position independent of any ideology or nation."

Hutchinson noted that WILPF observers representing different national sections at times had disagreed with each other and thus had conveyed a blurred image of the WILPF. There also had been cases of such observers acting as if they represented the WILPF officially, which created the impression that the WILPF was in full agreement with the political alignment and objectives of these congresses. While disagreements on domestic issues had begun to surface in several Communist countries, there was still very little freedom to dissent from the government on matters of foreign policy. "Political pronouncements from Communist dominated conferences which deal with international affairs must still be practically identical with Soviet foreign policy. It seems, therefore, that the WILPF cannot associate itself with such pronouncements and still retain the independence and objectivity which are essential to our work."[4]

This discussion within the WILPF took place against the background of a growing New Left, committed to a policy of nonexclusion and anti–anti-communism, and the steady radicalization of the antiwar movement. The American section of the WILPF was not immune to these new currents, and thus Hutchinson's views failed to prevail. In vain did the organization's executive director, Jo Graham, plead for the old sense of responsibility and question the wisdom of sending delegates to international peace conferences independently of the international parent organization. "It is this sense of responsibility that has kept us consistent in the application of our principle that if the use of violence is wrong in the settlement of disputes, it is wrong under all conditions and for all nations and is not to be condoned on occasion in the interests of expediency; and that if civil rights and liberties are a right for citizens of one nation they are also the right of citizens of another nation."[5]

Ignoring Graham's sentiments, the 1966 annual meeting recommended to the international executive committee a new policy
that incorporated a few of Hutchinson's caveats but in the main
was clearly aimed at furthering the WILPF's contact with the World
Peace Council and other such organizations. "It shall be the policy
of WILPF (International) to be represented by observers, whenever
possible, at conferences of international organizations concerned
with world peace," the statement declared. National sections, too,
should be able to appoint observers with knowledge of and loyalty
to WILPF principles. The international appointee should be the
head of the delegation; all members of the group should agree on
points to be made and views to be presented in order to give a clear
account of the WILPF's way of thinking and working.[6]

The international executive committee met in Stockholm in August 1966 and accepted the policy statement proposed by the
American section. At the same time, the committee voted to with-
hold endorsement from the International War Crimes Tribunal organized by the Bertrand Russell Peace Foundation. International
chairman Hutchinson informed the Foundation that the WILPF
objected to the trial of only one side and to the obvious bias of the
proceedings. "A pseudo-legal Tribunal made up of well known but,
in many cases, legally unqualified persons (who are likely to accept
appointment to the Tribunal only if predisposed to declare the guilt
of the accused) proposes to hear evidence of persons from one side
of a war-in-progress against persons of the other side." There was
also the well-known difficulty of verifying reported atrocities while
a war was still going on. It was "for these reasons, and not from
any desire to shield members of the present U.S. administration
from legitimate accusations, that WILPF has declined to associate
itself officially in any way with this War Crimes Tribunal project."[7]

Divisions within the international executive committee were so
pronounced that it took three days to work out a statement on
Vietnam acceptable to most of the members.[8] In the American section, meanwhile, elements sympathetic to the New Left and the
radical antiwar movement were gaining in strength. This faction
favored cooperation with anyone opposed to American policy in
Vietnam and was willing to overlook the participation of violent
fringe groups in these coalitions. Opponents warned that such coalition politics confused the WILPF position in the public eye with
that of organizations and individuals whose methods and goals were
markedly different from those of the League. In a column in *Four
Lights,* the official magazine of the WILPF, Graham complained

that the antiwar movement was increasingly acting in a self-defeating way. This kind of frantic, indiscriminate, and irrational endeavor failed to have a positive effect upon public opinion. "Instead," Graham noted, "it often seems to seek nothing more than a momentary release of personal tensions and frustrations."[9]

The issue became joined over participation in the Spring Mobilization to End the War in Vietnam, and the supporters of full involvement won out. Guidelines voted for at the meeting of the national board in February 1967 required that local branches have a share in planning the call to the demonstrations and the slogans to be carried, but these demands proved difficult to enforce. The radical faction also proposed the adoption of a new policy on civil disobedience. In the past, the WILPF, as an organization, had not officially endorsed or sponsored acts of civil disobedience. The League had maintained that unwise or unjust laws were to be changed through legal methods, though it recognized the right of individuals to refuse to obey a law that offended their conscience. Under the new policy, the WILPF was to be able to support and participate in mass civil disobedience or resistance. Final action on this proposal was to be taken in 1968.[10]

At the annual meeting held in June 1967, the WILPF went on record in favor of a withdrawal of all foreign troops from Vietnam. "Recognizing the possible internal chaos which might ensue following the withdrawal of our troops from Vietnam, we nevertheless feel that this would be minor compared with the death and horror wrought by the present conduct of the war." The statement also called for a cease-fire and withdrawal of support from the military government of South Vietnam "in order to permit the South Vietnamese to form a national coalition government."[11] Hutchinson was among those who recognized the unrealistic character of these demands, but the American section by now was controlled by elements that supported the NLF and sought an unconditional American withdrawal from Vietnam.

Executive Director Jo Graham Resigns

In her October column in *Four Lights,* Graham once again warned that the forces of extremism and anarchy in the country were growing steadily stronger, and she appealed to the WILPF, an organization traditionally committed to nonviolence and opposed to all forms of totalitarianism, to exert its influence in order to preserve democratic values and the possibility of peaceful change. "Recent experience in many cities has shown that reliance upon violence does not solve problems but tends to polarize positions," Graham noted.[12] When, after some hesitation, the executive committee of the WILPF voted to support the Fall Mobilization in the nation's capital on 21 October and that event, like earlier such mass demonstrations, led to violent outbursts and mass arrests, Graham decided to resign her post as executive director.

In a lengthy letter addressed to the national board and the branch chairmen of the WILPF, Graham explained the reasons for her resignation. She noted that she had reached this decision most reluctantly after fifteen years of close involvement with the League. However, conscience and personal integrity required her to object to conditions in the League that she could not condone or ignore. Because she cared deeply about the principles for which the WILPF had stood for fifty-two years, she found it necessary to dissociate herself from the current controlling power bloc within the organization. "During the past months of intimate association with the affairs of the WILPF, it has become increasingly clear that over a period of years a small, vocal and well-organized force in the organization has consolidated its strength by gaining control of most of the national committees, and has exploited the unwary within our membership as well as the many new members who have been frustrated beyond endurance by the inability of thousands of dissenting Americans to end the immoral and infamous war in Vietnam." Extremists of the Far Left, Graham claimed, had seized upon "the genuine desire of sincere and well-meaning people to cooperate in a common goal, to pressure for coalition efforts which further their own selfish propaganda aims and lend an aura of respectability to their cause. But such coalitions weaken, if not completely destroy, the witness of reasonable groups and affect negatively the policy-making governmental leadership and the general public, both of whose support is needed if policy is to be changed." Actions like the rally in front of the Pentagon on 21 October and similar attempts to resolve issues of foreign policy in the streets tended to stimulate the Far Right to increased activity and could usher in a fascist dictatorship.

The issues facing the WILPF, Graham continued, were clear-cut. The question was whether the League was going to be controlled by those who despaired of democratic change and therefore sought the destruction of the present social system, whether the WILPF would "follow the philosophy of those within our membership who are prone to condemn our own government in its conduct of the

Vietnam war as the epitome of all evil, and condone the same wrongdoing when committed by another nation," whether the WILPF would continue to work "within the framework of law or yield to the demands of those members who would endorse general resistance to law." The country faced serious problems, but there was "no crisis, no hysteria so urgent as to justify abandoning the moral and ethical principles for which one stands." The current trend within the WILPF demanded of its staff "a willingness to go along with constant attempts to promote positions and actions contrary to our stated policy. The only other alternative is to resign." To promote the WILPF on the basis of its unimpeachable past record was to mislead innocent and sincere people, Graham declared. "Nor can I remain silent and be used as an instrument in the furthering of a philosophy which I believe to be alien to that of WILPF." Bringing these problems out into the open, Graham concluded, might enable "the great majority of our members, whose basic commitment is to democracy and non-violence, to assert their control."[13]

It is not clear whom Graham had in mind when she spoke of "a small, vocal and well organized force" that had gained control of the League. Communist attempts at infiltration had been a problem for the WILPF during many years, but it appears that both the executive committee and the national board in 1967 were dominated not by Communists but by individuals adhering to the anti-American philosophy of the New Left. In the course of the following years, as we will see, the WILPF did indeed move from a position of anti – anti-communism to an outright pro-Communist stance. Could it be that Graham was able to detect the controlling influence of those responsible for this gradual ideological change already in 1967? We do not know, and those few who may know have wrapped themselves in a tight veil of silence.

The executive committee, meeting on 6-7 December, accepted Graham's resignation with regret. President Katherine (Kay) L. Camp stated that she did not doubt the sincerity of Graham's belief that the WILPF was being undermined, but she regretted the charges made, which might cause the loss of members. Camp felt that the League was committed to the principles of nonviolence and democracy, but the WILPF was also firmly convinced "that methods must be responsive to the times in which we live." It was decided that when the board met in February 1968, they would discuss the policy issues raised in Graham's letter of resignation.[14]

In preparation for this discussion, the board was given a paper prepared by the policy committee, chaired by Naomi Marcus, which denied that the WILPF had taken positions and actions contrary to basic League principles. The paper pointed out that, according to the international constitution of the WILPF, adopted in 1959, one of the aims of the League was "to study, make known and help abolish the political, social, economic and psychological causes of war, and to work for a constructive peace." Therefore, it could be concluded that the WILPF was indeed committed to a change (not the destruction) of the present social system. Whether this change could be carried out within the framework of the law or through civil disobedience and resistance was a subject under study. So far, the WILPF had cooperated only with organizations committed to nonviolence. "I hope," Marcus wrote, "the WILPF will never draw up a 'black list' of organizations with which it will not participate or indiscriminately impugn [sic] 'selfish propaganda aims' to the 'Far Left.' " The WILPF would continue to condemn vigorously the actions of the American government in Vietnam. "We recognize the fact that the violence of war is never confined to one party in the conflict. We can never condone wrongdoing by any nation, but neither can we equate our military action in Vietnam with the actions of the North Vietnamese or the NLF."[15]

The report of the policy committee was discussed at the meeting of the national board on 10 February 1968. In her summary of the report, Marcus stressed that the WILPF did and should include different philosophies. "Some philosophically and honestly believe the present system must be got rid of — are revolutionaries in a good sense." Some favored radical demonstrations and civil disobedience; others sought change through persuasion. A few participants in the discussion warned against working with those in the protest movement who "have been obstructing our government to achieve their ends. Results of their program would be anarchy." The majority, however, favored continuation of the present course of working within the existing coalitions. A motion to "approve the report of the Policy Committee, finding a value in diversity," was approved.[16]

A Process of Radicalization

The 1968 annual meeting, attended by 160 people from sixty-two branches, reflected the growing radicalization of the League. A report entitled "The Politics of Dissent," prepared under the chairmanship of Elise Boulding, urged that the WILPF not isolate itself from "student movements and other radical groups [which] are increasingly committed to direct confrontation of the authorities, and to disruption of establishment functioning as expressions of political dissent." These disruptive activities were engaged in "out of a conviction that traditional methods of orderly dissent are not effective in bringing about changes in our foreign and domestic policy." When WILPF goals were the same as those of such groups, the report recommended, the League "should express support of their aims, even when we cannot in conscience agree with their methods. In our public activities in support of peace and freedom, we should not shrink from confrontations which may, independently of our own intentions, lead to violence by the police or others." A working paper on civil disobedience noted that civil disobedience was likely "in a society which does violence to conscience and represses the aspirations of some of its citizens." However, there was disagreement about whether the WILPF itself should become the organizational sponsor of specific actions of civil disobedience, and a decision on this issue was once again postponed.[17]

By the time of the next annual meeting, held in June 1969, support had crystallized for the adoption of a new policy on civil disobedience. The delegates voted "to permit local branches to sponsor non-violent civil disobedience when a majority of their members felt it necessary either to test the constitutionality of local laws or to give the most forceful possible expression to their support of peace and freedom." The national organization, too, could, after approval by the executive committee, plan or participate in such civil disobedience. That such resort to the violation of law in order to express "support of peace and freedom" effectively circumvented and denied the legitimacy and binding character of the democratic process no longer seemed to trouble the delegates.

The mood of the meeting was militant. It approved recommendations on "creative dissent" that called on the WILPF to "stay in the forefront of the Movement" and to "create new ways of demonstrating the need for total commitment to peace and freedom." Among the actions proposed were "a physical blockade of entrances to several government buildings in Washington, D.C. (i.e. Pentagon, Capitol, Department of Treasury)" and participation by all members in "a national strike, being planned by a coalition of peace groups. In October, we will strike for one day; in November for two, and so on, until the war is over." A resolution on Vietnam noted "that the American military presence and U.S. support of the Saigon regime deny the people of South Vietnam the right to self-determination. We therefore urge that the U.S. withdraw support from the Saigon government, cease military action at once and immediately return all American sea, land and air armed forces and material to the United States."[18]

The process of radicalization continued during the following year, and by 1970 the WILPF had become an integral part of the New Left and the antiwar movement, with most of its pacifist principles in disarray. The motto of the 1970 annual meeting was "Confronting War and Repression"; the keynote speaker was Sidney Peck, co-chairman of the New Mobilization to End the War in Vietnam, whom an advance notice described as "a brilliant speaker who goes to the economic roots of the problems we face."[19]

WILPF president Katherine Camp gave a rousing address in which she noted that the "individual horrors of My Lai, of Kent and Jackson State, of the Cambodian incursion are not matters of chance or caprice but are predetermined by policies of the military mentality in power and predominant in the country, and on the rise throughout the world due largely to the overwhelming influence of the United States of America." This mentality, she said, resulted in the subverting of basic constitutional rights in order to suppress effective threats to the status quo, spurred and exploited racism, and ignored the poor. "It is exploitation by uncontrolled economic enterprise and the planned-for deprivation of the unequal. It is the anti-human attitude which has forged a world-wide anti-communist military alliance and which supplies most of the nations of the world with the machinery of death, in defiance of mankind's best hope for peace, the U.N. It encourages the growing number of military dictatorships throughout the world. Its logical conclusions are apartheid, genocide, and war."

There was a need, Camp continued, for a social revolution in order to change "the System." The WILPF had to make clear its commitment to nonviolence without cutting itself off from those who believed that violence was necessary. "We must be clear in our definitions, recognizing the difference between destruction of property or things and the destruction of lives or people which is the correct definition of violence." Camp insisted that the impetuous acts of America's youth, saturated with violence by consumption and the television culture, should not be equated "with the institutionalized violence of our government in the deliberate, premeditated massive murder that is warfare."[20]

The 1970 annual meeting featured panels on U.S. imperialism, racism, repression and resistance, and women's liberation, but for the Caucus for Radical Economic Change, this did not go far enough. This group of about forty delegates "felt a certain frustration in that they felt the Annual Meeting was addressing itself to symptoms rather than causes." The caucus stated its belief that "our imperialistic policies, our racist society and increasingly repressive reaction have their roots in our economic system. Having economic control in the hands of a few causes the exploitation of the many. It has been pointed out by numerous economists that capitalism depends on a work force that can be exploited. Without basic changes in our economic structure, without changing the profit motive, we can only change the symptoms, not the causes of the problems." The caucus proposed that the WILPF consider adopting projects aimed at changing America's economic system, including the development of contacts with working-class women and "a campaign to get Congress to set a maximum limit on income, for example, $15,000 per person."[21]

Among the actions taken by the League at the meeting was the adoption of a statement on world revolution. In a "period like the present," the statement read, "when society is basically military and exploitative, 'peace' people and organizations rightly find themselves on the side of those who feel oppressed (women, students, Blacks, poor, for example) advocating rapid change (revolution)." But whereas the oppressed focused entirely on the end of liberation, pacifists believed "that ends are inextricably bound up with the means employed, that violence begets more violence and . . . that non-violent means are more apt to result in less violence and at least a chance for the development of brotherhood. Hence the insistence of WILPF on *non-violent* methods of change. But it is more important to right wrongs and stand with the oppressed than to insist on method. Even Gandhiji, master of non-violence, insisted that it was better to oppose evil by any means than supinely to accept it and cooperate with it."

The delegates voted to send this statement, which effectively abandoned the organization's overriding commitment to nonviolence, to the international executive committee of the WILPF.[22] That body discussed the statement of the U.S. section at the end of July 1970 and decided that since it related "to the opposition to violence which has been basic to WILPF work," the subject should be taken up by the 18th International Congress of the WILPF scheduled to meet in New Delhi in December 1970. To this end, the committee adopted its own statement on world revolution, which followed the formulation of the U.S. statement with regard to the link between means and ends but then continued with a new paragraph:

It is essential to resist injustice and to be neither silent witness nor passive victims of oppression. We recognize the necessity for the active resistance of the oppressed, and we do not condemn them for using violent means when they see no other alternative. However, the Women's International League for Peace and Freedom, which has no faith in violence, must seek to share the experience of those who are striving for their freedom and should explore with them non-violent resistance techniques and take an active part in any resulting non-violent campaigns.[23]

When the international congress of the WILPF met in December 1970, it had before it the draft of resolutions of the U.S. section and of the international executive committee as well as a third resolution submitted by the Norwegian section. The Norwegians termed both draft resolutions on "world revolution" contrary to the WILPF constitution and instead proposed the following statement: "The recognition of violence in the social and national liberation movements will weaken the peace organizations' efforts to find alternatives to violence, and their future work in order to find ways and means of peaceful settlements of disputes."[24] The resolution that was finally adopted by the congress was ambiguous, although, like the American draft, it leaned toward accepting the legitimacy of revolutionary violence:

A society that is military and exploitative generates movements for rapid change toward social justice. It is a human right to resist injustice and to be neither silent witness nor passive victim of repression. We recognize the inevitability of violent resistance by the oppressed when other alternatives have failed even though we recognize that violence creates more problems than it solves.

The WILPF has a duty to make the public aware of the problems of the oppressed and exploited; to analyze the structure of power in society and the use made of it; to study and work towards developing methods for the effective use of non-violent means, [and] to engage ourselves actively in non-violent movements for change.[25]

Within the American section the debate over the question of revolutionary violence continued, although this dispute over a theoretical principle did not prevent the WILPF from continuing its active involvement in the radical antiwar movement. The WILPF participated in the April 1971 demonstrations organized by the National Peace Action Coalition, dominated by the Trotskyite Socialist Workers party, and by the People's Coalition for Peace and Justice, in which the Communist party played a strong role. The Biennial Meeting of the WILPF in June 1973 once again took up the issue of violence and national liberation movements, but by that time the direct American involvement in the war in Vietnam had ended, and the militants within the WILPF, many of them openly sympathetic to Marxist ideas, had moved into a commanding lead.

CHAPTER 5

The War Resisters League and United Front Politics

Of the four major pacifist organizations in the United States, the War Resisters League (WRL) has always been the least cohesive. The WRL has sought to combine radical pacifism, democratic socialism, and philosophical anarchism, and this ideological mix does not lead to very coherent positions or provide the basis for a tightly run organization. Often WRL policy has been simply what some of its leading personalities have written in the pages of the magazines supported by the League — *Liberation,* founded in 1956, and *WIN* (Workshop in Nonviolence), established in 1965. When, in the middle of the 1960s, the WRL began to embrace also the tenets of the counterculture, the freewheeling character of the League became even more pronounced.

Divisions over Revolutionary Nonviolence

The WRL has always taken pride in its commitment to revolutionary nonviolence and its support of a decentralized, egalitarian, and classless society. It was therefore not surprising that from the beginning of the Vietnam war, many members of the WRL and its close ally, the Committee for Nonviolent Action (CNVA), expressed sympathy for the NLF and took an active part in the unfolding antiwar movement. The WRL was a participant in the planning and preparation of the March on Washington organized by Students for a Democratic Society (SDS) on 17 April 1965. In an article reflecting on the march, Dave Dellinger, editor of *Liberation,* noted the danger that students and others would turn toward the acceptance of violence. The United States, Dellinger conceded, was "the chief threat to the freedom, dignity, economic advancement and self-government of underprivileged peoples," while support for these

89

aspirations came from various guerilla movements. Accordingly, students might conclude that guerilla warfare provided the best hope. Believers in nonviolence, who regarded *all* war and violence as a trap, had to oppose this tendency and show that one could be "both adequately revolutionary and genuinely nonviolent."

This did not mean, Dellinger insisted, that radical pacifists should see liberation movements that resort to violence as being on a par with the Pentagon and the American military-industrial complex. "Those of us who believe in the revolutionary potential of non-violence should become more actively revolutionary, and in the process of becoming so, have a great deal to learn from heroic forces like the Cuban Fidelistas and the Vietcong, even though we are saddened by, and must speak out against, bloodletting, intolerance, and all failures to recognize the fact that our worst enemies are still human beings, not too different from ourselves."[1]

Dellinger's position drew sharp criticism from Robert Pickus, a member of the CNVA and the West Coast director of Turn Toward Peace, a coalition of some sixty national organizations organized in 1961 in order to build momentum for disarmament without surrendering democratic values. Pickus called Dellinger "a former pacifist" because, in the conflict between the demand for justice and the commitment to nonviolence, Dellinger had abandoned his ad-herence to nonviolence and supported political forces that used mass violence to advance a conception of justice that he (Dellinger) favored. "Political integrity requires that pacifist tenets be applied to all power centers engaged in a violent conflict," Pickus claimed. A pacifist could not condemn the violence of one side and ignore or apologize for the violence of the other.

Dellinger's indulgent view of revolutionary violence, Pickus wrote, was part of a trend that had been developing in pacifist circles for several years. "It is in good part the fruit of a romantic attachment to revolution and an inaccurate perception of the realities of the third world along with a blind and unthoughtful anti – anti-Com-munism as foolish and mistaken as the ritual anti-Communism of America it is designed to correct." The deep alienation from Amer-ican society accompanying this attitude, Pickus suggested, was the result of "a vulgarized quasi-Marxist political analysis which locates the whole problem of twentieth-century international conflict in the structure of American economics and evil motivations of an Amer-ican power elite." The March on Washington, with its policy of not excluding anyone, marked the first significant reappearance of United Front politics in the American peace movement. This policy of nonexclusion, popular with the New Left and a new generation of young people whose first political lesson was that anti-communism was McCarthyism, was a mistake. Pacifists could not cooperate with those who regarded murder as a legitimate way of pursuing political objectives. It should be possible, Pickus argued, to distinguish between those who opposed American violence in Vietnam because of their principled opposition to all violence and those who opposed American policy because they wanted a Vietcong victory. These distinctions were crucial, and pacifists had to make clear their goals and values.[2]

A. J. Muste, a member of the WRL executive committee and of the editorial board of *Liberation,* wrote an article in the same issue of the magazine. He took a position somewhere in between Dellinger and Pickus. Muste agreed that it was politically naive to welcome the collaboration or co-sponsorship of any organization that accepted the objectives and slogans of a particular demonstration and was willing to adhere to a nonviolent discipline regardless of what other objectives it might have or what its behavior might have been on other occasions. Pacifists should not engage in joint activities or co-sponsorship with organizations that condoned revolutionary violence, although no individual should be excluded from actions under nonviolent discipline. At the same time, Muste argued that pacifists had to be aware of the danger of "fronting" with questionable groups on the right as well as on the left. Moreover, the Communist world now was different from that of the Stalin era, and one had to be on guard against McCarthyite attitudes and practices. "I firmly believe that the 'dialogue' with the Communist elements and Communist countries must be maintained," he stated.[3]

The debate started by Dellinger in May 1965 continued during the following months. Robert Gilmore and Bayard Rustin, both members of the CNVA executive committee, sided with Pickus; Staughton Lynd, a newcomer, supported Dellinger. In a reply to his critics published in the August 1965 issue of *Liberation,* Dellinger denied that expressions of sympathy for the Vietcong represented a betrayal of nonviolence. Was it not possible "to look approvingly on the *struggle* of the National Liberation Front without endorsing or applauding its violence?" Instead of adopting a "plague on both sides" stance, Dellinger argued, American pacifists should commit themselves to the historic struggle for liberation. "[We should] step up the tempo of our nonviolent action here in the United States, to try to stop American aggression at its source rather than leave the whole burden on those who suffer its impact." Pacifists might also consider offering "nonviolent assistance to those who are struggling in their own way for freedom and justice, dignity and self-liberation from Western domination."[4]

In a letter to the editors of *Liberation*, Charles Bloomstein, vice chairman of the WRL, raised the question about whether *Liberation* was still fully committed to pacifism, freedom, and justice as defined by the first group of editors in 1956. Some recent articles had reflected "a form of revolutionary barricade psychology which declares that failure to go along with this [or that] particular self-avowed radicalism means coalition with the Marines and reactionary politics." Criticizing Muste, Bloomstein insisted on the difference between "fronting" with liberals who opposed the war in Vietnam and with Marxists like those belonging to the DuBois Clubs and the Trotskyite Young Socialist Alliance, groups that sought to continue the war until a Vietcong victory had been achieved. "They seek goals embodying values quite opposed to those originally sought by *Liberation*. From the moral point of view it is difficult to justify joining a common cause with these elements." Such an alliance would also make it impossible to bring the American people into the peace effort.

Pacifists, Bloomstein argued, had to be clear in their attitude toward Communist regimes. The logic of supporting a revolutionary regime like Castro's Cuba, as Dellinger had proposed, was "inexorable — one either overlooks the violence or eventually excuses it." Dellinger had done just that. He had slurred over the violence, and his deploring it was mere lip service, since he supported the revolution despite its serious faults. Dellinger had described Communist regimes as experiments worth watching. "By what stretch of the imagination," Bloomstein asked, "can the regimes of the Soviet Union, China, Hanoi, the satellites, Cuba, and so on be called experiments? Does one suppress opposing political parties in an experiment? Does one imprison and execute political opponents in an experiment? Does one regiment an entire population in an experiment?" Dellinger had called these regimes experiments, Bloomstein claimed, because his excuses were thus prepared in advance — any experiment can go wrong. "No, I am afraid that Dellinger really does not support the revolution's aims while opposing its methods. He supports the revolution."[5]

During the course of the year 1966, CNVA leaders Muste and Bradford Lyttle were in the forefront of those who urged radical pacifists to become actively involved in mass antiwar protests and civil disobedience. Muste now had fully embraced the New Left's principle of nonexclusion, which he defended as "necessary to the political health of the nation. People of the Left (Communists with or without quotation marks) should be permitted and expected to function normally in the political life of the country." One could not effectively combat the deep-rooted anti-Communist psychology of the American people, Muste argued, if at the same time one excluded Communists from the antiwar movement. A non-Communist coalition, moreover, would seek allies to the right and thus become too moderate and restrained in its resistance to the war. Finally, there was the pragmatic consideration that the Old and the New Left represented the most activist core of the radical antiwar coalition. "What clinches the matter is that if we were to abandon the 'non-exclusion' principle we would quickly disintegrate," Muste claimed.[6]

While Muste continued to affirm his commitment to nonviolence, he now argued that "politically sophisticated pacifists" had to make "a distinction between the violence of liberation movements (of people who, in a situation where they have no real possibility of democratic means, resort to violence) and the violence imposed upon these countries by the imperialist powers, for example, the violence which the United States is carrying out in Vietnam at the present time." The U.S. was the main obstacle to peace and human development in the world, and Americans, whether as pacifists or as revolutionaries, had to oppose U.S. military and foreign policy to the utmost. What this came down to, Muste acknowledged, was that pacifists had to be on the side of the NLF and North Vietnam, even though they engaged in violent struggle, because they were in a morally superior position. One had to be "for the defeat of the United States in this war," Muste insisted. "I just don't see how anybody can be for anything except withdrawal or defeat." It was to be hoped that the coalition government that would emerge in South Vietnam after the end of American support for the Saigon government would give non-Communists and Buddhists a strong voice. But even if some kind of Communist purge were to take place, it was not up to the Americans to decide how the Vietnamese were to run their political affairs.[7]

A very similar position was taken by David McReynolds, a WRL field secretary and an influential figure in the day-to-day operation of the League. Pacifists, McReynolds argued, should not condone the terrorism of the NLF, but neither should they condemn it. Absolute pacifism might be a mistake. In some situations it was the violent position that was in fact the moral position. Only an American withdrawal from Vietnam might make possible a nonviolent solution. With the Americans there in force, pacifists had no non-violent answer to the problem of Vietnam. Pacifists had to be "less judgmental about those who are not following the pacifist position. We must accept the fact that there may be times and places when what is for us a personal imperative may not be for them a personal imperative and also may not be a political reality. And in that sense we would not be absolute pacifists." A broad-based coalition against the American role in Vietnam, even if it included some Communists and Trotskyites, was less of an evil than a coalition with liberals who were critical of the war but still supported President Johnson.[8]

Many West Coast leaders of the WRL were opposed to the de-mand for an unconditional American withdrawal from Vietnam, and they opposed the alliance with the New Left urged by Lyttle, Muste, and McReynolds. However, at a meeting of the executive committee held in November 1966, a set of principles was approved that went a long way toward accepting the kind of coalition policy favored by most of the East Coast leadership. The statement that was adopted in principle but was to be subject to further discussion affirmed the WRL's opposition to violence and forms of totalitari-anism. "We know that there are differences between wars and that the aim of the violent revolutionist is often more just than the cause of those violently defending the status quo. But we are convinced that means and ends cannot be separated: terror, violence and repression will not result in a free society."

Within this context of a commitment to nonviolence, the state-ment continued, WRL members could display a wide variety of religious, philosophical, and political beliefs. "The absence of a nar-row political program in the League encourages the widest exper-imentation with the theories and practices of nonviolence." WRL members in a given area should use their own judgment about whether to take part in a particular coalition effort against the war in Vietnam. Coalitions with Communists were not ruled out in principle—"we do share with the Communists a deep concern for profound social change"—and a creative dialogue with the Com-munist party had to be continued, the statement urged, despite the Communists' willingness to use violence. Association with the New Left, too, could be mutually beneficial. "For all its faults it is one of the few inherently healthy and exciting developments in the U.S. of the last decade." The New Left had "a sense of enthusiasm and innocence some of us have lost and should regain." In any such coalition, WRL members should make an effort to present the pacifist position and affirm that the League was for peace in Vietnam, not for a victory of the NLF. Demonstrations should reflect the WRL's belief in nonviolence and not be "ultramilitant."[9]

Vice Chairman Charles Bloomstein Resigns

A final draft of this statement was discussed at a meeting of the WRL executive committee on 13 June 1967. Vice chairman Bloomstein was unable to be present but submitted lengthy critical comments. Bloomstein found the opening portion unexceptional but objected to the idea that pacifists could work with Communists and adherents of the New Left as well as with liberals and democrats. Violence was central to Communist ideology; they did not seek the same kind of social change as pacifists. "Like all authoritarians, they seek a society in which the individual is not liberated but basically exists to serve the larger mass, defined as the state." The New Left, Bloomstein argued, was not a "healthy" development but rather an influence that diverted and distorted the healthy instincts of young people. "The extremism with which the 'new left' castigates American society is the reverse of pacifism, which seeks to reconcile not to polarize, . . . not to denounce evil men and stress a devil theory. The 'new left' is based on loving, but oddly it loves only its friends — it reserves the vilest contempt for its opponents." Such tactics strengthened the Right, Bloomstein claimed, and would "eventually drive the left into conspiratorial underground romanticism or, more likely, into desertion and apathy." Pacifists had to work with these young people, but they could do this best by holding up their own standard, "by confronting them with clarity and sharpness, highlighting our differences, rather than fawning and pandering."[10]

When Bloomstein realized that his views had no chance to prevail within the WRL, he withdrew from any active involvement. On 27 June he submitted his resignation as a contributor to *Liberation*. The magazine, Bloomstein wrote, had indirectly but consistently accepted violence as a legitimate alternative in the struggle against oppression. "I no longer consider *Liberation* to be a pacifist magazine and feel that its present trend is taking it further away from that position."[11] On 6 October Bloomstein resigned as vice chairman of the WRL and as a member of the executive committee. After twenty-nine years of active membership, he noted, this had not been an easy decision. "But I am convinced that the course the

Executive Committee seems firmly set on is damaging to pacifism. I cannot in honor be a part of it."

Bloomstein insisted that pacifists should seek to bring a genuinely radical thrust to peace activity instead of supporting spurious and emotional catharsis that passes for radicalism. The WRL had failed to confront the New Left and the advocates of Black Power with a principled, developed pacifist position. Major problems of style, tone, politics, and program were glossed over in order to facilitate cooperation. "Pacifists, specifically the WRL, did not see it as their responsibility to hold up their own flag, to force discussion on root issues and values, to resist hostility and alienation as the main thrust. The result might very well have been the same, but we shall never know since the effort was never made."

With regard to Vietnam, Bloomstein argued that the pacifist objective should be to stop the killing as soon as possible, not to favor a military victory of the NLF. Simplistic and ambiguous slogans about immediate or unilateral withdrawal were of no help. "Despite lip service to the need for a variegated pacifism, it is clear that the WRL Executive Committee believes that the answer to LBJ's escalation of the war is our escalation of protest and civil disobedience. I find both escalations equally irrational and mindless. Neither deals with what is essentially a political problem, and neither will be effective or constructive." In order to end the war, Bloomstein insisted, pacifists had to win over the middle class of America, which constituted the majority of the people. Seeking allies only among the young, the hippies, the Black Power advocates, and the dispossessed was a guarantee of failure. "The generalized alienation and hostility they represent may be effective in a revolutionary situation (in which case I would hope that pacifists would oppose a revolution based on such emotions), but surely no one in his right mind would even dream of describing America as on the brink of revolution."

Present WRL policies, Bloomstein maintained, were basically irrelevant. "Protest and civil disobedience are essential elements in any well-rounded program, but when they become the sole thrust, the use of oversimplified slogans dominates and real educational possibilities are lost." The WRL had not even found a way of functioning in a constructive, pacifist manner in the Mobilization to End the War in Vietnam and instead simply went along with whatever happened there. Useful and necessary work to achieve a military withdrawal from Vietnam had to be done, but the WRL was not the vehicle for it. "I am a pacifist and wish to retain my membership in the League. But my activity will have to be expressed elsewhere, and I can no longer, in good conscience, be a League officer or serve on the Executive Committee."[12]

Bloomstein's views were seconded by Lawrence Scott, a Quaker activist close to the CNVA and a member of the national advisory council of the WRL. In a paper entitled "Harmony of Ends and Means," Scott criticized the antiwar movement for its routine reliance on civil disobedience. This means of protest was a very serious matter. "It should be entered only as a last resort and then in a spirit and manner so as to enhance and bear witness to the need for more moral and equitable laws and governmental practices." Moreover, the widespread use of the tactic of noncooperation with arrest and court procedures tended to divert the witness made against a specific law or an immoral practice of government into a witness against the principle of government itself. Pacifists were not anarchists. They sought to build a viable community with a democratic government based on the rule of law; they favored the elimination of international anarchy, which was one of the primary causes of war. By resisting arrest and refusing to cooperate with the courts, pacifists undermined their own end.

Scott also took exception to the tactic of obstructing and blocking access to war plants, induction centers, and other government installations. Such obstructions did not work, he claimed; to try to force people to do something against their will misses the whole meaning of the power of nonviolence. "Nonviolence morally disarms the opponent. Obstruction morally arms the opponent and increases his will to continue doing what he is doing. Nonviolence speaks to the rational in the opponent; obstruction enhances the irrational. In the final analysis nonviolent action at government and military installations must be an appeal to the citizens of a country for a change of heart and policy. Attempts to obstruct and deprive citizens of military means which they think is their security only increases their fear and delusion." By resorting to such tactics, Scott noted, radical pacifists had antagonized the large majority of the American people. "Noncooperation with the principle of government, laws and courts, attempts to obstruct and the creation of disorder and chaos make men cling the tighter to armed nationalism." Feeling irrelevant and isolated, pacifists of late had begun to make common cause with violent groups. The first aberration involved "a mistake in tactics, the latter a loss of integrity."[13]

The Drift toward Confrontation and Resistance

The views of Bloomstein and Scott failed to prevail, and the WRL continued on its course toward more militancy. Occasionally, WRL and CNVA members, acting as marshals, were able to prevent violence at antiwar demonstrations, but more often radical pacifists were unable or unwilling to halt the steady drift of the antiwar movement in the direction of confrontation and resistance. Frustrated by their inability to halt the deepening involvement of the United States in the Vietnam conflict, pacifists increasingly grabbed any allies they could find, and the principle of nonexclusion served as the theoretical rationale for this policy. The strategy of exclusion, wrote Bradford Lyttle in May 1967, represented a violation of the principles of love, brotherhood, and community. "A pacifist should be willing to associate publicly with anyone, communist, liberal or right winger for the purpose of achieving common goals."[14]

The death of A. J. Muste at age eighty-two in 1967 removed the one person whom both sides in this controversy had respected and who might have acted as a conciliator. After the CNVA merged with the WRL in December 1967, the League increasingly lost its distinct pacifist identity and came to be perceived as simply one of the many militant factions in the antiwar movement.

The question of what Vietnam policy pacifists should support was debated once more in early 1968 in the pages of *Fellowship*. David McReynolds defended the policy of an immediate and unilateral withdrawal of American forces from Vietnam. The struggle there, he argued, was basically a struggle of Vietnamese nationalism against foreign domination. The fact that the leadership of this struggle was Communist was irrelevant because it was a Vietnamese communism, independent of Moscow and Peking. McReynolds acknowledged that an American withdrawal would most likely lead to a Communist takeover, followed by the suppression of religious and political minorities. "But I am utterly opposed to using the armed forces of the United States to prevent the Vietnamese from following this course," he declared. The U.S. had no right of any kind, legal or moral, to determine the political future of Vietnam.[15]

Robert Pickus rejected the view that the war was simply a struggle of Vietnamese nationalism against foreign domination. "That is Hanoi's view of the war and, given present leadership, it is common fare in the American peace movement. But such a view ignores those nationalists who oppose foreign domination but *also* the N.L.F." Hanoi and the NLF sought to impose their will upon the

South by force. Pickus argued that pacifists should not simply regard this violence as none of their business and urge the U.S. to walk away from it. Such a withdrawal would not end the killing. Instead, Pickus proposed a cease-fire and negotiations leading to free elections, supervised by an international authority, that would give the people of Vietnam the opportunity to determine their own future. Such a policy not only was in the interest of the people of Vietnam but also was an important step toward increasing the peace-making capability of the international community, a step in the direction of a world without war.

The American pacifist movement, Pickus warned, was in serious trouble. The recent resignations of Jo Graham as executive director of the WILPF and of Charles Bloomstein as vice chairman of the WRL were indications of this crisis. "In community after community, I see some pacifists providing a cover of genuine moral indignation for activity that strengthens the very evils they would resist: hatred, violence, the resolution of conflict by the contest of alternate armed camps, each seeking to kill its way to power." Such pacifists adopted the slogans and lies of one side in the war, that of Hanoi, and followed leadership committed to a victory for that side. "It is not surprising that American liberals of past popular front experience, or that people new in politics and rightly reacting to the horror of present U.S. policy, should take this course," Pickus noted. "But it is deeply depressing when it is taken by experienced pacifists."[16]

While McReynolds and other WRL leaders affirmed their continuing commitment to nonviolence and expressed their regret at the violence perpetrated by the Vietcong, they at the same time believed that the NLF represented a movement for liberation that deserved their support. In their view, the Vietnamese Communists were different from Soviet and Chinese Communists. Consequently, radical pacifists seeking a world free of all subjugation and exploitation could not be neutral in a conflict between capitalist, imperialist America and the Vietcong, who sought to liberate their country from all foreign influence and bring land reform and other measures of social welfare to their people. In this situation American pacifists had a positive duty to remove the United States as a participant in the conflict. Pickus, therefore, was correct when he saw little difference between the position of the Left in the antiwar movement, who openly favored a military victory of the NLF and Hanoi, and the position of pacifists like McReynolds of the WRL and Stewart

99

Meacham of the AFSC, who sought to promote the same result by working for a unilateral American withdrawal from Vietnam.

The intellectual premises of the WRL position were well articulated in a working paper entitled "On Wars of Liberation," adopted by the council of the War Resisters International (WRI), the parent body of the American WRL, at a meeting in Vienna in August 1968. The WRI, the statement began, "is first of all a freedom movement. We work for man's right to freedom: freedom to live without hunger, war, pestilence: freedom to live without economic, social, racial, and cultural exploitation." From the belief in freedom stemmed the WRI's "opposition to war, and to systems, which exploit and corrupt, such as colonialism, capitalism, and totalitarian communism." In addition to the direct violence of guns and bombs, "there was the silent violence of disease, hunger, and the dehumanization of men and women caught up in exploitative systems." The WRI therefore worked for "nothing less than a total nonviolent revolution. Our pacifism and the war resistance take their place in this total vision of liberated man."

The experience of the twentieth century, the paper continued, had shown that violence, whether used in war or in revolution, failed to bring about human liberation. Fifty million people had perished in the war against the Fascist axis, a war that culminated in the dropping of two atomic bombs and left the American people brutalized and insensitive to guilt. The violent struggle in Vietnam had been going on for twenty-two years, and the revolution had not been won. The Russian revolution, which began as a heroic experiment, "eventually produced a State which killed millions of its own citizens in purges and forced labor camps, oppressed the nations of Eastern Europe, and to this day is still imprisoning writers who seek to exercise the most elementary freedoms." These consequences were in large part due to "the basic mistake of thinking that violence, both during the revolution and in solving economic and social problems, could bring justice and freedom."

After this principled condemnation of all forms of violence came a qualified endorsement of liberation movements even though they used violence—the kind of non sequitur common in the radical pacifist camp. The statement affirmed that men "should not organize violence against one another, whether in revolution, in civil war, or in wars between nations."

But our unwavering commitment to nonviolence does not mean

that we are hostile to the revolutionary movements of our time, even though on certain fundamental issues we may disagree with some of them. It is impossible for us to be morally 'neutral,' for example, in the struggle between the people of Vietnam and the American Government, any more than we were able to be morally 'neutral' 12 years ago in the struggle between the people of Hungary and the Soviet Union. We do not support the violent *means* used by the NLF and Hanoi, but we do support their *objective* in seeking the liberation of Vietnam from foreign domination. . . . Clearly one has to distinguish between the violence of the Americans — which is criminal — and that of the people of Vietnam — which, by contrast, is tragic.

Pacifists could make the greatest single contribution to the liberation movements "not by becoming entangled in the debate over whether or not such movements should use violence, but by actively working to bring an end to colonialism and imperialism by attacking its centers of power in the West." The statement ended with a salute to those who used nonviolent action in their struggle as well as to "our brothers and sisters in the various liberation movements." The WRI would work with them when possible, but without abandoning the belief "that a society without violence must begin with revolutionists who will not use violence."[17]

The advice that the WRI statement gave to pacifists — not to become entangled in the theoretical debate over the legitimacy of revolutionary violence and instead to aid the liberation movements by working against their opponents in the Western democracies, especially the United States — had been followed by Dave Dellinger, editor of *Liberation,* from the beginning of the American involvement in Vietnam. In 1967 Dellinger became chairman of the National Mobilization to End the War in Vietnam. Here he found support for his view that traditional methods of civil disobedience were no longer adequate and that new, more militant tactics were necessary. In the summer of 1968, Dellinger participated in planning a series of demonstrations to be held around the convention of the Democratic party in Chicago. Rennie Davis and Tom Hayden, the two veterans of the SDS who drew up the plans for this campaign, emphasized that the demonstrations were to be nonviolent, but they also spoke of "a massive confrontation with our government" and an "attack on the Democratic convention," which seemed to encourage more militant actions.[18]

The Refusal to Disavow Violence

After the demonstrations had indeed ended in violent clashes with the Chicago police, Dellinger was questioned about his role in these events by the House Committee on Un-American Activities. He described himself as a "nonviolent revolutionist," devoted to revolutionary change as well as opposed to violence. At the same time, Dellinger stressed that he was willing to work with anyone who could help bring the war to an end. The Mobilization, he informed the Committee, included groups whose beliefs ranged from pacifism to militant self-defense. The coalition was not owned by any one segment and did not dictate the tactics to be employed by its different constituents. Dellinger explained that he personally took the same position. "I advocate nonviolence. I practice nonviolence, but I do not repudiate or oppose what I sometimes call the violence of the victims." Considering the menace posed by "the American imperialist aggression throughout the world today," it was not surprising that some people would resort to violence. The traditional nonviolent movement, Dellinger told the Committee, "has been much too passive and much too ineffective and I am not interested in the purity of the movement. I am interested in social effectiveness."[19]

By 1969 the leadership of the WRL had come to share fully Dellinger's militant views, including the need for pacifists, liberals, hippies, yippies, New Leftists, and Old Leftists to work together in order to stop the war. When the unifying factor, as Dellinger explained, was "the dynamic one of individual actions jointly undertaken, questions about political reliability and future loyalty recede into the background."[20] The WRL embraced the slogan "From Dissent to Resistance," including the promotion of resistance in the armed forces. In May 1971 the League was the only national peace group to endorse fully the week-long demonstrations in Washington organized by Rennie Davis's "May Day Tribe," which had the avowed purpose of bringing the activities of the government to a halt. The League assigned a staff member, Jerry Coffin, to work full-time with the May Day Tribe and to produce its tactical manual.[21]

Ironically, Dellinger now found himself in the position of the sorcerer who could not control his apprentice. In a letter to Bloomstein written in April 1969, Dellinger noted that until now he had tried "to educate the pacifists on the violent nature of American institutions. And now we have entered a period when it is more and more crucial to educate the new 'revolutionists' on the traps of violence and on the necessity for nonviolence." In the future, Del-linger said, *Liberation* "will be increasingly stressing the importance of nonviolence as 'infantile leftism' tends to become more and more of a current danger in the movement."[22]

Yet Dellinger's apprehension about the drift of the Movement into violence was mainly a prudential concern that these tactics would not work. "There are serious arguments that can be made for the uses of revolutionary violence," he wrote in *Liberation* in the fall of 1970. The question of "whether or not there are times when it is productive for some groups to use the gun as a carefully controlled supplement to other methods of struggle" was one he was willing to leave open. The whole issue of violence had arisen because of the nature of the violent society and system in which Americans were forced to live. "All the violence of the movement in the last five years," he wrote, "had not equalled the violence of a single B-52 bomber vomiting death and destruction on Laos."[23]

WRL staffer McReynolds, reflecting on the "Spring Offensive" of 1971 in the nation's capital, was gratified by "the largest single nonviolent action in American history," which had been a success despite certain blunders by the organizers. "The most hilarious and inexplicable snafu of the entire Spring Offensive came when the May Day Tribe was trying to block the 14th Street bridge at exactly the same time a contingent from the People's Coalition [for Peace and Justice] was trying to march across it to the Pentagon." Yet despite these and other problems, the May Day collective and the People's Coalition had won — "they forced 13,000 arrests and left a clear warning to the government of resistance yet to come. They trained thousands in the tactics of nonviolent disruption, which can be used in many cities, not just in Washington, against tax offices, draft offices, etc. The idea of closing down Washington through civil disobedience is entirely sound and justified when the govern-ment no longer respects the . . . [people], but without their consent and against their will, commits crimes against humanity." Mc-Reynolds expressed the hope that the People's Coalition could "de-velop to the point it can offer America an alternative to continued control of our national life by the corporate and military establishment."[24]

Reading these lines years later and removed from the apocalyptic temper of the early 1970s, one is struck by the political arrogance and wishful thinking that characterized McReynolds's comments on the political situation in the U.S. in the spring of 1971. On the basis of what, one is inclined to ask, was McReynolds justified in concluding that the elected government of the United States no longer represented the American people and that a mob of several thousand acted legitimately in closing down Washington? What court other than the openly partisan Russell Tribunal had convicted the U.S. government of crimes against humanity? A year and a half later, the Nixon administration, committed to seeking an honorable settlement of the Vietnam war, was to receive an overwhelming mandate from the American people, and the antiwar movement had become a sideshow. Support for an unconditional and unilateral American withdrawal from Vietnam, as provided in the Hanoi-sponsored People's Peace Treaty endorsed by McReynolds, was no greater in 1971 than in 1972. Yet the antiwar movement claimed a mandate for nullifying the regular political processes of this country and sought to impose its solution to the Vietnam problem by coercive actions in the streets. To call such a campaign of resistance to the democratically elected government "nonviolent" clearly represented a half-truth at best.

After the Paris Peace Agreement of 1973 had ended the direct American involvement in Vietnam, the WRL, together with the AFSC and other segments of the antiwar movement, participated in the Indochina Peace Campaign to cut off American aid to the Saigon government. President Thieu, as the North Vietnamese later put it gloatingly, was forced "to fight a poor man's war." Two years later, heavily armed North Vietnamese divisions entered Saigon, and the long agony of Vietnam had seemingly ended.

The issue of *Christian Century* published on 3 December 1975 carried an article by Paul Marx, a professor of English, that was sharply critical of McReynolds and other like-minded pacifists. These members of the peace movement, Marx charged, had been more interested in a defeat for the hated American "system" than in an end to the killing. "For those many in the movement, what happened this spring was a dream come true. Hence the jubilant victory celebration in Central Park. The fulfillment of that dream had led to new dreams. In a world in which almost all the evil is seen as the result of U.S. imperialism, there is now the dream of a continuous string of victorious wars of liberation throughout the Third World. Former peace movement people are working for further military victories! . . . The pacifist message is in danger of dying out."[25]

During the following years, Marx's fears for the future of the pacifist gospel proved all too warranted. In the third part of our study, we will look at the ways in which American pacifism has pursued its support and promotion of revolution in the Third World and beyond.

PART III

Making the World Safe for Revolution

CHAPTER 6

Vietnam and Cambodia: The Search for Communism with a Human Face

Pacifists Celebrate a Military Victory

The quick and unseemly death of the Paris Peace Agreement of 1973 at the hands of heavily armed North Vietnamese divisions was a bit of an embarrassment to some American pacifists. On a visit to Hanoi in early May 1975, John McAuliff, head of the AFSC's Indochina program, asked his hosts "why and when the decision was made to go all the way rather than negotiating with a neutralist government in Saigon. Their answer," he reported, "which I find credible, is that they had no alternative because the U.S. would not give up its intervention until the very last minute."[1]

It remains a mystery to this day what kind of U.S. intervention McAuliff was referring to, but, in any event, the AFSC staffer did not let this minor public relations problem spoil his mood of jubilation. McAuliff extended his stay in Hanoi in order to be able to attend the celebration of the great victory that the revolutionary forces had won. The *Indochina Program Newsletter*, which he edited, made the following note under the headline "Celebrate": "As American citizens we can all celebrate that a nationwide grassroots movement played a crucial role in defeating the combined power of the Pentagon, CIA, FBI and five successive Administrations, not to mention the ostensible wisdom of the 'best and the brightest' of the elite in the media and the academy."[2] When the Coalition to Stop Funding the War held its last formal session on May 13, 1975, the meeting was opened with three bottles of champagne, and several toasts were proposed.[3]

In its 1 May 1975 issue, *WIN* magazine, the organ of the War

Resisters League, published a series of reactions to "the imminent victory of liberation forces in both Cambodia and South Vietnam." Most of the contributors who were members of or close to the WRL welcomed the North Vietnamese victory. Barbara Deming, a feminist and a member of the editorial board of *Liberation,* expressed her joy that the United States had been thrown out of Vietnam and Cambodia, two countries it had tried to dominate. Marty Jezer, one of the founders of *WIN,* called the victory of North Vietnam "a victory for the human spirit" and "a triumph for revolutionary politics." The struggle, however, was only just beginning. "We must still work to dismantle the corporate military machine and transform American society in order to make other American adventures . . . impossible," Jezer urged. David McReynolds noted that the war had cured him of any liberal illusions about American society. "I entered the war years a moderate Marxist and left it a hardened one. It is only my nonviolence which separates me from the Weatherpeople. The war was no error. . . . Vietnam was deliberate. It *is* our foreign policy. True, to kill the oppressor makes us one with him, and so we lay aside the gun. But this *system* must be killed." There should be no amnesty for those who had killed American youth and Vietnamese people in order to secure corporate profit, McReynolds declared. "Vietnam was a spotlight focused on the councils of power in this country. Let us wed our love to our anger, our morality to politics, and recognize that protest is only the beginning. Revolution is the goal." Pete Seeger gave his "deep thanks to the heroic women and men of Indochina, who have exposed and expelled American imperialism."[4] On 11 May Dave Dellinger and Norma Becker, a member of the WRL executive committee, were among the sponsors of a "War Is Over" festivity in New York's Central Park where participants celebrated because the people of Indochina had become free and independent.

A few individuals in the pacifist community recognized the moral absurdity of pacifists applauding a military triumph. In an article entitled "Military Victories Are Not Cause for Celebration," written during the final days of the North Vietnamese offensive and published in *Peacework,* the organ of the AFSC's New England regional office, Ed Lazar, the region's peace education secretary, regretted the failure of the antiwar movement to protest the massive military drive under way against the South that was leading "to still more destruction of life and suffering for millions of people." The offensive, Lazar argued, represented "a major violation of the Paris Peace Accords." To cheer the advancing divisions and to regard the invasion as liberation was "a position as pro-war as that of those who urged the invasion of Cambodia and North Vietnam. How can anyone, let alone peace people, celebrate the new set of dead bodies along Highway One?" It was easy to be opposed to war when the military advantage was with the bad guys, "but it is just as important to be opposed to war when the military advantage is seemingly with the more sympathetic side. To do otherwise is to support the concept of the just war." Tanks and guns could never be instruments of liberation; any armed victory represented "a setback to the ending of war and the creation of peacemaking instruments and institutions."[5]

Lazar's article drew criticism. His "polemic against the revolutionary Vietnamese was out of place in a newsletter called *Peacework*," wrote the authors of a letter to the editor. The article was also factually inaccurate and morally dubious, the authors claimed. "Ed Lazar's attempt to impose his pacifist sensibility on the Vietnamese struggle is arrogant and inappropriate. This rigid outlook has distorted the facts of history in pursuit of a certain purist conception of change. We respect the decision of individuals to adhere to pacifism, but it is dismaying to see a spokesperson for an organization with a long record of opposition to the war attacking the very people who have finally restored peace to Vietnam." The actions and goals of the revolutionary Vietnamese were just and heroic, and there was no reason to attack "them and those of us who share their joy and celebrate their victory." Ed Lazar, the letter concluded, "might consider stepping down from his post to ponder these issues and the Vietnamese experience."[6]

A somewhat more nuanced critique came from Marjorie Swann, the executive secretary of the New England regional office. The last few weeks of the war in Indochina, she acknowledged, had been painful. She had not doubted that the powerful military drive against South Vietnam had represented a violation of the Paris Peace Accords, yet at the same time it was clear that liberation was being accomplished. She could not cheer the victories achieved by violence, "yet I *could* rejoice at the lifting of oppression, at the return of refugees to their villages, at the release of political prisoners, most of all at the ceasing of the war with all its suffering and destruction." As a pacifist, Swann believed that the use of nonviolence would bring about more lasting, beneficial results than any war of violence, but at the same time one had to "understand the anger, frustration and resorting to violence which many Third World people in this country (and other countries) advocate and use to express their drive toward independence, equality, dignity and justice." Nonviolence was not the only valid means for dealing with injustice. The dilemma of the pacifist, Swann concluded, was that being for peace and nonviolence did not always correlate with being for justice and freedom.[7]

In a response to his critics, Lazar reminded them of the Quaker declaration of 1660: "We utterly deny all outward wars and strife, and fighting with outward weapons, for any end, or under any pretense whatever; this is our testimony to the whole world." This denial of *all* wars, he insisted, was basic to the philosophy of Friends and to the pacifist position, yet many in the peace movement, seeking to relate constructively to struggle for liberation, had forgotten what guns and war are all about. "Those 'just' bullets in wars of liberation kill—and they kill civilian women, men, and children as well as other combatants; and the combatants are victims as well." Pacifists should "actively support peaceful struggles for radical change and liberation. I do not believe that we should support wars of liberation. . . . The public and the media have every reason to be sceptical about a peace movement that opposes war only when the war is going the wrong way."[8]

Jim Forest, editor of the FOR's magazine *Fellowship,* similarly expressed doubt that it made sense for pacifists to speak of a "victory." He could not help but think of "the brother and sister-in-law of Vietnamese friends killed with their three children by a 'liberation' rocket. I think of the human toll of the supposed 'liberation.' " Instead of rejoicing with *WIN* over "the collapse of America's Indochina Empire," Forest wondered whether "we aren't also observing the collapse of our faith in the pacifist insight: that the means control the quality of the end." One could not know what the future held for the Vietnamese, but Forest expressed his "hunch that the future isn't going to be as utopian as fans of the PRG and the North Vietnamese have advertised." He ended his letter by noting that it would be interesting to see "how much elbow room pacifists in Vietnam will be given in a 'liberated' country. Hopefully a great deal more than they got from Thieu and his predecessors. And yet I wonder. . . ."[9]

Forest's fears that the new Vietnam might merely substitute a new, even more ruthless tyranny for the old system of arbitrary power were soon to be confirmed. Indeed, the pacifist Buddhists were among the first victims. After the fall of Saigon, the Unified Buddhist Church had gone out of its way to demonstrate its good will toward the new regime. Uninvited, nine hundred monks and nuns had participated in the victory celebration held in Saigon on 15 May 1975. A few days later, on 19 May, twenty thousand Buddhists had gathered in front of the An Quang Pagoda for a tribute to President Ho Chi Minh in celebration of his birthday. Quite a few of the Buddhist monks were sympathetic to socialist ideas, and they looked forward to participating in the building of a new society of social justice. Yet little justice was to be forthcoming, and the Communists soon demonstrated that they had no use for these would-be allies. Pagodas were seized or destroyed, religious statues smashed, orphanages confiscated, and social service centers closed. Thich Tri Quang, the monk who had led the Buddhist movement of protest against Ngo Dinh Diem and who as recently as 31 May 1974 had participated in a demonstration calling for the resignation of President Thieu, was arrested on 12 August after giving a sermon that queried the government about its promise of concord and reconciliation.[10]

In late July of 1975, the AFSC peace education secretaries met for their yearly "Roundup." The group had before it as one of the topics of discussion a memo from John McAuliff, head of the Indochina program, outlining his views on the lessons of Vietnam and what the AFSC should do next. The U.S. war of aggression in Vietnam, McAuliff argued, had not been a mistake. "Instead it was the direct consequence of post World War II policies and of persistent U.S. policies and economic interests." The task ahead, therefore, consisted of preventing future Vietnams, other "outrageous events and instruments of intervention. But preventing future Vietnams requires a fundamental reordering of U.S. relationships to the Third World," McAuliff claimed. "This cannot happen without radically restructuring political and economic power in the United States." Another lesson to be pondered was "the role of Marxist-Leninist ideology in Vietnam's success and consequently its application to our own and other struggles. . . . It is not in the interests of the American people (though it does benefit our political/economic leadership class) to oppose socialist/communist revolutions in other countries. Moreover, if we try to understand what is in their best interests, we are likely to often support such revolutions in the Third World."[11]

Similar views were voiced at the AFSC New England regional office. The issue before us, declared an editorial in *Peacework* in June 1975, "is not the tip-of-the-iceberg aggression in Indochina but the violent economic and political system in this country that caused it."[12] What was needed, argued AFSC program consultant

Russell Johnson in the same issue, was a "second American revolution which changes the institutions of American society toward an economy which serves the people." An end had to be put to "the massive waste which in turn drives the corporations to intervene abroad and defend their profit-making by the CIA and American armed force. This is the lesson of Vietnam as yet dimly understood by the victims of American imperialism at home. This is the present task of the peace movement."[13]

In November 1975 Russell Johnson was one of the coordinators of a conference organized by the AFSC New England regional office on Third World repression and resistance. Attended by a thousand participants from about twenty activist groups, the conference focused on the role of the CIA in instigating and supporting repression and the forces that were behind such interventions. When, in January 1976, *Peacework* ran a symposium on the question "Do you believe capitalism has got to go?" all nineteen respondents answered affirmatively. There was general agreement that the war in Indochina, Watergate, and the revelations about recent U.S. intelligence activities had created a favorable climate "for the move towards people's power," and that the end of capitalism was a prerequisite for world peace.[14] The October 1976 issue of *Peacework* took note of the death of Mao Tse-tung by printing in a commemorative box a lengthy quotation from Mao's "On Practice" that ended, "If you want to know the theory and methods of revolution, you must take part in revolution. All genuine knowledge originates in direct experience."[15]

The peace education secretaries attending the summer 1975 roundup were pleased by the events of the spring of 1975. "Not only were people joyful that there was peace, but also almost all felt that Vietnam had been liberated." There was agreement on the need to encourage U.S. reconstruction aid to Vietnam and other solidarity projects, but no clear consensus emerged with regard to the AFSC attitude toward the Vietnamese evacuated during the final days of the collapse and now in the United States. The Pasadena office had become involved in sponsorship activities, but this move was criticized by almost everyone else. Two AFSC staffers who had served in Vietnam observed "that our friends in Vietnam would find it hard to understand AFSC helping the U.S. government resettle evacuees." Most agreed that the only role the AFSC should assume with regard to these people was to give them information about the situation in Vietnam and to help them gain repatriation.[16]

In June 1976 the AFSC board approved a campaign to collect

one million signatures on a petition calling for normalization of relations with and reconstruction aid for Vietnam. The petition also made reference to amnesty for American draft-law offenders and rehabilitation support for veterans. The "Appeal for Reconciliation," coordinated by John McAuliff, was supported by the distribution of AFSC publications that described how the new government of Vietnam was implementing the democratic freedoms guaranteed by the Paris Peace Agreement but denied by the Thieu regime. Inconvenient facts — for example, that reunification had been forced only one year after the fall of Saigon, that the promised autonomy for the South had failed to materialize, and that the PRG had been unceremoniously liquidated — were ignored. A thirty-minute slide show, "Peace Comes to Vietnam," which was designed to put "a human face on liberation," stressed the unmet needs of the country as it worked to rebuild and repair the ravages of war.[17] The petition was co-sponsored by several other organizations and was signed by former doves like Senator George McGovern and Representatives Bella Abzug and Ronald Dellums. By September the appeal had raised $11,000 in contributions.

An Appeal to North Vietnam to Observe Human Rights

The Appeal for Reconciliation began to run into resistance when foreign news stories and accounts of refugees started to cast doubt on the AFSC's glowing reports about "liberated" Vietnam. In the fall of 1976, two former antiwar activists, Richard Neuhaus and Jim Forest, began to draft and circulate an appeal to the Democratic Republic of Vietnam (DRV) in which they mentioned reports of widespread violations of human rights, including the detention of large numbers of people in so-called re-education camps. They also wrote to the Vietnamese observer at the United Nations, asking for a response to these charges.

Jim Forest published an article called "Vietnam: Unification without Reconciliation" in the October 1976 issue of *Fellowship*. The past eighteen months, Forest pointed out, had brought "a rising tide of profoundly disturbing news that is hard to square with the grace, civility and kindness that American peace activists continuously encountered when meeting with representatives of Vietnam's revolution." Jean Lacouture, a French journalist and author long stationed in Vietnam and an admirer of the Vietnamese revolution, had reported his estimate that there were 300,000 prisoners. Eighty percent of the activities of the Unified Buddhist Church, ranging from seminaries to various service projects, had been closed down by the government; leading monks were under house arrest or surveillance. In protest against the seizure of pagodas and the barrage of anti-religious propaganda, twelve monks and nuns had immolated themselves in November 1975. Forest maintained that members of the American peace movement had given up years of their lives to end America's intervention in Vietnam, "nourished by the hope that, despite every cruelty, the insurgent leadership was sincere in its pledge to create a decent and tolerant society." Surely, the peace movement had earned the right to a hearing from Vietnam's new government.[18]

In a letter to Paul Quinn-Judge, an AFSC staffer who had sought to rebut the *Fellowship* article, Forest acknowledged that for a long time he had been "hopeful that despite everything the new government of Vietnam would be as unique as many of its supporters predicted it would be: an example of that long-awaited society in which communism would have a more human quality." Unfortunately, developments since the fall of South Vietnam indicated otherwise. Forest mentioned that he had been taking "a rather merciless thumping" from some of his colleagues in the peace movement; allegations had been circulated that he was on the payroll of the CIA. Still, he was determined to persist. "I hope," he told his addressee in the final sentence, "that the AFSC's conscience about these things proves more sensitive than the voice that speaks in your letter."[19]

The AFSC staff in Philadelphia, meeting on 13 October, agreed after some discussion that the Neuhaus-Forest appeal had to be opposed. The evidence cited in the appeal was said to be insufficient. "In fact, the preponderance of evidence points to the opposite conclusion.... Obviously, religion will not play the same role in the public life of post-war socialist Vietnam as it did previously, but it is premature and uninformed to have much of a perspective as to whether this is over-all to the advantage or disadvantage of religion." The Neuhaus-Forest appeal contributed to "the hostile atmosphere in the U.S. towards Viet Nam. Regardless of the intentions of its sponsors, it plays into the hands of the U.S. government and others which oppose UN membership, normalization of relations, etc."[20] In a memo to peace education committee members, John McAuliff noted that he regretted the time that had to be spent on discussing this entire matter, which detracted from achieving the goals of the Appeal for Reconciliation.[21]

Yet the issue of human rights in the new Vietnam was not so easily swept under the rug. Several AFSC regional and area staff members and Friends questioned the position of the national office. Ian Lind of the Hawaii area office found it offensive that McAuliff considered the success of the ongoing campaign for reconciliation more important than questions concerning human rights. In addition, he said, "I am concerned about the argument that we should be silent in order to avoid playing into the hands of reactionaries either intentionally or unintentionally. It seems to me that this is the argument that AFSC normally gets, but in reverse."[22] Ed Lazar urged that the AFSC "fully support this Human Rights concern which I find consistent with traditional Quaker concerns."[23] Bob Vogel of the Pacific Southwest regional office suggested a mission of inquiry in order to ascertain the truth and warned against hiding facts. "If the AFSC is to retain its own credibility, it must be faithful to the truth."[24] Charles Bloomstein of the New York Friends Group felt that a prima facie case of violations of human rights had been made. "And given the Communist societies' tendency to be totalitarian, to subjugate the individual to the society, it seems to me that whatever evidence does exist must be given the presumption of validity. In what Communist country are human rights not violated? Do you know of any? Why should Vietnam be different?"[25]

The AFSC's endeavor to undermine the Neuhaus-Forest effort included the circulation of charges that the Buddhist monk Thich Nhat Hanh was a CIA agent. In response to one of the letters sent out by John McAuliff to a wide array of peace activists, a letter in which he sought to persuade them not to support the Neuhaus-Forest protest, Alfred Hassler, former executive secretary of the FOR, protested to McAuliff against the technique of character assassination used by the AFSC. Hassler maintained that the insinuations against Thich Nhat Hanh represented the "shameful support of a smear against one of the most decent, self-sacrificing pacifists I have ever met." There are "few things that can happen in 'the movement' capable of surprising or shocking me any more, unhappily, but your letter did both." McAuliff had defended the right of the Vietnam government to exclude from public life people suspected of involvement with the United States. Hassler asked McAuliff if he thought that the U.S. government, using the same rationale, would be justified in excluding those who had opposed the war in Vietnam. "Is the Vietnamese government also then justified, on the basis of its own unilateral, unproved, convenient 'suspicions,' in suppressing all free speech, the free exercise of religion, and so on? If so, friend, what exactly are the good ends for which the precious revolution is working?" Hassler conceded that his letter was not very reconciliatory, but when character assassination emerged from "the Quaker-pacifist-human rights movement milieu, it is not easy to package one's outrage in polite sentences."[26]

Following another discussion of the Neuhaus-Forest appeal in the national peace education committee, Lou Schneider, the AFSC's executive secretary, sent a letter to all the signers of the appeal in which he explained the AFSC's refusal to be associated with it. The documentation of the particular instances of repression cited was either open to serious question or insufficiently substantiated to support the allegations. "The overwhelming impression from experience in Vietnam of both American Friends Service Committee and Mennonite Central Committee staff, all of whom have now returned from Vietnam, is that the government is carrying out the awesome task of post-war reconstruction of their society, which was so shattered by the long and bitter war, with extraordinary humaneness."[27]

The "Appeal to the Government of Vietnam," signed by about a hundred former opponents of the war in Vietnam, had been delivered to the Vietnamese observer at the United Nations on 16 November. When no response had been received by the end of December, the appeal was made public at a press conference held by the International League for Human Rights on 29 December. With the appeal now out in the open, Stewart Meacham decided to send another letter to the signers urging them to reconsider their "support of the imperialists in our land against whom we once joined hands in common struggle" and to withdraw their signatures, as Dan Berrigan and several others had already done. "It is not easy," Meacham's letter began, "to get religious and humanist radicals and pacifists to make life easier for those engaged in military aggression, economic imperialism, and political tyranny but Jim Forest and Richard Neuhaus have come close to doing it." In the name of political and religious purity, they had misled a number of good people and made them falsely denounce Vietnam. "Our Vietnamese friends have displayed both grace and courage in a prolonged, bitter and successful struggle, and now they are seeking to heal the wounds of war, restore their ravaged land, and move ahead toward a just and confident society. We ought to remember our debt to them and do what we can to help."[28]

Vietnam's human rights record was also defended in a full-page ad in the *New York Times,* coordinated by Corliss Lamont, and

John McAuliff was one of the signers. The ad acknowledged that "some Saigon collaborationists have been detained in re-education centers, perhaps 40,000 at present." But such a number was surprisingly small in view of the savagery with which the Saigon regime had pursued its war policy. "The present government of Vietnam," the ad declared, "should be hailed for its moderation and for its extraordinary efforts to achieve reconciliation among all of its people."[29]

Normalization of Relations or Pressure for Human Rights?

Meanwhile, the Neuhaus-Forest appeal was beginning to run into opposition also from within the FOR. A memo of understanding, drawn up after a meeting of the staff, took note of the "tremendous amount of correspondence, animosity and vituperative discussion [that] has been generated by the affair" and called for "an end to the 'charges and countercharges' discussion as rapidly as possible. Little strength can come to the peace community from a continuing exchange of vituperative and sarcastic comments." The appeal had been perceived as an inspired effort by the FOR while in fact it had originated with staff members Jim Forest and Tom Cornell acting on their own. Some members of the staff had signed it; most had not. "Staff gives strong approval to a joint approach of a number of groups to Amnesty International, asking them to explore the truth or falsity of the allegations being made." The memo ended with the staff making it clear that the FOR supported the normalization of relations between the United States and Vietnam, the entrance of Vietnam into the United Nations, and the payment of American compensation to the government of Vietnam.[30]

Hassler, still a member of the FOR advisory committee and carrying the title of emeritus executive secretary, took exception to the staff memo in a letter addressed to Barton Hunter, the FOR's new executive secretary. The agreement seemed to imply that the FOR was not and should not become involved in this issue. "For me the contrary is the case. The matter of political prisoners surely is not a new one for FOR to confront: we were literally the first to holler about it under Thieu and Ky. I would assume, moreover, that FOR would hardly be comfortable with the position of Jim's critics: that persecution for one's political or religious beliefs, on a massive scale, is sanctified by the 'revolutionary' claims of the persecutors." Hassler pointed out that the numerous reports on human rights violations in Vietnam came from the same reliable sources which had caused so much trouble for the previous Saigon government and which nobody in the peace movement at the time had challenged as untrustworthy. These sources were superior to anyone else's, including those of Amnesty International. "For the Fellowship to pass the buck under these circumstances would be very disheartening."

The "charges and countercharges" that had characterized the discussion so far, Hassler maintained, were "not the accidental consequences of overheated emotions." The vituperative accusations came almost entirely from those opposed to the appeal. The people who suggested that Forest and Nhat Hanh were CIA agents did so because they feared and resented them, "because their fondest beliefs in what they call revolutionary justice have been bound up in the present Vietnamese government, and they cannot bear to have those beliefs shaken. To tell them that this kind of argument will not strengthen the peace movement would leave them convulsed: the 'peace movement' is something to be manipulated for an end that is not peace except on the terms they define." Hassler admitted that all this did not sound very loving and reconciliatory, but, he insisted, "reconciliation and love become mere sentimentalism if they are the reflection of an unwillingness to confront truth." Those who had made these "utterly contemptible" charges "must be opposed, openly and vigorously."[31]

The FOR executive committee, meeting on 6 December, took up the controversy but failed to reach agreement on how to resolve it. A motion to refer the substance of the Neuhaus-Forest appeal to the national council was opposed by McReynolds and Hunter on the grounds that Vietnam was now a closed issue in the peace movement; they did not see any point in the council's spending time on it. Others expressed the view that the issue of human rights in Communist Vietnam was part of the larger problem of how pacifists should relate to violent liberation movements, but a proposal that the council take up this broader topic also failed to win approval.[32]

McReynolds continued his attack upon Forest in a confidential memo that he circulated to the leadership of the War Resisters League (WRL) and others, including the Vietnamese observer at the UN. McReynolds argued that Forest had compromised the FOR by not clearing his appeal, sent out on FOR stationery, with the executive committee. More basically, the Forest appeal had revived the sharp divisions within the FOR that had developed during the years of the Vietnam war between those who demanded an unconditional American withdrawal and those, grouped around Hassler, who wanted to ensure that the Buddhists would have a role in a democratically governed South Vietnam. Hassler's grasp of what was happening in Vietnam, McReynolds charged, had been "warped by the memories of the Cold-War—he could never transcend a kind of reflexive anti-Communism." If the Fellowship during those years did good work on the Vietnam issue, it was largely despite Hassler and because of Ron Young and Allan Brick. "The Fellowship was a house badly divided—and this is one reason I am so pained that Jim, by his actions, has raised up the past."

McReynolds went on to note that the evidence for Forest's charge of "grievous and systematic violations of human rights" was not conclusive, but what "did we expect the Vietnamese to do with the legacy we left behind?" Most people will turn to violence when they see all other doors closed, he argued, and the French and Americans did indeed close the doors to normal democratic change in Vietnam. Any revolution involves heartbreaking experiences; it is an earth-quake in which helpless and innocent people are trapped by rubble. "In the midst of all this, it is pointless to stand with a stick and beat the ground to punish it." McReynolds did not expect Communist Vietnam to have the kind of bureaucratic and insensitive regime that had emerged in the Soviet Union, but neither did he think that it would have freedom in the way that America has it. Whatever the facts were about human rights in Vietnam, he declared, after what the United States had done to Vietnam—"the best and closest comparison is Germany and the Jews"—I "cannot and will not at *this time* publicly call to account the Vietnamese, much of whose soil is barren now, many of whose forests are stark and dead, and more than a million of whose people are no more."[33]

In a reply, addressed to "Dear Friends in the WRL," Forest conceded that his use of FOR stationery might have been poor judgment, though he had not claimed to speak on behalf of the organization. "Let him who hasn't used his letterhead for personal concerns cast the first typewriter." Forest charged that McReynolds's remarks about Hassler involved "abusive verbal violence." Hassler was not "a closet Cold Warrior in pacifist wrappings" but an anti-totalitarian. Given the reality of Marxist states, there was no reason to apologize for this position. That Vietnam had not experienced a bloodbath at the end of the war was a fact to be welcomed, but one could not be glad that the new regime treated "masses of people like pawns, 're-educating' them under lock and key and rifle site [sic]" and that it generally had chosen the familiar repressive path of the total state. McReynolds seemed to think that "whenever an historical process calls itself a Revolution that one no longer need protest what he rightly calls, 'the heartbreaking experiences' that come in its wake. . . . Equate these violations of human rights with earthquakes? If that's what it means to be a pacifist, then I need to find another tag to indicate to others something of my value system." Finally, Forest questioned McReynolds's sharing of a supposedly confidential letter with the Vietnamese observer at the UN. "Is Dave fishing for a visa for a Vietnam trip? A gold star on their Friends list?" It was extremely inappropriate "to curry favor from government officials at one another's expense."[34]

At its meeting in February 1977, the FOR executive committee once more took up the contentious issue. After some discussion, it was agreed to let the controversy die down but also to insert an item into *Fellowship* to indicate the FOR's concern over the dispute.[35] Such a statement, signed by executive secretary Hunter, appeared in the March-April issue and now publicly dissociated the FOR from the Neuhaus-Forest appeal. The question of political and religious repression in Vietnam, Hunter explained, had been raised by two members of the FOR staff acting on their own. "The F.O.R. has chosen not to involve itself in the controversy. To many of us on the staff and in the Executive Committee, the evidence has not seemed to be clear." Moreover, the entire discussion had not been helpful. "It has tended to divide and disrupt the peace community. It has used up untold hours of time. Both the original statement and the responses have tended to greatly exaggerate and heighten public doubt about the stability and good intentions of the Vietnamese government." There should be no misunderstanding regarding the FOR's consistent "support of Vietnam's sovereign right to determine its own policies without interference from other nations"; regarding the FOR's support of a normalization of relations between the United States and Vietnam, including financial aid from the U.S. for reconstruction and repair of damages "caused by our invasion of Vietnam"; or regarding the FOR's commitment to civil and religious freedom. If and when the evidence about the allegations of official political and religious oppression in Vietnam became reasonably clear, the FOR would take a position. "Meanwhile," Hunter declared, "we wish to get on with the major business of peace which, for us in these times, seems to be the matter of disarmament."[36]

In his contribution to the May 1975 *WIN* symposium on the end of the war in Vietnam, Staughton Lynd, an editor of *Liberation,* had counseled the peace movement to "apply the same tests of lawful and humane behavior to all governments, and . . . [to] expect that a revolutionary government in Vietnam, like all governments, will imprison people unjustly, will betray the rhetoric which brought it to power, and will need to be resisted."[37] Yet when in 1976 reports began to accumulate about gross violations of human rights in the newly unified Vietnam, most of the WRL leadership denied or minimized these abuses. Jim Peck was the only one of the six-person WRL staff to sign the "Appeal to the Government of Vietnam" authored by Forest and Neuhaus. Only two other members of the twenty-four-person WRL executive committee lent their support to this appeal, even though Jim Forest and Tom Cornell, the originators of this intervention, were members of the committee.

In January 1977, prodded by McReynolds, who strongly opposed the Neuhaus-Forest appeal, the executive committee voted for a resolution that formally dissociated the WRL from the appeal. The resolution went on to reaffirm the League's support of UN membership and U.S. recognition of the Socialist Republic of Vietnam as well as of U.S. aid to repair war damage and to heal the wounds of war. The committee also expressed its support for the planned AFSC mission to Vietnam in order to investigate allegations of violations of human rights.[38] WRL chairwoman Norma Becker and executive committee member Grace Paley were among the signers of the full-page ad, coordinated by Corliss Lamont, that appeared in the *New York Times* of 30 January 1977. The ad maintained that many of the forty thousand Vietnamese detained in re-education camps had engaged in terrible crimes against their own people and that the new government of Vietnam should be hailed for its moderation.

An AFSC Delegation Takes a Guided Tour of Vietnam

In late January 1977 a six-person AFSC delegation left for a two-week visit to Vietnam. The group included Stewart Meacham and Wallace Collett, a Cincinnati businessman and chairman of the AFSC board of directors. In a meeting with former leaders of the Third Force in Saigon, the delegation was assured that human rights were well protected in the new Vietnam, and it was asked to convey this message to those who had signed the Neuhaus-Forest appeal. Ly Chanh Trung, a professor of philosophy at the University of Saigon who had been previously identified with the Catholic Left, explained that the construction of socialism in the South would guarantee the most basic human rights like the right to live, to have work, to receive health protection and education — all rights not protected in the capitalist societies of the West. "We'd like our friends to understand," Trung explained, "that we ourselves cannot rely on the norms and standards of capitalism to criticize socialism. The two societies are very different in nature, in purpose and in concrete experience."

Trung declared that the rumors that had been spread about conditions in the detention camps were false; the purpose of detention was not revenge but re-education. "The people living under the old regime here were influenced by anti-communist propaganda. If there was no re-education, there would be no way whatsoever of bringing them into the new society with their fellow countrymen." There was a need, Trung said, to create "a change in ideology and feelings" so that these people could see the truth and understand the nature of socialism. The maximum time for re-education was three years, "but those people who show appropriate development can be released earlier." At the same meeting, Lou Kubicka, an AFSC representative in Laos, indicated how impressed he was by "the human decency that we've seen in the approach of the society to all the problems that are confronting it: the balance between compassion, tolerance, and strictness where it's necessary." Kubicka responded to Professor Trung's explanation of the purposes of re-education: "I think what you've said here will do a great deal to help clarify things for some people who had conscience, that perhaps lacked some perspective."[39]

On 6 February 1977 Wallace Collett was interviewed by the Voice of Vietnam Radio, and he described his impressions of the country. One of his most interesting experiences had been the visit to a "new economic zone," where the delegation had seen the "homes of the pioneer families who have moved out of the city and are dedicating themselves to reclaiming the land [and] to building a new life of productive work. It reminded me of the American pioneers who moved into the forests and plains of our country and who created farms and homes and communities. There are so many ways in which American and Vietnamese experience [are] similar." Collett was also impressed by the decency of the policy of reconciliation. "We have sensed it keenly in the humane policy you are following to reconcile all the elements of your people." The delegation had met with former officers of Thieu's army, leaders of the churches and temples, and intellectuals and peasants, and it was able to "sense the commitment to granting full opportunity to all, regardless of past associations, to belonging and participating in the life and development of your country." Once back in the United States, the delegation would convey to all the expressions of friendship toward the American people that they had experienced — "a message of the decency, the sincerity, and the humaneness of Vietnam."[40]

At the meeting of the national peace education committee held on 18-20 February, two members of the delegation reported on the visit to Vietnam. Carol Bragg, peace education secretary of the Rhode Island regional office, described the wide range of the sights seen and the meetings held and spoke of "the honor and privilege it had been to represent AFSC on the trip to Vietnam." Stewart Meacham reiterated that the delegation had seen no signs of repression. "Stewart raised the question of whether it is possible for socialism to emerge with a human face. Is Vietnam the place where that can occur? He made a plea that resources be made available in order to help bring that about."[41]

AFSC publications also carried detailed reports from the members of the delegation. Writing in the *Quaker Service Bulletin,* the AFSC fund-raiser Wilmer Tjossem described his meeting with four Catholic priests in Saigon, who told him, "Since liberation we Christians have better conditions." One priest declared, "Socialism is the way for Vietnam." In Hanoi the vice foreign minister had assured the delegation, "There has been no bloodbath in the South, as predicted by some. When you visit there you will see with your own eyes whether there are violations of human rights." Tjossem added, "Indeed, we did not see any signs of political repression when we visited Saigon, although, of course, we could not literally see everything."[42]

Carol Bragg wrote a two-part article in *Peacework* that painted a similarly positive picture. In the first part she confirmed that "there is no serious effort under way to discourage or suppress the practice of religion in Vietnam." Some violations of human rights had probably occurred, and some excesses had taken place, but these were not sanctioned by the government. "The Catholic, Protestant, and Buddhist churches — with the exception of a few congregations — seem to have come to terms with the new government and are working hand-in-hand with that government to build a new society." Members of the Patriotic Buddhist Association in Saigon had told her that the alleged self-immolations of twelve monks and nuns in November 1975 had actually been "the act of a deviant monk who put to death the two male novices and 9 nuns who were accomplices or witnesses to his debauchery; he then committed suicide." Bragg argued that since twelve simultaneous immolations were imaginable only in the face of the most severe repression, and since the deaths occurred in the absence of other forms of protest, the authenticity of the alleged self-immolations was doubtful.[43]

In the second part of her article, Bragg wrote that the number of detainees in re-education camps had declined from 200,000 in the spring of 1976 to fifty thousand in February 1977. The purpose of re-education was to orient people who had committed vicious crimes to the policies and goals of the new government and to prepare them for building the new society. It could be argued that "re-education camps — even without the benefit of trials — represent far greater respect for human rights than did the war crimes tribunals after World War II, which strictly observed due process but terminated in life imprisonment or execution for most of the defendants." Human rights "can be a relative thing," Bragg claimed. "Certainly the re-education camps and the reconciliation they seek to achieve stand in sharp contrast to the bloodbath the US State Department so enthusiastically predicted."[44]

Two Friends Dissent

Not everyone in the Quaker family was convinced by these reports about the humaneness of the new Vietnamese regime. Kenneth E. Boulding, a well-known economist at the University of Colorado and a member of the Society of Friends, had been one of the signers of the Neuhaus-Forest appeal. In January 1977 he wrote to both Louis Schneider and Stewart Meacham expressing his distress at the way the AFSC staff had responded to the appeal. No serious attempt had been made to refute it, he pointed out. "If the communist government of Vietnam is an exception to the general rule that communism involves centralization of power, corruption of information systems, and an intolerance of diversity, I would be most happy, but also I confess somewhat surprised." The way in which the Committee had reacted to the appeal confirmed his "deep anxieties about the AFSC and the nagging feeling, which almost everything that has happened recently has reinforced, that the Committee has departed a long way from its original conception as a politically impartial agency for the diminution of human suffering. These suspicions are very corrosive, but unless they can be faced and be brought into the open, I think both the American Friends Service Committee and the Society for Friends are in grave danger."[45]

On 31 January Boulding informed the board and staff of the

AFSC that from 9-11 A.M. on 31 March 1977 he would stand in a personal silent vigil in the entrance hall of the AFSC office in Philadelphia in order to give testimony to his deep spiritual anguish. For some time the fear had been building up in him "that the AFSC is departing from the light of the Gospel and of science, and is following an ideology that is both secular and untrue to the scientific ethic." The AFSC's attempt to discredit the Neuhaus-Forest appeal had turned these anxieties into certainty, Boulding said. It "suggests to me that the AFSC has lost touch with that 'religion of veracity rooted in spiritual inwardness' which William James described as the essence of the Society of Friends." Boulding stressed that he had no intention of embarrassing the AFSC or of obstructing its valuable work in the relief and cure of human suffering; he wanted no outside publicity. "This is strictly an internal matter between the conscience of an individual Friend and the AFSC."[46]

Boulding's critique of the AFSC was endorsed by another well-known Friend, John P. Powelson, also a professor of economics at the University of Colorado, Boulder. Powelson communicated his concern to the Colorado General Meeting of the Society of Friends. He charged that the AFSC had "adopted a secular ideology that puts an aura of propriety on whatever the third-world socialist countries may do or say." This included an uncritical acceptance of proposals for "a new international economic order." Gunnar Myrdal, an early supporter of the aspirations of Third World countries and a proponent of programs to transfer resources from rich to poor, had now become convinced by his own research that the cause of poverty in the Third World was rooted in the social, cultural, and economic deficiencies of the Third World countries themselves. By ignoring these and other scientific findings, Powelson claimed, the AFSC was endangering its credibility.

Furthermore, Powelson noted, the AFSC had adopted "an apology for third-world repression, which might even be construed as a Quaker endorsement of it." Before the six-person AFSC delegation left for Vietnam in January 1977, they had promised to make inquiries about a number of Vietnamese who according to reports had disappeared or been detained. Yet when in Vietnam the delegation had been so impressed by the VIP treatment extended to them that they had decided it was "inappropriate" to inquire about these people. Upon their return to the U.S., the delegation had affirmed their conviction that there was no repression in Vietnam. However, given the censorship and other restrictions on the gathering of information that existed there, it was at least questionable

how they could make such a statement authoritatively. "In our Society of Friends, which has such a strong tradition for *helping* the
imprisoned and the sick and the tortured, I find it *shameful* that the
organization we have loved and trusted for so long should become
a conduit through which government-controlled information is
spread to the American people, to urge them to turn their backs on
the *many, many*, reports of political repression in Vietnam." These
reports had not been confirmed by investigation because the government of Vietnam would not allow it, but they were far too numerous to be denied out of hand as the AFSC had done. "For some
of us, it is going to take a lot of adjustment to the fact that our
American Friends Service Committee no longer represents the spirit
we loved and trusted so much and for so long."[47]

In a letter addressed to the Colorado General Meeting, executive
secretary Lou Schneider denied that the AFSC had adopted a new
secular ideology:

> It is true that the AFSC and others have added to, rather than
> shifted away from, their emphasis on the relief of human suffering
> and war, the task of understanding of their causes. The addition came
> largely as the result of the inner leadings of those who were engaged
> in contact with suffering victims. They found themselves asking: Is
> binding up the wounds of war enough? Must we not also try to
> prevent war? It was from such a leading that AFSC added peace
> education and international conferences and dialogues to its
> agenda. . . . We feel that an enormous challenge of our times is to
> discover how people can be assured not only of political and civil
> rights but also of social and economic rights. We believe that Quak-
> ers, including us, are deeply concerned about all of those rights for
> all, and not some for some.

Without touching directly on the issue of repression in Vietnam,
Schneider noted that he had joined Kenneth Boulding in his recent
vigil in the national office because he, too, had a concern for veracity. Afterward, Boulding and several staff and board members
had held a long discussion. "I believe Kenneth may have modified
some of his judgments about us," Schneider reported, "but that is
for him to say."[48]

Schneider's speculation about a change in Boulding's critical attitude toward the AFSC was mostly wishful thinking. In April 1977,
Boulding addressed the Society of Friends with "A Friendly Clarification: One Quaker's Contribution to World Social Philosophy."

Without mentioning the AFSC specifically, Boulding once again distanced himself from the kind of "half-baked Marxism" that he felt had come to prevail in the AFSC's peace education work. The Society of Friends, Boulding affirmed, not only was concerned with the full realization of the divine potential of each individual but had always been mindful of poverty, oppression, and violence in society, which could impede individuals' improvement of their hearts and minds. For three hundred years the Society had sought to develop "a peaceable and democratic social capitalism" — progressive taxation, social legislation, and limits to the prerogatives of private property. The world now faced the challenge of a new secular religion — Marxism. However, Boulding noted, because of a legitimate concern with the means by which Marxism has been opposed, "we have failed to develop a prophetic critique of Marxism, and hence we are exposed to having our own identity and witness subtly undermined by it. For fear of being anti-communist, we have failed to establish our own prophetic faith and mission in regard to the evolution of world social institutions."

Marxism had links to the prophetic biblical tradition of equality and justice, Boulding pointed out, but in many respects it was in deep conflict with the Christian faith and had to be criticized "in a resolute and friendly spirit." Friends could not accept Marxism's denial of the validity of religious thought and practice, the ideal of the class war as a path to peace and justice, the personal oppression that has hitherto always resulted from the coercive power of a centrally planned economy, or the claim of a small political party to represent the diversity of individuals that constitute the people. As a group that cannot survive in a communist society, Friends should seek to modify these societies from the outside through research, thought, prayer, and personal contact. They should utterly reject any forceful overthrow of communist states, but by being faithful to their own insight and witness, they might be able to make some contribution to human betterment.[49]

The AFSC staff, including its executive secretary Lou Schneider, politely listened to these expressions of anxiety about the future of the organization, but continued to do as they pleased. A member of the Colorado area office complained to Schneider that the trend toward the right in the U.S. was also "reflected in Quaker meetings here and elsewhere." Still, this member happily reported a little later, the Colorado General Meeting had all but disregarded Jack Powelson's complaints and had spent a mere five minutes on the paper he had submitted.[50] At a consultation on the AFSC's Indochina program held in April 1977, Lou Schneider expressed the view that "a relationship to Viet Nam as a developing socialist country, if it can be continued, is perhaps the most important work we have to do now." Carol Bragg of the Rhode Island office stressed the importance of educating the American people about socialist thought and the realities of socialism in order to undermine the fear of communism.[51] The Colorado office, after reading the report on the consultation, wrote that they were "*very* excited about the continued focus on North Vietnam as a socialist-experiment model. It's very important here in Denver."[52]

In July, Schneider distributed an essay on Quakerism and socialism by Terry SoRelle, a member of the peace team of the Pacific Northwest office in Portland, Oregon. SoRelle argued that there was no contradiction between these two systems of belief and that they were indeed complementary to each other. "Without a socialist transformation of the economic system, the prospects for economic democracy are dubious at best. Without economic democracy, peace and social justice is a faraway dream." In order to help anti-capitalist national liberation movements to be nonviolent, the AFSC had to do "everything in our power to restrain the repressive power of the United States. This is morally incumbent upon us as Friends and Americans." Neither the AFSC nor socialists should be apologists for socialist governments, but "our first priority should be to address those conditions of oppression which our country supports directly or indirectly."[53]

Hassler and Forest Plead for the Buddhists

But the defenders of human rights in Vietnam refused to accept these evasions. After a trip to Paris, where he met with various people concerned about the situation in Vietnam, Alfred Hassler renewed his plea that the FOR not wash its hands of these new victims of persecution. The kinds of facts that Americans were accustomed to regard as "hard evidence," he wrote, were difficult to come by when independent newsgathering or neutral investigative teams were not permitted. Nevertheless, the evidence for the serious charges made against the government of Vietnam was substantial and manifold. There was the evidence of flight—many thousands of ordinary folks abandoning their ancestral homes and risking their lives in flimsy boats in order to escape life under the new regime. There was the evidence given by the refugees. While these accusations had to be examined with care, it was absurd to suggest that no evidence from refugees was acceptable. "We had no difficulty believing the stories of refugees from Hitler's Germany," Hassler reminded his readers, "and left-liberals do not object today to finding refugees from Chile, Argentina, Rhodesia and South Africa credible sources of information about conditions in these countries." Furthermore, there was a stream of messages pouring out from the FOR's friends in Vietnam to friends in France. Since these messages came from those who during the years of the war had acquired a reputation for accuracy and care, this evidence was the most convincing. A special committee of the Unified Buddhist Church in Paris had just released a list of forty-eight artists and writers arrested between November 1975 and March 1976. Many of these people had been vigorous opponents of the Thieu government. Since the war's end, nineteen leaders of the Unified Buddhist Church had been taken into custody.

In addition, Hassler continued, there was the evidence collected by reputable journalists like Jean Lacouture, a consistent supporter of the NLF during the entire war. And finally, there was the evidence of history. "It is the practice of totalitarian regimes, and especially of Communist totalitarian regimes, to behave in this fashion, suppressing all dissent and enforcing conformity throughout the country. . . . There is no reason to be surprised that it should be occurring again." Hassler conceded that it was impossible to prove how many people had been sent to re-education camps and the new economic zones, but the evidence of massive persecution of dissenters was persuasive. "The peace movement has the right to remind the victorious Vietnamese of the promises it made to us that it has not honored."[54]

After these nonpublic interventions had failed to produce results, Hassler took his case to the readers of *Fellowship*. In a letter published in the September 1977 issue, Hassler once again raised the predicament of the FOR's friends in Vietnam, "who are in prison there, often because of their attempts to win democracy for *their* society." The FOR had decided to do nothing and to acknowledge the right of the Vietnamese government to make its own decisions on internal matters. This did not represent his views, Hassler wrote. He did "not acknowledge the sovereign right of *any* government to imprison and otherwise harass people because of their conviction." Hanoi might have the *power* to imprison his friends and colleagues, but it did not the *right* to do so. The evidence about imprisonment and intimidation came from sources the FOR had long relied upon, including Thich Nhat Hanh, one of its vice presidents. The fact that

131

the United States had inflicted much suffering on Vietnam did not preclude the right and duty of Americans to speak up about these sad developments. "My primary vision of an effective FOR," Hassler declared, "is of a body that will speak for the oppressed of all varieties to *any* oppressor—to resurrect a neglected phrase, to speak truth to power." There was a chance that the Vietnamese authorities might listen to the American peace movement, and the FOR should not miss this opportunity.[55]

The executive committee, which met on 19 September, once again failed to take the forthright stand that Hassler recommended. It issued a statement concerning Vietnam in which it maintained that "working for the normalization of governmental relations and providing immediate and long-term reconstruction aid are the best contributions to human rights in Viet Nam that we as Americans can make." Such assistance would mitigate the suffering caused by U.S. military intervention and create "a climate for greater respect for human rights." There existed no "collateral corroboration" of the reports about arrests of Buddhist monks. The statement repeated the suggestion that Amnesty International investigate this and other allegations of human rights violations by officials of the new Socialist Republic of Vietnam.[56]

In December 1976 Jim Forest had resigned as editor of *Fellowship* and had assumed the post of coordinator for the International Fellowship of Reconciliation (IFOR) headquartered in Holland. Unhampered there by the close identification with Socialist Vietnam that dominated the American branch of the Fellowship, Forest continued his efforts on behalf of the persecuted Buddhists. In April 1977 the council of the IFOR appealed to Prime Minister Pham Van Dong to release the arrested leaders of the Unified Buddhist Church. At the same time, Forest and his IFOR colleague Geoffrey Pope, at the request of Richard Chartier, the new editor of *Fellowship,* prepared another article for the FOR magazine that reported the latest developments in the situation of the Vietnamese Buddhists. When Chartier decided to hold the article until he could obtain a "balancing response," Forest and Pope objected and termed this procedure "unethical." They had not been told that their article was going to be part of a symposium; the individual chosen to deliver the rebuttal would have the last word. An exchange of views should have been planned in advance with a precise formulation of the issues to be addressed. Without such a structure, whoever was going to be invited to direct potshots at their article would undoubtedly tend to evade the real problems. "To put it as bluntly as I can,"

Pope wrote Chartier, "I'd like those who favor or condone political imprisonment, anti-religious repression, the denial of basic rights of speech, movement, association, etc. and one-party rule to be out front about it."[57]

Much to the chagrin of Forest and Pope, their article, entitled "Speaking Up for the Vietnamese Buddhists," did not get published until October. Half a year would pass, Forest wrote a friend in the U.S., before the readers of *Fellowship* would be permitted to know how many of their former friends in Vietnam were now in jail and what they might do "on their behalf equivalent to what we routinely suggest for political prisoners in every other country. This matter still sends a chill up my spine—a dread for the conscience of the FOR."[58] The rebuttal was written by David Elder, coordinator of Southeast Asian programs at the national office of the AFSC, who composed his essay with the help of other AFSC staffers. John A. Sullivan, associate executive secretary for information and interpretation, expressed concern about "the numerous traps set by the Forest letter," but urged that the AFSC use this opportunity "to recover some of the ground we lost in the last round. By that I mean we should try to dispel some of the doubts raised about our veracity, our partisanship, our pacifism, our ability to speak with one voice."[59]

Elder's article, "Another View on Human Rights in Vietnam," published in *Fellowship* alongside the piece by Forest and Pope, began with the insistence that the author, too, was "very concerned for the human rights of Vietnamese." Yet he saw the need to add some considerations to the concerns expressed by Forest and Pope. Elder related that a report written by a Mennonite who had been in Vietnam until April 1976 spoke of "the willingness of religious people to put their service orientation to work in the new society, whether in new economic zones or social welfare institutions directed by the government." The new government was "impressively successful in making services available to ordinary people." The issue that had resulted in the arrest of five Buddhist leaders was not freedom of worship or participation in society but a dispute over the management of educational and welfare institutions. It was to be hoped that this disagreement would soon be resolved and the Buddhists released.

On the whole, Elder stated, American visitors "have been struck by government efforts to work for internal and external reconciliation." No bloodbath had occurred. "There appears to be a genuine atmosphere of reunion and reconciliation." Shortages of food and medicines were the result of what America had done to Vietnam,

Elder claimed. "How credible to the ordinary, hungry, ill-equipped Vietnamese would a protest about human rights in Vietnam be that failed to focus on the massive and gross violations of human rights caused by the U.S. denying them food, medicine, and the means to recover from the war?"[60]

The FOR thus had demonstrated its evenhandedness in the matter of human rights in Vietnam: it had given space to and provided publicity for both the accusers and the defenders of Communist Vietnam. But that was not what Hassler and Forest considered an appropriate FOR role, and in December 1977 Hassler attended as a guest a meeting of the executive committee in order to make still another attempt at galvanizing the FOR into action. He provided the committee with several documents recently smuggled out of Vietnam, and described the suppression of human rights and religious practices that had become a "fact of life" in that country. The FOR, Hassler suggested, should renew the close relationship it had had during the war years with the Buddhists. The Fellowship should provide them with a base in the United States in order to help them communicate what they had to report and say. After a lengthy debate, it was decided that the FOR staff would be willing to meet with a delegation of Buddhists, would approach the Vietnamese delegation at the UN, and perhaps would look into further steps such as organizing a trip of inquiry. But the minutes "stressed that F.O.R. is not a spokesman for the Buddhist Church but is simply focusing on the issue of human rights insofar as they are related to peace people in the Unified Buddhist Church."[61] Hassler's plea that the FOR demonstrate full solidarity with its former Buddhist allies and friends had apparently once again fallen on deaf ears.

And yet the persistent prodding of Hassler and Forest was gradually having some small impact. In February 1978 the question of what to do about the disturbing news out of Vietnam was once again on the agenda of the executive committee, and this time both staff and committee displayed a limited openness to the ideas of their critics. A staff memo noted that it seemed appropriate for the FOR to show "a special interest in Vietnam following years of wartime concern for the Vietnamese people in general and cooperation with the Unified Buddhists in particular." While knowledge about events in Vietnam was incomplete and insufficient for taking some types of action, it was adequate for taking other initiatives and actions, the memo declared. Vietnam was now governed by a Communist regime, "acting on the presuppositions and in the manner of such governments. This means, among other things, that rumors of limitations upon religious freedom and civil liberties have a certain presupposition in favor of their truth." Religious freedom seemed to be greatly limited, re-education camps had been in operation for two years, and the exodus of the boat people suggested considerable dissatisfaction with the new regime. "Whatever our attitude toward Communism, the best that we may hope for in the near future is that Vietnam may become a nation exemplifying 'Socialism with a human face.' " The most promising way of liberalizing this regime was that of normalizing relations, the memo declared. In a more relaxed and friendly climate, concerns of religious and civil liberties might be heard and exercise some influence. "This is not to say that we ignore or play down evidence of oppression. It is simply to say that we do not expect that merely by detailing charges of religious and civil oppression, we will accomplish our goals of improving the conditions for human life in Vietnam."[62]

After a lengthy and involved discussion, the committee approved a series of actions that once again represented a compromise of conflicting impulses and intentions. The FOR would seek to convince the U.S. government to admit a larger number of boat people, it would enhance its efforts to develop a Buddhist Peace Fellowship in the United States, it would maintain an ongoing friendly working relationship with the Vietnamese Buddhist Peace Delegation in France, and it would welcome to its national office any and all people with knowledge about the situation in Vietnam.

These friendly gestures to the Buddhists were counterbalanced by a paragraph that stressed the importance of establishing a personal relationship with the Vietnamese mission to the UN "so that F.O.R. may, in the best tradition of reconciliation, speak out of friendship rather than out of an adversarial relationship when we are raising questions about governmental practice." Members of the mission could be invited to the national office "for friendly conversations." An FOR team should be sent to the Vietnamese mission to express the Fellowship's traditional support for the freedom and welfare of the Vietnamese people, to inquire about the truth or falsehood of the allegations made about religious intolerance and mistreatment of Buddhist religious leaders, and to express the hope that these allegations were not true. At the same time, the committee resolved, discussions should be held with the American authorities about normalization of relations with Vietnam, about allegations of political and religious repression, and about U.S. aid to Vietnam. The FOR was to support the efforts of Amnesty International and other independent bodies to seek information and document reports about *specific* human rights violations. *Fellowship* was to publicize factually sound information about both good and bad conditions in Vietnam. However, a recently issued appeal of the Unified Buddhist Church that contained disturbing information on human rights issues and asked for help was to be published as a news item only.[63]

In the spring of 1978, several exiled Vietnamese Buddhists visited the United States. At Hassler's request, they were given the opportunity to make a presentation to the FOR staff, at which time a pronounced disagreement developed over the issue of food aid to Vietnam. The Buddhists argued that the peasants were not raising grain in large quantities because they were opposed to the Communist government. They felt that the U.S. should not weaken this resistance by sending food to Vietnam. The FOR staff took the position that Vietnam should be given American aid, including food. Shortly thereafter, Hassler requested that the FOR take responsibility for organizing a speaking tour for another Buddhist delegation from France, a group that included Thich Nhat Hanh. The proposal came before the national council in April 1978 but was turned down. One council member voiced the frank view "that the Vietnamese are not presenting a very progressive image."[64]

In a letter published in *Fellowship* in September 1978, Thich Nhat Hanh and another member of the Vietnamese delegation in Paris expressed their bitterness at the way the FOR had treated them and the cause of their persecuted brethren in Vietnam. It was understandable, they wrote, that the FOR sought to heal the wounds of war and therefore participated in efforts to send humanitarian aid to Vietnam. However, the FOR should know that very little of these aid shipments actually reached the Vietnamese people. Instead, the government used food and medicines as tools to strengthen its repressive grip. "Whatever else you find you must do," the two delegation members implored, "we hope you will at least find ways to express your concern and support for those you befriended so well in earlier years." The Buddhists were prepared to brave the government that oppressed them.

> But we would welcome the compassion and concern of our friends. For wanting to serve in our Buddhist way, for daring to challenge the present government as we have challenged earlier ones, we have been suffering for many months. Yet the peace organization closest to us, and to which we belong, is looking the other way. It finds something interesting and encouraging to say about the policies of

our government, but treats us who were sisters and brothers as if we were invisible or *dead*.

You are right when saying that you have no right to tell us what to do, whether we are in government or in prison. But you could still be our friends. You could be not only Americans but Earth citizens, protesting to our present government, as you have to other Vietnamese governments, the injustices we are suffering.

This is our hope in writing you, fellow members of the Fellowship of Reconciliation.[65]

Meanwhile, reports continued to accumulate about the worsening human rights situation in Vietnam. The government of Vietnam began to expel Vietnamese of Chinese descent. A large-scale exodus was now under way, with tens of thousands of Vietnamese of all class backgrounds seeking to flee the country in flimsy boats. The AFSC reaction continued to be one of denial that anything was amiss. John McAuliff, who visited Vietnam in August 1978, reported on his return that the "rebuilding and reunification is being carried out in a responsible and effective fashion." There were severe economic problems, caused by the failure of the United States to pay reparations for the damage it had caused, but most people maintained "a real spirit of change, social idealism and hope for the future."[66]

In September 1978 Charles Bloomstein of the New York Friends Group drew attention to the tragedy of the boat people and inquired whether Lou Schneider still thought that Vietnam was now "extraordinarily humane." In his reply to Bloomstein, John Sullivan, associate executive secretary for information and interpretation, pointed out that because the AFSC, determined to see people as people, made "the courageous effort to go to and relate to places where left ideology is institutionalized in government and society," it was often characterized as soft on communism. The AFSC had become vulnerable to this charge also because it refused to reinforce "the dishonest manipulation of anti-radicalism, anti-leftism, anti-communism." Moreover, noted Sullivan, "it is patently difficult for us to maintain relations with left societies, which I believe we should, and to be in the forefront of negative criticism of them." All this created a "tricky problem," but the AFSC had to persist on "this difficult course, trying to keep communications lines open, but with integrity."[67]

Joan Baez Speaks Out for Human Rights

On 30 May 1979 Joan Baez and other former antiwar activists placed large ads containing an "Open Letter to the Socialist Republic of Vietnam" in the *New York Times* and other major newspapers nationwide. The letter denounced the continuing detention, mistreatment, and torture of thousands of innocent Vietnamese in prisons and re-education camps. "For many, life is hell and death is prayed for." Among the signers of this new appeal on behalf of the victims of the Vietnamese Gulag were Staughton Lynd and Bradford Lyttle as well as Daniel Berrigan. Philip Berrigan signed but then changed his mind.[68] Dave Dellinger refused to endorse the appeal because it involved "wildly inflated charges from discredited sources." There was the strong possibility, he wrote, that the former student leader Doan Van Toai, one of Baez's main sources, was a CIA agent.[69]

In a letter sent to David McReynolds and other "pacifist friends" who had declined to sign the appeal, Baez accused her former antiwar colleagues of "behaving like guilt-ridden stooges of the Hanoi regime." That regime "seems to have you and certain outspoken members of the American Friends Service Committee, War Resisters League and the Mennonites in its pocket, and there is not enough light in there to see properly." The totalitarian government in Hanoi ran "one of the smoothest public relations operations since the Russian Politbureau of the 30s." Baez wrote that she was furious with those who had abandoned their social conscience and had let their ideological attachments become ideological blinders. "If you are against all violence, then speak up against violence anywhere and everywhere it takes place. If you justify, accept or support the violence of the left, then do so openly. If you tow [sic] the same line as Pham Van Dong, then defend him openly as Nixon defends the Shah."[70]

McReynolds replied in an equally angry tone and also circulated his letter to a large list of individuals. He accused Baez of being "possessed of a uniquely arrogant mind." Was it not possible, McReynolds asked, that he and others on the Left had looked at the same facts and drawn different conclusions and perhaps even had had access to additional facts Baez did not have? He still considered himself a pacifist and not a supporter of Hanoi. He had never called Baez an agent of the CIA. "I didn't even call Forest an agent, despite his close link with Al Hassler who retired to Franco's

Spain with a mysteriously acquired permanent visa." McReynolds added that while "Hassler was a tragic figure, and not a terribly pleasant or honest one," he did not think Hassler had worked for the CIA. "Some of your co-workers have links with the CIA — I assume you are aware of that." McReynolds closed his letter by inviting Baez to talk things over, although he thought it unlikely that she would "sit down face to face with some of us you call Hanoi's agents."[71]

McReynolds and other pacifist leaders refused to associate themselves with the Baez appeal for several reasons. There was first their strongly held conviction that after what they believed America had done to Vietnam, they were morally obligated not to attack the new regime or support any action that might discredit it. More important was the mystique of revolution that surrounded the Vietnamese Communists and legitimated their "defensive violence." For over ten years pacifists like Dellinger, Meacham, and McReynolds had closely identified with the Vietcong and North Vietnam and had met with them on numerous occasions, and now they were simply unable to cut the strong emotional bonds that had developed between them and the Vietnamese. An American pacifist close to Dellinger, who in 1967 spent eight days exchanging ideas with a small delegation of NLF and North Vietnamese representatives, expressed well why he could not get himself to condemn the revolutionary violence of his Vietnamese friends: "There is one crime worse than murder: to retire from the revolution."[72] McReynolds, too, considered himself "a comrade" of the NLF and Hanoi. "What makes us comrades is that we are joined in a struggle and our disagreement is over the tactics we use."[73] A revolution, like an earthquake, was the result of natural upheavals and therefore, presumably, beyond moral criticism.[74]

A rebuttal to the Baez "Open Letter," sponsored by the U.S. Peace Council, appeared in the *New York Times* of 24 June 1979. This reply, "The Truth about Vietnam," asserted that the government of the Socialist Republic of Vietnam had sent "some 400,000 servants of the former barbaric regimes" to re-education camps, and only forty thousand of these individuals remained incarcerated. This program of re-education was "absolutely necessary" and was conducted with a "remarkable spirit of moderation, restraint and clemency." There was no evidence to back up charges of torture. "Vietnam now enjoys human rights as it has never [before] known in [its] history as described in the International Covenant on Human Rights: the right to a job and safe, healthy working conditions, the right to join trade unions, the right to be free from hunger, from colonialism and racism." The Peace Council statement was such a crude exercise in apologetics that hardly any leaders of the peace movement were willing to subscribe to it. It was signed by Marjorie Boehm and Vivien Myerson, the president and vice president of the WILPF; Ruth Gage-Colby, the League's UN representative; Vivian Hallinan of the San Francisco branch; and Dorothy Steffens, the WILPF's former executive director.

By 1979 the WILPF in effect had become an integral part of the international Soviet propaganda network. A few weeks after the appearance of the Peace Council rebuttal, the WILPF received an appeal for additional support from the Vietnamese Women's Union. "We send you this letter as one of those who have long devoted strenuous efforts to the lofty struggle toward progress against oppression and exploitation. . . . We always bear in mind your great contribution which has helped us to gain final victory and to reunify our country." The letter asked for the WILPF's help against "a campaign of slander aimed at undermining Vietnam's international prestige, isolating the country and destroying the Revolution." The charges of gross violations of human rights were false, the Vietnamese women insisted. The ethnic Chinese were not being expelled but were leaving on their own accord because they no longer fit into Vietnam's socialism. These middle-class people had the choice of going to the new economic zones to work in agriculture or leaving the country. The government merely facilitated this choice.[75]

In January 1980 several WILPF members toured Vietnam and Cambodia at the invitation of the Vietnamese Women's Union. Their report, published in *Peace and Freedom,* provided the kind of publicity requested by the Vietnamese. According to the report, there was evidence of impressive social accomplishments in the South. "The aim of the socialist revolution is to bring equality to society and to do away with exploitation. Insofar as it has succeeded, that success has caused the exodus of those who will not live with the changes." The American women visited a re-education camp and a new economic zone — "all parts of the nation-building policy that incorporates the concept of 'reconciliation' with attempts to reform and even enlist otherwise alienated members of society." The re-education effort appealed to pride and nationalism and called for "participation in a nation where economic, social and human rights are a part of the fabric."[76]

The Horrors of Kampuchea

We find the same wishful thinking and the denial of painful realities in the AFSC's attitude toward revolutionary Cambodia (Kampuchea). In the spring of 1975, as resistance to the advancing Khmer Rouge was collapsing, AFSC program coordinator Russell Johnson assured his readers in *Peacework* that the Khmer Rouge leadership was "capable and committed" and that there was no reason to fear a "bloodbath." "Americans who are concerned about [a] 'bloodbath' should understand that communists ordinarily use violence for political purposes (apart from actual combat situations) and that in both Vietnam and Cambodia the major political intent once the war ends will be to consolidate their position and rally support from the population at all levels, including those who have hitherto been in opposition."[77]

There followed in quick succession the fall of Phnom Penh on 17 April, reports about the forced evacuation of the Cambodian capital carried out with ruthless determination that did not spare even patients in hospitals, and the first accounts of large-scale massacres. Cambodian radio broadcasts monitored in the West spoke of plans for a total revolution. However, John McAuliff, head of the AFSC's Indochina program, saw all that as part of an American attempt to discredit "the example of an alternative model of development and social organization" that could have a powerful impact on all of Southeast Asia. The U.S., he maintained, was well practiced in the art of spreading misinformation and creating false atrocity stories such as the "Hue massacre myth." "These precedents should encourage a healthy scepticism about the articles on Cambodia which appear in the U.S. press based on refugee stories and intelligence sources." There was need for "a sense of historical perspective," McAuliff declared, "both with the harsh events which followed our own Revolution and Civil War, and with other third world countries facing similar challenges of economic development and external subversion by a hostile superpower."[78]

McAuliff's apologia for the unfolding horrors of revolutionary Kampuchea drew a forceful reply from a member of the War Resisters League. This "long-time reader" of the *Indochina Program Newsletter* expressed his shock and distress at McAuliff's essay, especially the argument that refugee stories were to be regarded as unreliable. There was a time, he reminded McAuliff, when the Movement had "leaned exclusively on refugee stories and a few rumors to tell of what was happening on the Plain of Jars." Why should such accounts now be disregarded? "Refugee stories do not become reliable when they say what we want to hear and unreliable when they say what we don't want to hear. The Indochina Program has become intellectually dishonest — saying whatever is politically expedient to say at a given moment. . . . I want nothing more to do with you."[79]

AFSC old-timers like Russell Johnson had no problem with the Indochina program line on Kampuchea. Writing in *Peacework,* Johnson took note of "the intensification of 'bloodbath stories' purporting to be those of refugees of Cambodia which have appeared recently in *Time* and the *Wall Street Journal*" and attributed them to "a new wave of anti-communism" that was abroad in the land. He had known "this kind of brainwashing in the fifties and sixties." The U.S. government and other interested parties exploited apprehensions of totalitarianism "as a cover for objection to nations deciding to close their boundaries to exploitation by multinational corporations seeking raw materials, markets for surplus and cheap labor."[80] When, in March 1977, a reader of *Peacework* who had read the condensation of the book *Murder of a Gentle Land* by Anthony Paul and John Barron in *Reader's Digest* inquired why there was no public outcry over the mass killings in Kampuchea, another reader responded that *Reader's Digest* was simply out to discredit the revolution. The accomplishments of the new regime in Kampuchea, according to this reader, were "a source of inspiration and admiration."[81]

By the summer of 1977 only loyal admirers of the Indochina Communists like Gareth Porter of the Indochina Resource Center still persisted in disbelieving the recurring reports of mass executions of educated people and the systematic uprooting of traditional Cambodian culture and religion by the Khmer Rouge. In July 1978 Amnesty International informed the UN Commission on Human Rights that "an impartial examination of all available information indicates that fundamental human rights are being grossly violated in Democratic Kampuchea."[82] Yet the AFSC maintained a discreet silence. Only after Vietnam had invaded and seized Cambodia and had begun to publicize the atrocities of the Pol Pot regime, its former ally, did the AFSC finally acknowledge that these horrors had indeed taken place. AFSC board member Edward F. Snyder, who had been to Kampuchea as part of a five-person AFSC delegation to ascertain relief needs, reported after his return that Pol Pot had "reduced Kampuchea to a primitive agrarian society built on intimidation and death. An estimated one third of the population has died or been killed in the past four years."[83]

The Vietnamese invasion itself and the Chinese attack on Vietnam that followed were a bit of an embarrassment to an organization which had always argued that wars between nations occurred because of the sway of capitalism. Also, as Stewart Meacham and Russell Johnson had never tired of affirming, the intentions of the Vietnamese Communists were peaceful, and they would never threaten the other nations of the region. But the AFSC quickly recovered its composure by way of the time-honored device of blaming the new war in Southeast Asia on America. "As a pacifist organization," wrote the Rhode Island field secretaries of the AFSC in February 1979, "AFSC deplores the use of warfare to settle international disputes and, in particular, cannot condone the invasion of one country by another." Nevertheless, one had to understand the causes of this armed conflict, which included — in addition to long-standing historical animosities between Vietnam and Cambodia — past U.S. policy. There was, first of all, the devastating and brutalizing American bombing of peaceful and neutral Cambodia in order to deny the Vietnamese guerillas the use of Cambodian territory — "one of the worst war crimes in history." Furthermore, the U.S. could have prevented the invasion by providing food and reconstruction aid to Vietnam, thus easing substantially Vietnam's acute economic and food problems.[84]

John McAuliff was instrumental in preparing the document called "Statement on the Crisis in Southeast Asia," which expressed grave concern over both China's invasion of Vietnam and Vietnam's invasion of Kampuchea. The statement argued that the U.S. could play a role in achieving a political settlement of this conflict if it took a truly evenhanded approach. "To do this, the United States needs to understand and correct the manner in which its own military and diplomatic role in the region had contributed to the present disaster." The U.S. should establish normal diplomatic relations with Vietnam, lift the trade embargo, and contribute humanitarian aid to help "all people victimized by the current and previous wars."[85]

Russell Johnson, ready as always to see a U.S. hand in any world calamity, took these arguments still further. In an essay entitled "The Meaning of the Cambodian Tragedy," Johnson suggested that "one should hesitate to rush to judgment and must strive to have some empathy with the Khmer revolutionaries." One had to bear in mind the isolation of the new regime when it took power in 1975 and the earlier terrible American bombing that may have driven thousands out of their minds. Most important, it was necessary "to help concerned Americans understand why there may well be more Cambodian tragedies in the future unless we dedicate ourselves to making fundamental changes in the system which is betraying our best values and in the foreign and military policy designed to protect that system." It was the capitalist system that ever since the Bolshevik Revolution of 1917 had sought to destroy socialism based on the common ownership of the means of production and the abolition of private profit to corporate stockholders. It was the capitalist system "which led to American intervention in Vietnam following World War II, which in turn led to intervention in Cambodia and the resultant destruction and suffering inflicted on that once peaceful kingdom and its people."[86]

In 1979-80 the AFSC participated in the worldwide effort to ship relief supplies to Cambodia. The Cambodian Relief and Reconciliation Fund was established, which, according to *Peacework,* used "funds on a 50/50 basis for food support and political interpretation."[87] Presumably the effort to communicate to the American people the explanations developed by Russell Johnson and others in the AFSC about the deeper roots of the Cambodian tragedy was as important to the AFSC as the actual relief of starvation.

On the whole, during the last few years Indochina has received only limited attention from the AFSC's peace education effort. In part this undoubtedly has been due to the difficulty of continuing to describe Vietnam as a model of development and as a country practicing "socialism with a human face."

In 1981 Amnesty International published a report on the Socialist Republic of Vietnam, as unified Vietnam now was called, which sharply criticized the detention without trial of thousands of former members of the Saigon administration and its armed forces, in clear violation of the Paris Peace Agreement of January 1973, which prohibited such reprisals. Others incarcerated included former members of the Third Force, individuals accused of anti-government activities, and people arrested for attempting to flee the country. As of September 1980, the number of detainees was still said to be twenty thousand. Amnesty International concluded that compulsory detention for purposes of re-education — without trial and a regular review procedure, without inspection of the facilities by an independent body like the international committee of the Red Cross, and without adequate safeguards against mistreatment and torture — violated "basic principles of justice."[88] Other reports have been even more critical. Truong Nhu Tang, one of the founders of the NLF and later minister of justice of the PRG, after his escape from Vietnam in late 1979 described the North Vietnamese Communists as "architects of one of the world's most rigid regimes" who had introduced a system of oppression "unparalleled in Vietnam's history."[89]

Vietnam-occupied Cambodia, too, continues to receive bad press. In November 1984 a three-member group representing the Lawyers Committee for International Human Rights criticized the involvement of Vietnamese in the arrest and torture of Cambodian citizens. The noted civil rights lawyer Floyd Abrams told the *New York Times* in an interview that Cambodia today is a country "in which people are arrested without charges being made and jailed without being convicted, in which confessions are forced and torture seems to be commonplace."[90] In June 1987 Amnesty International issued a report which charged that Cambodia was holding thousands of political prisoners without charge or trial under "cruel and inhuman" conditions and that "many do not survive the ordeal."[91] In a rare instance of candor, *Fellowship,* the magazine of the FOR, recently opened its pages to an American official of Amnesty International, who accused Vietnamese military and civilian officials of playing a role in political arrests and torture in Kampuchea. The article called on members of the U.S. peace movement to express their concern to the governments of the People's Republic of Kampuchea and Vietnam.[92] With all this negative publicity for the Socialist Republic of Vietnam, accusations that simply could no longer be denied or explained away, it is not surprising that American pacifists in recent years have sought to find other socialist revolutions to be admired and protected against "American imperialism."

CHAPTER 7

The Romance with Cuba and Grenada

Cuba as a Model of Popular Government

Almost from the start, American pacifist organizations have shared the New Left's romantic attachment to Castro's Cuba, and this fanciful picture of the Cuban revolution has remained intact in the face of all adverse information. In October 1969 a team of four Quakers spent four weeks in Cuba, and in 1970 the AFSC published a lengthy report on this "Visit to the Revolution," as the report was subtitled. The visitors noted "the absence of formal channels for . . . dissent in Cuba. There are no opposition parties or press. The Communist Party is the controlling political organization." They also were disturbed by the little children who chanted slogans as they marched to class and by the large number of uniformed men and women everywhere. "We fear that such martial patterns may become a way of life, difficult to pluck from the fabric of society." The Committees for the Defense of the Revolution, established on each city block, were described as protection against "any effort to pull Cuba away from socialism," though the visitors saw them also as "a powerful influence toward political conformity." Still, the team was satisfied that the country was not "the sort of 'police state' many Americans imagine Cuba to be," and they believed that there were good explanations for the controls that had been imposed. "We recognize the reasons for strict vigilance in the country — U.S. government hostility and the antagonism of Cuban exiles."

The visiting Quakers found that there was no provision for conscientious objection to the three-year military service obligatory for all young men, but there were said to be few such conscientious objectors anyway. As a young Cuban Quaker explained to the visitors, "Pacifism in the United States with the war in Vietnam is completely different from the defense of a country like Cuba." The churches operated under various restrictions: their schools and colleges had been confiscated; they could not hold outdoor services; they had great difficulty in printing their materials; foreign publications sent to clergymen by mail often did not arrive. But, the visitors thought, the poor relations between church and state that had existed in the early years of the revolution were being overcome. The government did not want to infringe on anyone's religious beliefs; it merely wanted the churches to participate more fully in the constructive social program of the revolution.

On the whole, then, the overall impression was positive. The problems that existed were not systemic, the visitors claimed, but had to "be seen within the context of a country only ten years into very radical change. . . . Mistakes, some severe, have been made and admitted, and the leadership seems to have been learning. Our impression is that the Cuban Revolution is today a going concern." Despite rigorous rationing, there were no signs of hunger. The new holders of power were not out to enrich themselves at the expense of the population. "We feel that the Revolution has strong support from the majority of the people," declared the visitors. We cannot judge, they noted, "conditions or practices with which we have had no direct encounters. We cannot comment on the numbers of or living conditions of political prisoners, for instance, or on the possibility that Cuba may be training 'revolutionaries for export.' "[1]

An internal summary report submitted to the peace education division was still more commendatory. "The Cuban Revolution appears dedicated to meeting the needs of the majority of the people." The Communist party had dominant political influence. However, the report stated, "we feel that Party policies are determined with sensitivity to the interests of the society as a whole. Through unique social and political institutions, the Cuban Revolution is attempting to eliminate the gap between the constituency and the government."[2]

In a letter she wrote to Lyndon B. Johnson in October 1962, WILPF president Dorothy Hutchinson told the vice president that the WILPF agreed with him "in deploring the totalitarian characteristics of the Cuban regime and the role which the U.S.S.R. is now playing in Cuba."[3] Seven years later, in October 1969, WILPF president Kay Camp described her trip to Cuba as part of a WILPF delegation in quite different language. The American visitors had been guests of the Federation of Cuban Women, who had escorted them "to observe the many impressive achievements of the Revolution." They had also seen "some serious restrictions on freedom of which most North Americans are aware." However, Camp noted, "most North Americans are not aware of the seriousness of the challenge Castroism presents to the concept of Western democracy throughout the Third World."[4]

Relations between the WILPF and Cuba continued to become closer during the following years. In her report to the national board meeting in October 1973, executive director Dorothy R. Steffens described her recent visit to the island — "the amazing strides in education in Cuba, how living and working conditions have changed and the new role(s) and status of women." She eagerly looked forward to speaking about all she had seen in visits to WILPF branches and regions. "It's hard to postpone talking about how it feels to be inside an unalienated society — a country where people speak glowingly, yet openly and with humor, about the new world they are building together, . . . and are supremely confident they hold the future in their own hands." Steffens reported that the Federation of Cuban Women (FMC) was eager to meet with the WILPF.[5] In December 1975 the WILPF sent the FMC a telegram that said, "New Year's Greetings to our Cuban sisters and congratulations on 1975 FMC Congress and Party Congress."[6] Such organizational ties clearly went beyond the romantic attachment to Castro's Cuba common among the New Left. It must be remembered that an organization like the Federation of Cuban Women in a Communist country, unlike the League of Women Voters in the U.S., is not an independent, voluntary group but is closely linked to the ruling Communist party. Some years later, in 1986, the head of the FMC was even given a seat on the Politburo.

In February 1976 Marjorie Boehm, who became president of the WILPF the following year, attended an "Angolan Seminar" held in Havana, her travel expenses paid by the Cubans. The seminar, Boehm reported to the national board in March, had been arranged at the request of the People's Republic of Angola. "I learned a great deal about Angola and about what other organizations in the U.S. are doing to help the MPLA [People's Movement for the Liberation of Angola] and stop U.S. intervention. I loved being in Cuba!" The WILPF board agreed to work for the support of the People's Republic of Angola and to offer WILPF hospitality to an Angolan delegation.[7]

In March 1977 the Federation of Cuban Women once again invited a WILPF delegation to visit Cuba. The invitation included the wish that the WILPF have "new and greater success in the important work in which your organization is engaged for peace, disarmament and international solidarity, work which unites all the women of the world in the struggle for a better future."[8] A solidarity resolution adopted by the national plenary of the FMC in April, sent to the WILPF, expressed "admiration, respect, fraternal friendship and unbreakable solidarity" to "the women of the glorious homeland of Lenin," to the heroic combatants of Angola, to all those fighting for national liberation, and to "those, who inside the entrails of imperialism, in the United States, fight for changing the ruling system and who act together with their sisters who all over the world struggle for gaining a future that is free of exploitation, misery and death, a different future."[9]

After a visit to Cuba in 1978, Patrick Lacefield, a member of the FOR executive committee, reported in the pages of *Fellowship* that Cuba held an estimated twenty thousand political prisoners but that Castro's Cuba also could boast of many genuine achievements. In a rare voice of dissent from the ranks, a reader of *Fellowship* pointed out in a letter to the editor that the equivalent number of political prisoners in the United States, allowing for the difference in population, would be 500,000. "It is painful," he wrote, "to see pacifists and self-proclaimed 'democratic socialists' like Lacefield buy the tired nonsense that material advantages can be purchased at the cost of thousands of political prisoners."[10] Two years later Paul Deats, the chairman of the FOR, returned from a visit to Cuba, arranged by the Cuban Ministry of Religious Affairs, with the impression that the Cuban churches were divided "between critical support and quiet opposition." Deats wrote that he had not seen or sensed the kind of deep poverty or political oppression to be found in many Latin American and Caribbean countries. "We felt that people walked with self-assurance and seemed happy."[11]

The infatuation of the AFSC with Castro's Cuba has likewise continued. In August 1981 AFSC staffer Ken Dossar praised the Cuban revolution for creating a "new person" and for "moving toward the goal of constructing a new society aided by a process called Popular Power." In Cuba, Dossar pointed out, more than 95 percent of the citizens participated in elections, whereas in the last American presidential election, only 29 percent of all registered voters had actually cast their ballots. The Cuban Communist party, he claimed, "has the basic objective of the widest possible participation of the people in the government."[12] AFSC veteran staffer Russell Johnson has defended even the longtime presence of Cuban mercenaries in Angola. In April 1976 he wrote that Cuba was "making a substantial contribution to another people" who seek liberty, independence, and "socialist economic growth."[13]

By the early 1980s the Cuban revolution had lost much of its early luster. Human rights organizations like Americas Watch and Amnesty International have reported that the number of political prisoners in Cuba, arrested solely on account of their ideological opposition to the country's Communist regime, is proportionately among the highest in the world, and that some of these prisoners are also among the longest serving prisoners. Upon completion of their original sentences, many have been resentenced without any legal defense or other due process of law. So-called "deviants," including homosexuals and members of religious sects, have been harassed and imprisoned. Reports of mistreatment in jails and detention camps, including torture and lack of medical attention, are numerous. Amnesty International has made one visit to the country, but all other requests for visitations — made by the International Committee of the Red Cross, the UN Human Rights Commission, the Inter-American Commission on Human Rights, and Americas Watch — have been refused.[14] On examination, the much-touted social advances of the Castro regime turn out to be no greater than those of several other Caribbean and Central American societies; in fact, in some cases Cuba is actually lagging behind.[15] Since Castro's assumption of power in 1959, Cuba has dropped from fourth in Latin American nations in per-capita income to twenty-first or twenty-second. Shortages of basic foodstuffs and clothing continue to bedevil the Cuban economy.[16] Regimes that purport to provide bread at the expense of liberty end up providing neither bread nor liberty. Castro's Cuba — which, according to the AFSC, has strong popular support — has experienced the flight of 1.2 million of its people, more than 10 percent of its total population.

By now, the eyewitness stories told by former close associates of Castro like Huber Matos, Carlos Franqui, and Fidel's sister Juanita have led many former supporters and admirers of Castro to desert his cause. Prominent men of the Left like Jean-Paul Sartre, Noam Chomsky, and I. F. Stone have protested the imprisonment of Cuban educators, writers, and churchmen. Meanwhile, Castro's jailers make good use of the few remaining fans of the Cuban revolution like the AFSC, and for those imprisoned the effect is said to be crushing. The poet Armando Valladares, released in 1983 after serving twenty-two years in various Cuban political prisons, has told how he and his fellow inmates were regularly provided with translations of pamphlets and articles favorable to Castro authored by various American Christians. This was worse than the beatings or the hunger. "While we waited for the embrace of solidarity from our brothers in Christ, incomprehensibly to us those who were embraced were our tormentors." Thus, he went on to say, the Christians in Cuba's prisons today suffer not only the pain of torture and isolation but also the conviction that they have been deserted by their brothers in Christ.[17]

Despite all this negative publicity, most American pacifists appear to have remained loyal to Castro. In November 1985 Jim Antal, executive secretary of the FOR, participated in a religious delegation to Cuba, invited by the Cuban Ecumenical Council. His reactions were positive. Antal acknowledged that the Ecumenical Council, composed of seven Protestant denominations, was "quite progressive — it cooperates closely and enjoys friendly relations with the [Communist] Party." He noted without comment that several other Protestant denominations (Baptists, Pentecostals, Seventh Day Adventists) were not members of the Council. The fact that the people who showed him around were quasi-officials of the Communist government did not, in his eyes, detract from their trustworthiness.

Antal exhibited the same gullibility in a meeting with a local Committee for the Defense of the Revolution, about which he observed, "The most deep experience of the people is their gratitude for the improved conditions which the Revolution has brought about." While students of the Cuban revolution consider the primary function of these committees to be that of a network of watchdogs and informers for the government, Antal regarded them as "a well structured version of block organizations present in parts of the US." During a visit to the Isle of Youth, where Cuba hosts about fifteen thousand students from Third World countries in order to inculcate them with revolutionary consciousness, Antal was impressed by the education given these young people, mostly of high-school age. The Cubans, he related, were proud that they were "able to contribute to the struggle of countries' even poorer than themselves by helping to develop leadership in the youth of these countries." At the Namibian School, Antal and his colleagues were greeted with dances and songs. "My eyes watered as we all joined hands and joined the chorus," Antal reported.

But Antal had no tears for the fate of Castro's political prisoners. When this matter came up in a meeting with an official of the central committee of the Communist party, it turned out that "no member of the delegation was adequately briefed on the issue to press it." On another occasion, in a discussion with a member of the National Union of Jurists, the delegation was told that there were fewer than three hundred political prisoners, that the cases that had attracted so much public attention were "exaggerated," and that in the future religious delegations would be able to pay pastoral visits to prisoners. Altogether, there now were "fewer and fewer crimes, since the society is more and more just." That bill of goods, too, was accepted without challenge.

And so it went. The meeting with Castro was "electrifying," Antal reported. The delegates sat on the edge of their chairs because Castro "brings an excitement to the room that I had never before experienced." Cuban society, Antal summarized, was "a much more approachable place than the Soviet Union. There is an absence of ideological dogma, and a wonderful warmth that the people extend to North Americans. One has a sense of freedom and openness — partly due to climate, but fully manifest in social exchange. On an official level, the major concern is not control, but hospitality and responding to requests. Cuba has developed a distinctive form of Marxist-Leninist-Socialism, one that is more accessible to North Americans." Cuba had done all it could to improve relations with the United States, Antal claimed. It was up to the U.S. to acknowledge the right of the people of Latin America to determine their own form of government. This process had to begin soon "unless the US is willing to exact heretofore unseen forms of repression on the people of LA [Latin America]."[18]

The Communist Jewel in the Caribbean

Not surprisingly, American pacifists vigorously denounced the brief American intervention in Grenada in October 1983. The U.S. claim that the invasion had been undertaken to preserve democracy and American lives was rejected. An AFSC statement declared that "the real message to the world is that the present U.S. administration is prepared to use any means, including military intervention, to stifle any attempt at social change and to prevent any challenge to its power to control the terms of political and economic life in a region determined by it to be an area of U.S. interest."[19] A five-person AFSC delegation that visited Grenada and neighboring islands from 27 December 1983 to 10 January 1984 reported upon its return that a "deep feeling of cynicism and dependence" existed in Grenada, "which, before October, represented an experiment in new forms of social organization and development. Civil rights are curtailed. . . . Repression has spread to other Caribbean islands, and dissenters are being intimidated."[20]

It is difficult to take seriously the AFSC's concern for political freedom in Grenada in the wake of the toppling of the New Jewel movement. The few restrictions on civil rights imposed by the Americans, all short-lived, surely pale before the massive violations of human rights that occurred under the regimé of Maurice Bishop. The People's Revolutionary Government of Grenada, established in March 1979 by Bishop in a bloodless coup, had, by the time of the American intervention, shut down all independent news media and jailed several hundred Grenadians on political charges, keeping them in crowded, filthy prisons. As the documents seized by the Americans reveal conclusively, the leaders of the New Jewel movement considered themselves dedicated Communists. They spoke of building a "Marxist-Leninist vanguard party" that would "lead the people to socialism and communism."[21] In agreements signed "in the spirit of anti-imperialist solidarity and proletarian internationalism" with Cuba, the Soviet Union, and other Soviet bloc nations, they promised to carry on the "struggle against imperialism, neo-colonialism, racism and Zionism." In a report to his government, W. Richard Jacobs, the Grenadian ambassador in the Soviet Union, expressed his pleasure that the comrades in Moscow recognized the New Jewel movement as a fraternal "communist party." For Grenada to assume a position of prestige and importance to the Soviet Union, it was necessary that Grenada "be the sponsor of revolutionary activity and progressive developments in this region at least." The "most likely candidate for special attention" was Surinam; another possibility was Belize.[22]

It is true that the Bishop regime presented itself to the outside world as "progressive" and "non-aligned" and took a few non-communists into the government. As Bishop told a party meeting in September 1982, these deceptions were necessary "so that imperialism won't get too excited" and send in troops.[23] However, the AFSC had a special relationship with the New Jewel movement, and at least some AFSC staffers undoubtedly were fully aware of the true nature of the "new forms of social organization and development" that the Bishop regime had imposed on the people of Grenada.

In the spring of 1983, Ian Jacobs, a special assistant to Bishop, had been on a tour of the United States. After his return to Grenada, Jacobs listed the AFSC among the "key organizations" that had contributed to the success of his visit. When "a wealthy Jew who is very supportive of the Peace Movement" agreed to contribute from $1,000 to $2,000 toward the purchase of a word processor if a tax credit could be arranged for him, Jacobs spoke to a contact at the AFSC in Philadelphia so that "he [the would-be contributor] can send the money to them and then they will send it here."[24] We do not know whether the plans for this money-laundering operation were actually carried out. What we do know is that AFSC staffer Kaisha Brown, a member of the AFSC delegation to Grenada after the American intervention, visited the island at least two other times during 1983 and, in her own words, had a "close psychological, social, historical, emotional and political relationship to the people, the nation and the government of Grenada under the New Jewel Movement."[25] It is rather unlikely that a person so intimate with the New Jewel movement did not understand the real aims of the "progressive" Bishop regime.

Brown was not the only AFSC staffer to wax enthusiastic about the "new jewel" in the Caribbean. In an article published in 1983 in the AFSC's *Third World Coalition News,* former AFSC Caribbean staffer Atherton Martin hailed the fact that in 1979 two new countries, Grenada and Nicaragua, had "moved dramatically forward along the path toward liberation." Cuba now was no longer alone, and a triangular counter-offensive to the machinations of imperialism (the Soviet code-word for the United States) had been put in motion. In this triangular relationship between Cuba, Grenada, and Nicaragua, a cumulatively more powerful unit had been created that would share "the spoils of freedom, peace, justice, economic and political self-determination."

Martin ended his essay by expressing the hope that "soon new liberation triangles can be constructed in the region that would enhance the Caribbean/Central American process and overcome once and for all the real enemies of justice, peace and freedom."[26] Is it a mere coincidence that Soviet leaders used exactly the same language to describe the situation in this region prior to the overthrow of the Bishop regime? In March 1983 Marshal Nikolai Ogarkov, chief of the general staff of the Soviet armed forces, declared that two decades ago, "there was only Cuba in Latin America, today there are Nicaragua, Grenada and a serious battle is going in El Salvador." The U.S. would try to prevent progress, "but there were no prospects for imperialism to turn back history."[27] The statement that the AFSC board issued on Grenada in October 1983 used more moderate terminology, and most members of the board probably did not know much about the Marxist-Leninist character of the Bishop regime. But, of course, the AFSC board has generally functioned in this way. Its public pronouncements have promulgated a philosophy of "peace and justice" while the AFSC staff, many of them non-Quakers, have freely gone about their business of establishing close ties with revolutionary Marxist movements all over the world.

CHAPTER **8**

The Struggle for Central America

In the late 1970s Central America had reached a point of convulsive turmoil. The year 1979 saw the overthrow of the Somoza dynasty in Nicaragua and the toppling of Colonel Humberto Romero in El Salvador. Cuban-backed guerillas were mounting increasingly violent campaigns against the governments of Guatemala and El Salvador. Here, then, was another opportunity for American pacifists to demonstrate their commitment to the "struggle of the oppressed."

In El Salvador the Romero government had been overthrown by a group of reform-oriented officers because Romero had been unable to stem the tide of leftist terrorism and because he had refused to undertake needed political and social reforms. In March 1980 José Napoleón Duarte, a Christian Democrat who had won the 1972 presidential election only to be arrested and tortured by the military, returned from exile to a hero's welcome and joined the military-civilian junta that now governed the country. In the same month the new government announced a far-reaching program of land reform, yet the leftist guerillas stepped up their attacks in both the countryside and the urban areas. In April 1980, after the assassination of Archbishop Arturo Romero allegedly by right-wing terrorists, several dissident Christian Democrats joined an umbrella group of Marxist-Leninist organizations to form the Revolutionary Democratic Front (FDR). In November, at the urging of Fidel Castro, the various Marxist-Leninist guerilla groups coalesced into the Farabundo Martí National Liberation Front (FMLN). Significantly, to this day the political leadership of the FDR has no representation in the command structure of the FMLN, which consists of assorted Marxist-Leninists. The main function of the FDR appears to be to solicit political support for the FMLN.

Against Aid to the New Government of El Salvador

The new government of El Salvador, under pressure from both the Right and the Left, was weak, yet it had set the country on the path of political and social reform. The AFSC refused to acknowledge the legitimacy of this process and from the beginning took the side of the leftist insurgents. American military and economic aid to El Salvador was condemned as shoring up a repressive regime. In the summer of 1980, Ron Young, head of the peace education division, returned from a visit to El Salvador to report that the organizations opposed to the junta had significant popular support and represented a hopeful development toward the triumph of justice and liberty.[1] In an internal discussion paper, another AFSC staffer, Kenneth Dossar, who had visited Central America as part of an AFSC delegation in late 1980, argued that "the struggle in El Salvador is essentially for the same goals sought by the human rights movement that has flowered out of Dr. King's self-sacrifice." This conflict was part of a worldwide struggle against colonialism and imperialism; hunger, poverty, and illiteracy were "fueling the movement of the populace toward armed struggle." The U.S., Dossar insisted, had no right "to support efforts that would abort the natural process that is occurring in El Salvador."[2] In March 1981 Phillip Berryman, who until 1980 had been the AFSC representative in Central America, told the House Subcommittee on Inter-American Affairs that "a large popular insurgency in El Salvador, coordinated by a coalition of Marxists and non-Marxists," was attempting to overthrow a brutally repressive government. The land reform was merely "a pretext for and means to military control of the countryside."[3]

As the civil war in El Salvador heated up, the same forces that had pushed for the unconditional withdrawal of the U.S. from Vietnam and had successfully labored to cut American aid to the Saigon government now teamed up for the second time — to halt "U.S. intervention in Central America." American pacifists were once again an integral part of this coalition effort. Some of the activists were old-timers. For example, Fred Branfman, formerly co-director of the Indochina Resource Center (with much justification called "the Hanoi Lobby" by many in Washington at the time), now emerged as director of the Commission on U.S.-Central American Relations. The Commission included among its constituent organizations the Coalition for a New Foreign and Military Policy (which had evolved out of the Coalition to Stop Funding the [Vietnam] War), the Institute for Policy Studies, and the AFSC. A representative of the AFSC served on the board of the Washington Office on Latin America, another of the numerous Washington lobbies for the Central American Left. Among the organizations which, according to the AFSC, could "assist you in learning more about Central America and in organizing activities in your community, church or union,"[4] was the Committee in Solidarity with the People of El Salvador (CISPES), begun in 1980 with seed money from the American Communist party and its front, the U.S. Peace Council.[5] All of these groups, with varying degrees of militancy, oppose U.S. aid to the government of El Salvador while at the same time they minimize or deny Soviet-bloc support for the insurgents. They are part of what Suzanne Garment in the *Wall Street Journal* has called the American Left's new cottage industry, which "uses the language of human rights and social justice to delegitimize our imperfect efforts" to nurture democratic regimes in Central America.[6]

The AFSC is part of this industry. Writing in *Peacework,* Jerry Elmer of the Rhode Island regional office noted what he saw as a parallel between the American intervention in Vietnam and that in El Salvador — both were the result of the "underlying imperialism of American foreign policy," which aimed at protecting the interests of U.S.-based multinational corporations and their access to markets and cheap labor. "Like Vietnam, the growing conflict in El Salvador is not primarily a civil war between factions of El Salvadoreans, but rather is between Salvadoreans fighting for freedom and self-determination and the same foreign aggressor seeking to impose an unpopular government."[7] The widely hailed elections for a constituent assembly held in March 1982 were rejected as a sham, and the AFSC joined with SANE, CISPES, the National Lawyers Guild, the U.S. Peace Council, and other organizations of the Left in continuing to oppose U.S. military aid to the government of El Salvador.[8]

The other pacifist organizations have taken the same position. For example, the editor of *Fellowship* wrote an article on El Salvador in early 1981 in which he declared that the United States "has chosen to thwart rather than support the legitimate aspirations of an oppressed people." The opposition to the ruling junta had wide popular backing, and the U.S. supported a military regime "in its war against its own people."[9] In a replay of the Vietnam story, the FOR, together with the entire "peace and justice" network, has sought to promote peace by ending all U.S. aid to the government of El Salvador — a sure recipe for a victory of the Marxist-Leninist guerillas, who receive their arms from Nicaragua, Cuba, and the Soviet Union.

In 1982 the WILPF teamed up with the AFSC, the FOR, the WRL, SANE, CISPES, the National Lawyers Guild, and the U.S. Peace Council in the Campaign for Peace and Justice in Central America, which opposed all U.S. military aid to El Salvador, Honduras, and Guatemala. In an address to the northeast regional biennial in June 1984, Kay Camp, WILPF disarmament coordinator, denounced the American pattern of global intervention and observed that human rights deteriorated whenever the U.S. intervened.[10]

The strategy of getting the Americans off the backs of the revolutionaries by eliminating or reducing aid to a beleaguered government — a strategy that had worked so well in Vietnam — did not meet with the same success in El Salvador, and Congress has continued to fund economic and military aid to that troubled and war-torn country. The gradual reduction of right-wing death squad activity by the Duarte government undercut the American Left's denunciation of El Salvador's "repressive government." The rebels themselves agreed in September 1985 to form a Marxist-Leninist vanguard party to lead the way toward socialism, thus making ridiculous the argument of their American supporters that the FMLN represented a broadly based, popular coalition effort.

On the other hand, the pacifists' agitation against U.S. intervention fell on more fertile soil in connection with American policy toward Sandinista-ruled Nicaragua. Here, too, the pacifist community identified with the new revolutionary regime from the beginning and defended it against the charge of being communist.

Support for the Sandinista Revolution

After the Reagan administration had adopted a sharply hostile attitude toward the Sandinistas, accusing them of serious human rights violations and of subverting neighboring countries, the AFSC joined those who argued that it was U.S. policy which was pushing Nicaragua into the Soviet orbit. The implication was that more friendly treatment by the U.S. would have allowed the Nicaraguan revolution to evolve in a more democratic direction. The same argument had been pressed earlier concerning the Cuban revolution, but today knowledgeable students of Cuba agree that Castro's revolution would have turned leftward no matter what the U.S. did or did not do.[11] According to Tad Szulc, author of a new study of Castro based on previously secret or unavailable sources, a careful reconstruction of events in the weeks and months after Fidel Castro took power in 1959 "makes it clear how, from the outset, Castro went about turning Cuba into a Marxist-Leninist state, with the collaboration of old-line Communists and the new Communist cadres he was creating within the rebel army."[12]

In the case of the Nicaraguan revolution, the issue is even more clear-cut. During the eighteen months before Ronald Reagan assumed the presidency and while the Carter administration provided the new government of Nicaragua with $118 million in aid—more than it received from any other country—the Sandinistas began the systematic harassment of both the Catholic and the Protestant churches, turned toward the Soviet bloc for help in setting up a tightly organized internal security apparatus, introduced censorship, and established fraternal party-to-party ties with the Communist party of the Soviet Union. In August 1981, well before the "Contras" had received any aid from the new Reagan administration, minister of defense Humberto Ortega declared in a speech to army officers that the revolution was guided by the scientific doctrine of Marxism-Leninism. "A Sandinismo without Marxism-Leninism cannot be revolutionary." The alliance with the bourgeoisie, Ortega explained, was "temporary and exclusively tactical." The elections planned for 1984 would in no way decide who would hold power, for "this power belongs to the FSLN [Sandinista National Liberation Front], to our Directorate."[13]

During the following two years the Catholic bishops of Nicaragua, labor leaders, human rights advocates, newspaper editors, and many others reported the stepped-up repression practiced against any independent voice or institution in Nicaragua, and the country's ominous drift toward totalitarian rule. The AFSC saw no reason to worry and defended the Sandinista regime as practicing a largely homegrown, nonaligned Marxism, not dependent on either the Soviet Union or Cuba. In a pamphlet the revolution was said to serve "the basic needs of the majority." Like the socialism of North Vietnam, the Marxism of the Sandinistas was described as "indigenous" and aimed at building an authentically Central American form of revolution that would be "dynamic, open, and experimental."[14]

In a book published in 1984, Phillip Berryman, the author of the just-quoted AFSC pamphlet, elaborated on his view that Nicaragua not only was not totalitarian but actually was creating a new, superior kind of democracy. It was wrong, he maintained, to identify democracy with elections and other "Western forms." For a country like Nicaragua, grass-roots participation in the task of building a new, just order and "economic democracy" were far more important than the rituals of "bourgeois democracy." The massive mobilization of volunteers for such tasks as picking coffee and cotton, the Sandinista Defense Committees, and the popular militias were all examples of a new kind of democracy—"people's power." Moreover, Berryman argued, as long as the revolution was still fragile and vulnerable, it was probably necessary to curtail the privileges of those opposed to the revolution, including their use of freedom of the press. There were no ideal revolutions, and human rights had to be ranked in order of importance. "The basic issue might be stated this way: The Nicaraguan people have a right to their revolution, which is the means whereby the poor will achieve their rights to life and the basic means to life, to culture, to political participation, and so forth. Their rights are prior rights, both over the luxury consumption and further accumulation of wealth of the privileged and over the elites' right to 'pluralism' or to certain political forms."[15]

Berryman acknowledged that his categories of analysis—"bourgeois democracy" versus "economic democracy," the priority of the rights of the revolution over those of political pluralism, and the assumption that pluralism served merely the privileged classes—were Marxist. However, he insisted, it was wrong to equate Marxism with totalitarianism. The historical record of socialism was mixed, and even the Soviet Union, despite its forced-labor camps and the suppression of dissidents, did not simply embody totalitarianism. Certainly the foreign policy of the Soviet Union, which usually supported "the poor in liberation movements," was preferable to that of the U.S., which was "more apt to be allied with dominant elites and military regimes." The deformation of socialist societies had to be seen "in terms of their particular histories" and was not inevitable; the future was open. "Implied here," noted Berryman, "is an act of faith in the creativity of Central America, that out of their own resources, and learning from other experiences, they may be able to form a new kind of society, in which the needs of the poor will be better served and there will be a greater measure of real freedom for all."[16]

A representative of the FOR who, together with 150 other religious figures, journeyed to Nicaragua in 1983 in order to call for a peaceful end to the fighting on that country's borders was at first shocked by the degree to which Nicaragua had been militarized. He soon convinced himself, however, that this was due to U.S. policy and that in this situation pacifists had to support the Sandinista regime. "While I do not support the taking up of arms myself," he wrote in *Fellowship* in late 1983, "I feel that I must stand firmly in solidarity with the poor people who take up arms in revolutionary struggle." When speaking of peace in Central America, it was necessary first to speak of justice and liberation. "If we take time to listen to the poor in Latin America, we will hear that the most important step North American pacifists can take is to stop US military and economic intervention in their countries." Once American pacifists have more of an impact on U.S. policy, the representative claimed, "nonviolent struggle will become a more attractive and more possible option for the people of Central America."[17]

This indirect aid to the Sandinistas and other Marxist-Leninists in Central America was criticized as inadequate in a companion piece written by an Ecuadoran Roman Catholic theologian. The capitalist system represented "institutionalized violence," and those who controlled that system labeled any opposition to it as violent, subversive, or terrorist. "That is why the nonviolence stance called for by some US peace groups arouses suspicion. Could it be that nonviolence is one of the reactions permitted the victims by the system to prevent a radical change of its structures? Could nonviolence become an ideology that serves and protects the capitalist system?" The theologian went on to say that the Latin American bishops had realized that this could happen and therefore had placed the responsibility for the temptation to use violence to overcome the institutionalized violence in Latin America on the shoulders of those who supported and benefited from the status quo. The victims had a right to defend themselves — even using violence. "Those who struggle for liberation do not want the death of those in power," claimed the theologian, "but their conversion."[18]

While the FOR is not yet prepared to regard its commitment to nonviolence and pacifism as an ideology that "serves and protects the capitalist system," the Fellowship has done everything else possible to aid the Sandinista regime and other Marxist-Leninist movements in Latin America short of actually participating in armed struggle. In the face of massive contrary evidence, the FOR persists in portraying the Sandinista regime as a unique revolution that subscribes to pluralism and nonalignment. The Sandinistas, Sidney Lens wrote in *Fellowship* in June 1984, do not want to take the Cuban road to socialism or adopt Cuban foreign policy.[19] The FOR supports "Witness for Peace," which sends Americans to the border of Nicaragua and Honduras in order to provide a protective shield for the people of Nicaragua against Contra attacks. Richard Deats, executive secretary of the FOR, participated in such a vigil in December 1983 and January 1984.

The FOR has raised money and helped coordinate the shipment to Nicaragua of medicines, school supplies, fishing equipment, and other "instruments for health and life" in order "to support democracy and pluralism" in that country. The national council of the FOR has gone on record as opposing all military training and assistance for Latin American forces and as opposing any form of political or economic intervention "that may interfere with genuine self-determination for the people of Latin America or thwart the development of their economic institutions."[20] Together with CISPES, the National Lawyers Guild, the U.S. Peace Council, and other "peace and justice" organizations, the FOR has demonstrated in Washington to stop U.S. military intervention in Central America, the Middle East, and Europe.[21] In December 1984 the FOR, together with two North Carolina groups, published "An Open Letter to Soldiers at Ft. Bragg" in the daily newspaper of Fayetteville, North Carolina, which told the troops that should "the order to move against the people of Nicaragua come, you do have other options."[22]

The WRL's infatuation with the mystique of revolution may explain the almost compulsive support the League has expressed from the beginning for the Sandinista revolution in Nicaragua. Once again, it would seem, this support was granted primarily to the idea of revolution incarnated in the new revolutionary regime, for the League was fully aware of the Sandinistas' shortcomings and equivocations. Linnea Capps, chairwoman of the WRL, was part of a delegation of twenty-two American socialists who visited Nicaragua at the invitation of the Sandinistas in January 1983. When she returned, she reported that there were problems about such things as freedom of the press. "Answers about non-alignment and Nicaragua's lack of criticism of Soviet imperialism were less than satisfying," she noted. The delegation had received few replies to their questions about the mistreatment of the Miskito Indians. Nevertheless, she concluded, the accomplishments of the revolution were "evident," and there was reason to hope that political and economic pluralism could be preserved.[23]

The WRL has also been disturbed about the refusal of the Sandinistas to provide for the right of conscientious objection to military service. However, the League has not allowed this disagreement to interfere with its endorsement of the Sandinista revolution, either. When Joanne Sheehan, a member of the executive committee of the

War Resisters International (WRI), wrote to the ambassador of Nicaragua in Washington in February 1984 and pleaded for Managua's legal recognition of CO status, she prefaced her remarks with this statement: "I should begin by saying that the WRI is very much in support of the people's revolution in Nicaragua. . . . We are *not* in opposition to the ideals of your revolution."[24]

During the last few years the adoption of various repressive measures by the Nicaraguan revolution has tested the loyalty of its supporters. The mistreatment of the Miskito Indians, the organized attacks on Catholic priests, the confiscation of many Protestant churches and the closing of seminaries, the expulsion of the Salvation Army, the perversion of the legal system through the introduction of special tribunals that ignore basic rules of due process, the large-scale arrests of political opponents, the muzzling of *La Prensa,* a symbol of resistance to the Somoza dictatorship — all these repressive practices began well before the "Contras" became a serious threat to the regime and cannot be explained away simply as defensive in character. The leaders of the United Nicaraguan Opposition — Arturo J. Cruz, Adolfo Calero, and Alfonso Robelo, all of whom fought in the Nicaraguan revolution before it was appropriated and betrayed by the Sandinistas — have correctly pointed out that the crisis faced by Nicaragua "did not grow out of a confrontation between imperialism and the revolution, as the Sandinista Front pretends, but out of the contradictions which emerge from a clash between democratic expectations of the Nicaraguan people and the imposition of a totalitarian system such as that which is being implanted in our country by the Sandinista Front."[25]

Instead of avoiding the "deformations" of existing socialist societies, the Sandinistas have followed the examples set by Cuba and the Soviet Union, and they have made no secret of their admiration for the Communist model they intend to copy. In an interview with the Soviet news agency Tass on 4 March 1985, Socorro Galan, secretary general of the Nicaraguan Association for Friendship with the Socialist Countries, paid homage to the Soviet version of democracy: "The USSR's success in building communism, in bringing up a new man, [has] always been and will remain an inspiring example for the Nicaraguan people building a democratic society."[26]

Recent developments in Nicaragua have involved American pacifists in difficult mental acrobatics, especially pronounced in the case of the AFSC, the most vocal defender of the Nicaraguan revolution. While the Sandinistas have proudly proclaimed their commitment to "revolutionary internationalism," to the strengthening of the revolution in Central America, and have supported the main tenets of Soviet foreign policy, the AFSC insists that the Sandinistas are nonaligned and that there is no proof of Nicaraguan aid to the Marxist insurgents in El Salvador. While leading American Indian activists denounce the Sandinista regime as an "unconscionably racist, soulless Marxist experiment,"[27] the AFSC is satisfied that past mistakes in the treatment of the Miskito Indians have been corrected. A five-person native Indian delegation from the AFSC returned from a visit to Nicaragua to report that, despite deep differences, "it was clear that the Miskito leadership saw their future as being with the Sandinistas."[28]

While the Nicaraguan Permanent Commission on Human Rights — made famous in the 1970s by its courageous denunciation of the crimes of the Somoza regime — was ordered to submit its reports for censorship, and while the amount of censored news in *La Prensa* rose from 40 to 60 percent,[29] the AFSC praised the accomplishments of the revolution: "The country is struggling to be both free and democratic."[30] While the religious leaders of Nicaragua reported the interrogation and detention of clerical and lay religious figures, and while the government forbade outdoor religious ceremonies connected with the visits of Cardinal Miguel Obando y Bravo to provincial towns, the AFSC was pleased that many grass-roots pastoral workers and lay church members "see participation in the revolution as a practical consequence of their faith."[31]

On 10 July 1986, after *La Prensa* was completely closed down, the *New York Times* ran an editorial under the title "The Sandinista Road to Stalinism" which argued that the "pluralist revolution seems hopelessly betrayed" and that the Sandinistas "are well down the totalitarian road traveled by Fidel Castro." The activities of the Contras, the *Times* concluded, "neither justify nor explain the totalitarian trend in Nicaragua. More plausibly, it is the regime's loss of popularity at home that drives the suppression."

We find the same estrangement from the facts of life and an air of unreality in the AFSC's more recent pronouncements on El Salvador. During the last two years, the operations of the FMLN have increasingly antagonized the rural population. The guerillas' campaign of economic sabotage has destroyed countless passenger and commercial vehicles; numerous telephone offices and town halls have been burnt down. There have been several massacres of villagers, including women and children, as a warning of the cost of allowing the organization of local civil defense militias. Consequently, there now exists widespread doubt in the countryside that the guerillas are the liberators they claim to be. As one journalist on the scene has commented, "They have failed to offer a convincing new argument for revolution now that the armed forces have curbed the reckless slaughter of civilians." Whatever the shortcomings of the three elections held during the last two years, they have offered hope and provide the Duarte government with an aura of legitimacy.[32] By 1987 the government-sponsored land reform program had distributed 782,000 acres — approximately 22 percent of the country's scarce agricultural land — to 525,000 peasants and their families, an estimated 25 percent of the rural poor. Despite many problems, even the program's critics acknowledge that it has drained support from the guerillas.[33]

The evidence available today on the infiltration of Soviet-bloc supplies from Nicaragua is massive and has convinced even earlier Democratic doubters on the House Intelligence Committee. Yet the AFSC continues to insist that there is no credible information on Soviet and Cuban involvement in the region and that the outside influence that must be stopped is that of the United States. The U.S., declared an AFSC pamphlet on El Salvador in early 1984, "is committing itself to massive military intervention in El Salvador. The President, Congress and the media must hear the resolve of U.S. citizens to end U.S. support for repression and military terror in El Salvador and throughout Central America."[34]

Congress has been reading both developments in Central America and the mood of the American people in a somewhat different way. In 1984-85 strong bipartisan support emerged on Capitol Hill for increased economic and military aid to Duarte's government in El Salvador, and in 1986 Congress even approved a modest amount of military aid for the Contras of Nicaragua. At this writing it is unclear whether the agreement signed by the presidents of Costa Rica, El Salvador, Guatemala, Honduras, and Nicaragua on 7 August 1987 will indeed lead to the promised democratization of the Sandinista regime and bring peace to the region.

At times seeing the democratic process of this country result in unpalatable policies, the AFSC in recent years has again decided to take an important political issue to the streets and to call for massive civil disobedience. In June 1983 the AFSC board endorsed participation in a coalition effort involving civil disobedience against the shipment of arms to El Salvador. The fact that a majority of Congress, the duly constituted legislative body of the nation, had approved this policy was apparently regarded as irrelevant.

In September 1984 the AFSC board adopted a policy statement

that called on the people of the United States to "take nonviolent action to help stop the U.S. military involvement in Central America." The statement acknowledged that other countries, including the Soviet Union and Cuba, had also supplied military equipment to the belligerents. Nevertheless, and without insisting on a machinery of enforcement that would prevent the introduction of arms by all outside powers, the AFSC asked the U.S. government to "halt and reverse its military build-up and military intervention in Central America and the Caribbean and curtail arms shipments to the region."

The AFSC board statement of September 1984 affirmed the principle of political self-determination. "The American Friends Service Committee does not believe that it is a proper role for the United States to try to determine how other people and nations shall live and be governed." Every nation should be left free to choose its own form of government without outside interference, the statement declared.[35] But, of course, as John Stuart Mill pointed out more than a hundred years ago, "The doctrine of non-intervention, to be a legitimate principle of morality, must be accepted by all governments. The despots must consent to be bound by it as well as the free states. Unless they do, the profession of it by the free countries comes but to this miserable issue, that the wrong side may help the wrong, but the right must not help the right."[36]

In the 1930s the nonintervention of the Western democracies in the Spanish Civil War, at a time when Nazi Germany and Fascist Italy were generously helping the insurgents, was a crucial factor intervening in favor of Franco's victory. Given the AFSC's frequently stated pronounced sympathies for the Marxist-Leninist guerillas of El Salvador and the Sandinista regime in Nicaragua, could one be sure that the AFSC's demand for U.S. nonintervention was not similarly motivated by the wish to help one side in the conflict? Had not the AFSC developed and perfected the same strategy of getting the U.S. off the back of a Marxist regime during the Vietnam war? At a time when the AFSC was calling for American sanctions against South Africa and, even in the statement discussed here, urging the U.S. "to identify and support, or at least avoid interference with Third World movements for social justice," was the AFSC primarily concerned with self-determination and noninterference or, once again, with making another region of the world safe for a Marxist-Leninist revolution?

In late 1984 the AFSC was one of several organizations engaged in collecting signatures on "The Pledge of Resistance." Those endorsing this document pledged themselves to be "on call" to engage with others in nonviolent direct action and civil disobedience in the event of a U.S. military escalation in Central America. By December 1986 more than eighty thousand people nationwide were said to have signed the pledge. During the year 1986, more than 4,000 participants in sit-ins in federal buildings and other public facilities were arrested.[37] In each case, the alleged American escalation consisted of actions by Congress involving military and other aid packages to Central America. Once again, then, the AFSC and its allies decided to seek to circumvent and overrule the democratic process.

CHAPTER 9

Nonviolence, Liberation Struggles, and Civil Disobedience

Support for the Violence of the Oppressed

During the course of opposing the American involvement in Vietnam, all the major pacifist organizations had gradually come to support the armed struggle of the National Liberation Front of South Vietnam. Necessarily this meant a compromise with the pacifist values of reconciliation and nonviolence and eventually the open acceptance of the legitimacy of the revolutionary "struggle of the oppressed."

The first pacifist group to shed the burden of nonviolence was the WILPF. In her report to the 1973 biennial meeting, executive director Dorothy R. Steffens hailed the fact that the giant United States had been "defeated by a tiny, underdeveloped non-white nation. This has tremendous significance for the national liberation struggles now going on all over the world." The WILPF and other peace groups could be pleased by the role they had played "in turning the American people around and making it difficult for our government to again intervene in other people's independence struggles. . . . If, as our Vietnamese friends told us in Hanoi, revolutionary change is 'the tide of our epoch,' then we WILPF women are prepared to move with the tide and even be in its leading edge."[1]

Florence Luscomb, a longtime member from Massachusetts and a former executive secretary of the state branch, told the delegates that America was no longer a democracy. "Behind the screen of the ballot the real holders of political power, the people who decide national policies and laws and control public opinion by their ownership of all the mass media of information, are the great industrialists who under capitalism control our national economic life. The monopoly capitalists, who together with the armed forces form the military-industrial complex, are our real rulers . . . to achieve their dream of a worldwide economic empire, . . . must crush the aspirations of all humanity for freedom, and human dignity, and lives of well-being."[2]

In a speech he delivered at the meeting, Gene Sharp, author of *The Politics of Nonviolence,* appealed to the WILPF as a peace organization concerned with freedom to explore the evidence that in the past nonviolent tactics had often proven a more humane method of successfully resisting oppression than violence. After his speech there was a rush to the microphone, and several speakers denounced Sharp as naive and stupid for putting his faith in the efficacy of nonviolence.[3] Dorothy Hutchinson, no longer an officer of the WILPF but in attendance at the biennial meeting, was so shocked by this episode that two months later she declined to be listed as a sponsor of the League.[4]

The WILPF biennial meetings undertake the task of clarifying positions and mapping out programs for the following two years. The discussion of revolutionary violence at the biennial of June 1973 had been heated but inconclusive. Consequently, the October meeting of the national board once more took up the controversial topic. Hutchinson was still a person of considerable prestige in the League. Knowing her strong feelings on the subject, the board asked her to prepare a position paper, and Hutchinson agreed to do so. In a letter to executive secretary emeritus Mildred Scott Olmsted, Hutchinson informed her friend that she was making "a real attempt to draw WILPF back to what both you and I believe to be its traditional path."[5]

In her paper, "Statement on Liberation Struggles or Statement on Nonviolence," which she sent to the board on 15 October, Hutchinson explained that the "revealing experience of our Biennial has awakened me to the importance of ending the silence and equivocation which have beclouded basic differences of opinion among us." The WILPF, she noted, had never advocated passive submission to injustice. "We want to encourage the oppressed to act vigorously to achieve their freedom and we feel called to act vigorously to assist them. Imagining ourselves in the place of those struggling for their freedom, we do not condemn any who believe that they have no alternative but to use the traditional means of violence." However, Hutchinson pointed out, armed struggle, even in the best of causes, brings suffering and death to the innocent and creates more problems than it solves. "We, therefore, believe that it is not our function to participate in, encourage, or condone the use of violence but rather to seek, advocate and promote non-violent alternative means for achieving the same ends." There was no guarantee that nonviolent campaigns would succeed promptly, but violent rebellion also often failed to produce a prompt victory. The Vietnamese provided an example: after twenty-six years of violence against France and the United States, they had not yet achieved their goal despite the usual justification of violence as the quickest way to get results.

In recent years the WILPF had repeatedly taken sides in wars, and this tendency, Hutchinson warned, could have regrettable results. "If we not only endorse the *goals* of liberation movements, but also regard violence as the best or only possible *means* for achieving them, why is it not our duty to participate in and procure arms for 'just' wars and riots? Isn't it unworthy of WILPF to stand safely on the sidelines shouting, 'Let's you and him fight it out!'?" The WILPF had to remain loyal to its long-standing principle that peace requires a dedication to nonviolent means for the resolution of conflict, Hutchinson urged. "I still believe in the indivisibility of peace and freedom and am deeply concerned lest we lose our distinctive reason for existence as an organization by becoming the Women's International League for War and Freedom."[6]

The national board voted to forward Hutchinson's position paper to the branches for study, but otherwise proceeded unperturbed on the course it had charted for the League. It adopted guidelines on coalitions which permitted both the national organization and its branches to join coalitions that were in agreement with the WILPF's general aims and purposes, although it was recognized "that it is futile to seek statements from the coalition guaranteeing non-violence or other abstract and hard-to-define principles." Membership in these coalitions was to be nonexclusionary.[7] A shortened version of Hutchinson's paper, published in the WILPF magazine *Peace and Freedom*, left out all of the sentences directly critical of the WILPF. It was accompanied by a statement from the German section of the WILPF which argued "that 'uncritical idealist pacifism' could never offer a serious or permanent challenge to individual or collective violence and, even less, to structural violence." As a second rebuttal, the editor reprinted the declaration of the New Delhi Congress on World Revolution.[8]

The FOR has several times grappled with the issue of revolutionary violence, although its inability to formulate a clear theoretical position has not prevented the organization from expressing its

sympathy for various leftist guerilla movements. A statement—
"Justice, 'Liberation,' and Nonviolence"—drafted by the staff was
discussed by the national council at its March 1979 meeting. The
statement began with a lengthy indictment of America for causing
most of the world's ills. America needed to acknowledge "our responsibility for the oppression and injustices suffered by many people and groups in our world today." America was guilty of "national
complicity in the poverty of underdeveloped nations" and "complicity in the 'systemic violence' of our own and other national
groups." Any identification with the underprivileged and dispossessed people of the world, the statement argued, had to begin at
home—with "changing our own government and social structures,
as these are responsible for the sufferings of others."

It should be noted that in this catalogue of American and Western
guilt, there was no account of the fact that the desperately poor and
extravagantly rich are as likely to be found within a single state as
in the division between states. Still less could that fact be squared
with the abundant evidence that contact with the West has been
the prime agent of material progress in the Third World, and that
the poorest countries today are those with few or no external contacts. Multinational corporations, the alleged instruments of neo-
colonialism and exploitation, do not operate in the most backward
countries, while their presence helps explain rapid economic growth
and relative prosperity in nations like Taiwan, Korea, Singapore,
and Hong Kong.

The search for justice and freedom, the FOR draft statement
continued, had to be based on nonviolence. Pacifists could not justify or condone the use of violence in seeking to achieve even the
most reasonable of goals. The statement stressed the point that
pacifists "must [apply] the same standards of evaluation with regard
to the processes of liberation 'counter-violence' as we do to the
processes and practitioners of 'systemic violence' or those who support the use of international war as a means of settling disputes."[9]

The national council discussed the draft statement at great length
but failed to agree on its adoption. After a committee had tried its
hand at improving it, the entire issue was shelved. Since then, as
before, the FOR, unencumbered by theoretical guidelines or con-
ceptual strictures, has been able to follow its political and moral
impulses. These impulses have kept the FOR an integral part of the
"peace and justice" network and have led to the adoption of positions and policies fully supportive of the practice of revolutionary
violence.

The AFSC's desire to give assistance to the guerilla movements of Central America in early 1981 led to the adoption of a new formal statement on nonviolence. In late 1980 a staff conference of the Latin American program produced a consensus statement called "AFSC Commitment to Nonviolence in Latin America," which in its frank acceptance of the "violence of the oppressed" went beyond anything produced during the heyday of the Vietnam war. The principal forms of violence in Latin America, the statement declared, are "the oppression and exploitation produced by economic and political structures, both national and international. Direct repression is carried out in defense of these structures by governments linked to dominant groups." In this setting, the use of force by some oppressed groups in defense of their rights involved a violence that "is essentially reactive and aimed at justice and is therefore qualitatively different from the violence of the oppressors."

The AFSC's basic commitment in Latin America, the statement affirmed, "is to the poor and the oppressed. We support those groups engaged or potentially engaged in the struggle for profound structural changes which will bring economic and political justice." This support had to be consistent with the Quaker principle of nonviolence, but the commitment to such groups "must be complete" and maintained "to the end of their struggle, as long as they want our help and their goals remain those of equality and justice. We will do so even if a group has adopted or is led to adopt violent as well as nonviolent means to achieve its goals." Such support could take the form of humanitarian assistance, development of leadership, and "education, locally and in the United States, and internationally regarding the struggle and the conditions that make it necessary." One of the fundamental objectives of the AFSC was reconciliation, the statement pointed out. However, "this does not mean that people should reconcile themselves to their oppression. Neither does it mean that we should maintain neutrality in the confrontation between oppressor and oppressed." True reconciliation was possible only "between relatively equal parties. Therefore it requires a process which involves transformation of the structures of oppression that deny people equality and dignity."[10]

Never before had an AFSC policy statement so openly endorsed violent struggle. While the oppressed groups to be supported "to the end of their struggle" were not named, the context of the statement made it unmistakably clear that it included the Marxist-Leninist guerillas of Central America. The use of violence by these groups was defended by being declared "essentially reactive," and their claim to seek "economic and political justice" was accepted without questioning.

Because of its extreme language and the challenge it expressed to traditional Quaker principles, the statement drew protest from other AFSC staff members. The AFSC board therefore took up these issues in a lengthy session that lasted several days, and on 24 January 1981 they finally adopted a memorandum called "AFSC Perspectives on Nonviolence in Relation to Groups Struggling for Social Justice." This board statement toned down some of the more strident language used by the Latin American program staff, but otherwise, despite certain rhetorical disclaimers, it left the door open to the same cooperation with and encouragement of Marxist-Leninist guerillas enunciated in the earlier version.

The statement affirmed the AFSC's "commitment to work for social justice and to aid victims of oppression." The peace sought by the AFSC, it noted, "will not reign while patterns of inequity and oppression continue." How should the AFSC relate to groups that work for the same goals of justice and peace but do not maintain a principled refusal to use violence to advance their cause?

It had to be understood, the statement argued, that the violence of the oppressed against the "massive use of official violence in defense of a flawed status quo" was usually due to "despair at bringing change any other way." Nevertheless, the AFSC "cannot endorse the use of violence. The AFSC stands firm on its Quaker heritage in denying the legitimacy of violence however extreme the provocation. We have not [formulated] and will not formulate a theory of 'acceptable' revolutionary violence." However, the statement declared, "where basic human rights and social equity are at issue, Quakers and the AFSC need to be engaged in common cause to the limit of our beliefs, resources and program capacity. . . . When AFSC staff form personal and programmatic associations with groups struggling toward social justice, these relationships should not be terminated solely because acts of violence have been carried out in the name of such organizations, any more than AFSC should break off dealing in love with forces in power who turn to violence in the same setting." The AFSC should have compassion for people in every faction, but "respect for the humanity of the oppressor should not still the insistence upon movement toward social justice and the priority given to empowering the disadvantaged." The statement ended by affirming once again the basic strategy of keeping action and advocacy focused "on the American role in maintaining systems of oppression or promoting equity in other countries."[11]

The relative moderation of the AFSC board statement did not prevent publications on the Central American conflict issued by the national office from expressing full support for the leftist guerillas of El Salvador. We find the same disparity in regard to AFSC policy on the Middle East, a divergence between a series of reasonably restrained board statements on the one hand and pronounced sympathy for the Palestine Liberation Organization (PLO) and its goals on the part of AFSC staff on the other. A recent situation provides a good example. The AFSC's comprehensive study entitled *A Compassionate Peace: A Future for the Middle East,* published in 1982, insisted that all states in the region, as well as the PLO, had to recognize the state of Israel. The study supported the right of the Palestinian Arabs to have a state of their own but condemned the use of violence by all parties, including resort to terrorism by guerilla groups. Indeed, "acts of terror involve a special degree of inhumanity, particularly as these acts inflict harm and take the lives of the unarmed and the noncombatant." There may well be justice in the cause for which terrorism has been used, the statement noted, "but the acceptance of terror as the weapon—the choice of a technique that kills the innocent—perverts the very justice of the cause."[12]

After this forthright condemnation of terrorism, the AFSC proceeded—in the same publication—to tilt the balance against Israel and in favor of its enemies. Israel was asked to break the cycle of violence by a courageous refusal to retaliate. More ominously, the major supplier nations were urged to "declare a moratorium on the shipment of all new weapons and halt all current arms transfer agreements. The U.S., as the largest supplier, can take a crucial lead in freezing the arms race in the Middle East."[13] This seemingly evenhanded proposal cannot but have one-sided effects, for the AFSC has no leverage over Soviet policy in the Middle East, and the Soviet Union has repeatedly declared that it will continue to support the Arabs until they have succeeded in the liberation of the occupied territories. A unilateral freeze on American arms supplies to Israel thus would seriously handicap Israel.

Legitimizing the Palestine Liberation Organization

When it comes to the role of and appraisal of the PLO in the peace process, official AFSC statements and staff actions are on the same wavelength. The PLO is usually described as the most widely recognized organization representing the Palestinians that must be included in any peace negotiations. The acceptance of the PLO as a legitimate negotiating partner is unconditional—that is, there is no demand that the PLO acknowledge Israel's right to exist or forswear terrorism. In fact, for years the AFSC, against all evidence to the contrary, has stressed the alleged moderation of the PLO. "Much of the PLO and its leadership," declared the 1982 AFSC study *A Compassionate Peace,* "has moved from the maximalist positions of 1968 steadily if uncertainly in the direction of accommodation. They have dropped the insistence on the armed liberation of the whole of Palestine and have increasingly talked of and utilized political action as well as armed struggle to achieve their ends." The willingness of the PLO to meet with "progressive Jewish and Israeli groups" was said to be an indication of the organization's eagerness to find "acceptable paths to peace."[14] Not mentioned here is the fact that most of these "progressive" groups, in this country and in Israel, are in general sympathy with the demands of the PLO and thus find it easy to discover common terms of reference. If any further refutation of the AFSC's delusions about the peaceful intentions of the PLO was needed, in early November 1986 PLO spokesmen announced once again that the Palestine Liberation Organization under the leadership of Yasir Arafat had decided to give armed struggle against Israel priority over the peace process.[15]

Some AFSC staffers—like Joseph Gerson, the peace education secretary of the New England regional office, who belongs to the same "progressive" camp—have publicly acknowledged that they support the PLO's goal of a "bi-national or democratic secular state," which, of course, means nothing less than the abolition of the Jewish state and probably the expulsion of a large part of its population. Gerson has proposed a two-state solution that might serve as a possible interim basis for peace until both sides are ready to "embrace the harmony of a bi-national or democratic secular state."[16]

While official AFSC policy statements defend the legitimacy of the state of Israel and condemn acts of terror against it, much of the AFSC's activity in the field vilifies Israel because of its links to America's alleged interventionist designs in the Middle East, seeks to legitimize the PLO, and works at creating good will for the struggling Palestinians. Their anger cannot be expected to cool until what they perceive as justice has been achieved. Joseph Gerson of the AFSC New England regional office explained in 1984 that work for peace necessarily had to take different forms inside Israel and in the occupied territories where Palestinians "suffer the immediate and brutal consequences of military occupation. The work of 'peace activists' thus must be different in the communities of the occupied and the occupier." And that explained why the struggle of the oppressed Palestinians was not always nonviolent.[17] In short, once again we find pacifists discovering good reasons for sympathizing with a violent "liberation movement" while at the same time making efforts to prevent its victim from getting U.S. aid. The AFSC seeks to restrict Israel's ability to obtain arms essential for its survival while simultaneously Israel is put under pressure to make concessions to the PLO, who seek to destroy it. As Martin Peretz put it in a recent column in the *New Republic*, "These realists are the sort who, instead of backing the Czechs against the Nazis, would have pressed Eduard Benes to compromise with Hitler."[18]

Dialogue with Colonel Muammar Qaddafi

The WRL, ever since the late 1960s, has tried to solve the contradiction between pacifism and the support of revolutionary violence by avoiding the constraints of logic and consistency. In December 1984 the WRL started a new magazine, *The Nonviolent Activist,* to replace *Liberation,* which had folded in 1977, and *WIN,* which had ended publication in 1983. During their last years both of these journals had moved away from any explicit identification with pacifism and instead had emphasized their ideological ties to the Left and the counterculture. As the editors of *Liberation* had written in January 1975, "We admittedly no longer define *Liberation* by pacifist politics. We feel that violence takes many subtle forms which are not readily discernible as such, and have thus been overlooked by traditionial pacifism." The entire debate over the issue of violence versus nonviolence was outdated, the editors claimed.[19] The new WRL magazine featured an editorial that affirmed the League's roots in Western liberalism, Marxism, and classical anarchism and its endorsement of feminism, environmentalism, and pacifism. "We use nonviolence both because of our commitment to action and because of our recognition of our limits. If we use violence, we are likely to hurt others. If we do not act, we implicitly condone existing oppression and wish our own destruction." A new beginning had to be made, the editorial declared:

> We must stop giving a blessing to killing sisters and brothers by calling it revolutionary necessity. Yet even while saying this, we know we are on the side of the oppressed who use violence to overthrow

their subjugators, rather than the oppressors who use violence to subjugate others. In the struggle for justice, for freedom, for a human life with meaning, we stand with the African National Congress; we stand with the Sandinistas; we stand with the Polish people who struggle against totalitarian constraints; we stand with those elements of the Palestinian people who seek statehood without terrorism; and we stand with those Jews within Israel who reject the right of Zionism to crush the Palestinians.

The editorial concluded with the observation that the WRL was aware of the contradictions in its thinking. "We feel that by exposing contradictions, we may help achieve agreement; by exposing divisions, we may work toward unity."[20]

Of late the WRL's search for unity in the peace movement has taken it to rather unlikely allies. In March 1984 David McReynolds attended the First International Conference of Peace and Liberation Movements in Malta. The conference was hosted by the Malta Pope John XXIII Peace Laboratory, an organization receiving financial support from Libya, which also paid the airfare of some of the participants. Colonel Muammar Qaddafi's *Green Book* was distributed at the conference, and some of the European delegates complained that the Libyan influence was excessive. In his report on the conference in the WRL newsletter, however, McReynolds did not share this view. "Rather than being frightened by the Libyans, which was the reaction of a number of those from the West, should we not welcome the fact that revolutionary movements, including the Libyans, are interested in dialogue with the nonviolence movements?" Liberation movements, McReynolds argued, had to become peace movements, and peace movements had to become liberation movements.[21]

The Reverend Louis Farrakhan, leader of the Nation of Islam, which also has received financial support from Libya, has called the Libyan strongman "a fellow struggler in the cause of liberation."[22] On the other hand, Neil Kinnock, the leader of the British Labour party, in 1984 angrily denounced the striking National Union of Mineworkers for seeking aid from Qaddafi. "By any measure of political, civil, trade union or human rights, the Qaddafi regime is vile. Any offers from them would be an affront to everything the British labor movement stands for."[23] By what perverted reasoning, one is tempted to ask, can a pacifist like McReynolds rationalize the acceptance of an alliance with the godfather of contemporary international terrorism?

Going beyond the Democratic Process

While American pacifists, with varying degrees of frankness, have embraced leftist-led national liberation movements, they have at the same time frequently expressed their disdain for the "formal democracy" of capitalist America. In order to help their revolutionary friends, pacifists seek to prevent U.S. involvement in the Third World, and when ordinary political action does not produce the desired results, they go outside the democratic process. All the major pacifist groups from time to time have thus defied the law of the land, though few have taken the trouble to formulate a theoretical rationale for such tactics.

In April 1984 the AFSC board adopted a set of principles to guide engagement in civil disobedience. The AFSC, the statement declared, "believes in a society of laws"; it is law that enables the human family to live in justice and peace. The defiance of law and civil disobedience, therefore, "should not be undertaken lightly, but only when there appears to be no other practical option within the law. There should be no element of selfish advantage in the violation, a discipline of non-violence should be observed, and one should be willing to suffer without complaint the punishment that society may exact. Civil disobedience so undertaken does not subvert the rule of law." When rightly used, "civil disobedience strengthens the rule of law by making law more worthy of respect." According to the statement, civil disobedience would be justified under certain circumstances and for certain reasons: (1) in case of a conflict between one's obedience to God and one's obedience to government (e.g., when Friends, prior to the availability of alternative service, refused to enter the military service); (2) when, in an issue very deeply felt by an individual or a community, other options have been tried and have failed; (3) when the evil being perpetuated by government is felt to be of such magnitude that civil disobedience is the best moral response; (4) as a show of solidarity with a community engaging in civil disobedience; (5) when civil disobedience is perceived as the only way to focus attention on a wrong perpetrated; and (6) when a group responds to a special situation of injustice without premeditation.[24]

Several comments about this set of principles are in order. First, while the guidelines affirmed the principle that civil disobedience should not be undertaken lightly, in actuality the statement recognized a very wide variety of circumstances under which the defiance of law would be justified. There was no check on the conscientiousness of such an act, no recognition of the possibility that there could be what Catholic theology has called an "errant individual conscience." Those who enact the laws also have their moral reasons for doing so, and the individual who substitutes his moral judgment for that of the community should at least be reminded to search his mind most carefully and to engage in an inward wrestle for valid moral insights before he disobeys the law. In the nature of the case, there can be no impartial observer to adjudicate between an individual's conscience and the conscience of the law. However, an individual should accept the moral legitimacy of the law unless he has succeeded in winning his way to a clear moral decision establishing that the law is truly unjust. Such a decision should be based on a moral deliberation that uses all the sources of enlightenment available to an individual; it should not be the result of a mere intuitive feeling of moral outrage.

Furthermore, the AFSC made no allowance for the political and legal context in which the question of civil disobedience may arise. The statement recalled Gandhi's campaign for Indian independence and the U.S. civil rights movement without recognizing that in both of these cases no legal channels of redress had been available to the aggrieved Indians and blacks. In a situation where the democratic process is intact and where individuals or groups can work to change or repeal a law thought to be unjust, it is doubtful that there is a justification for civil disobedience simply because other options have been tried and have failed. Such a failure could be due simply to the fact that a majority has not been found for changing the law in question. During the late 1960s and early 1970s, many opponents of the war in Vietnam, including the AFSC, had convinced themselves that their opposition to the war was shared by a majority of the American people and that democracy had failed to work because their position did not prevail. Both of these assumptions were factually incorrect. At no time did a majority of the American people support the kind of unconditional, unilateral withdrawal from Vietnam demanded by the AFSC. Minorities must respect the legitimate decision-making processes of a democratic system even if the outcome seriously displeases or even disturbs them. Civil disobedience is not justified because one has lost out in the struggle for votes. To think otherwise is to subvert the very essence of democracy.

Last but not least, the easy resort to civil disobedience allowed by the AFSC's statement endangers the stability of a democratic society, for what is good for the goose is good for the gander. Once the supremacy of conscience is conceded, what is to prevent defenders of the separation of the races from interfering with social practices that offend their sense of morality? Would opponents of abortion on demand not be entitled to block access to abortion clinics? The way in which law resolves the disputed moral issues of a pluralistic society may not always be ideal, but it is difficult to think of a better alternative.

None of these considerations was taken into account in the AFSC statement on civil disobedience — or, for that matter, in the pacifist community's actions regarding the Vietnam war and the problem of Central America. The frequent disregard of the country's legitimate forms of political action in favor of extra-legal activities has been another symptom of the pacifists' alienation from the democratic tradition of the United States.

CHAPTER **10**

Pacifists and Communists

The Revival of the United Front

Until the 1960s the pacifist community shunned association with groups like the Communist party and the World Peace Council because these organizations were seen, quite correctly, as spokesmen and apologists for Soviet foreign policy. Cooperation was to be limited to organizations whose purposes and methods were in accord with pacifist ideals. When American pacifists embraced the New Left's principle of nonexclusion, however, these caveats were forgotten, and the urgency of achieving political goals like U.S. withdrawal from Vietnam took precedence over the lack of commitment of leftist allies to pacifist values. Today, these alliances with the radical Left are a commonplace feature of pacifist political action.

AFSC guidelines on the establishment of coalitions, reformulated in October 1979, stated that the AFSC would act jointly with groups "whose philosophy is compatible with ours in some respects but may be different in others." It was enough if the AFSC would have opportunities to make clear "that we wish to live up to Friends' testimonies of equality, of peace and nonviolence, of social and economic justice, of civil and religious freedom, and other principles central to Friends."[1] By this time, of course, the AFSC's understanding of the meaning of such key philosophical and political concepts as equality, social justice, and civil and religious freedom had become so similar to that of the Left that the affirmation of these principles in a coalition with the Left did not present much of a problem.

Not surprisingly, therefore, AFSC protest activities against U.S. policy in Central America have taken place in the framework of coalitions that are indeed fully nonexclusive. For example, a large rally held in Washington on 12 November 1983 to protest the American action against Marxist-ruled Grenada and against U.S.

intervention in Central America was organized by the AFSC with the endorsement of the U.S. Communist party, the Communist Workers party, the American Workers party, the U.S. Peace Council, the Christian Peace Conference, the Grenada Revolutionary League, CISPES, the National Council of American-Soviet Friendship, the National Lawyers Guild, the Committee for Marxist Education, the Young Socialist League, and dozens of other New Left and "peace and justice" organizations, as they have come to be called.[2] It is indicative of the AFSC's political values and place on the political spectrum that the philosophy of groups like the Stalinist U.S. Communist party or the Trotskyite Young Socialist Alliance is held to be "compatible" with that of the AFSC "in some respects."

National AFSC officials, when queried about such coalitions, have defended them as necessary in order to create a broad-based movement of protest against the Reagan administration's policies. The AFSC, it is said, has liberated itself from the repressive, red-baiting outlook of the 1950s. These relatively young AFSC officials are blissfully ignorant of the fact that the AFSC's earlier opposition to such coalitions was formulated in the 1930s and 1940s — that is, well before the anti-Communist hysteria of the 1950s — because of experience with the dire consequences of working with the Communists and not because the AFSC had succumbed to a cold-war mentality or compulsive anti-communism.

Against the "Myth of the Soviet Threat"

The AFSC's preoccupation with avoiding what it has often called a "pathological fear of communism" has led the organization to adopt a truly compulsive anti – anti-communism, which in turn has resulted in an indulgent and often outright sympathetic view of Marxist-Leninist regimes that are hardly supportive of Quaker values. As in the case of Communist Vietnam, such regimes are given every possible benefit of the doubt; practices and policies that would be sharply condemned if found in the U.S. are explained away or justified and excused.

While the AFSC has been in the forefront of those who have campaigned against the danger of U.S. interventionism, it has at the same time sought to convince the American public that the Soviet Union is essentially a "have nation" and that the American perception of a Soviet threat against the United States is mythical and unfounded. Indeed, in 1981 the AFSC disarmament program published a pamphlet entitled *Questions and Answers on the Soviet*

Threat and National Security, in which it was argued that the United States has led the arms race. The Soviet Union has been increasing its military power in order to catch up with the U.S., but "the Soviet military establishment is designed for different purposes than that of the US with far more of its budget directed toward internal security and defense and virtually no 'power projection' forces." The pamphlet described the U.S. as "the only nation capable of projecting and sustaining its power by military force globally." Altogether, the pamphlet argued, the Soviet Union "has been an imitator in acting like a superpower in global affairs. . . . Compared [with] the United States's network of 200 bases, alliances, aid programs and covert operations, the Soviet efforts outside its 'sphere of influence' are modest."

The pamphlet conceded that the Soviet Union's continued oppression of several East European countries had to be condemned, but this "expansion of territory and power into Eastern Europe by the Soviets was a direct result of their experience with two German invasions that brought incredible death and destruction to the Russians." Since World War II, the Soviet Union had not annexed any new territory, and, outside the border states of Hungary, Czechoslovakia, and Afghanistan, it had not sent any troops or intervened militarily in a direct fashion. During that same time period, the pamphlet declared, the U.S. had intervened militarily on the average of once every eighteen months by sending U.S. troops to such places as Guatemala, Lebanon, Vietnam, the Dominican Republic, the Congo, Iran, Laos, and Cambodia. All of these American interventions "were carried out to help put down disruptive revolutions"; the Soviet Union, on the other hand, provided military and economic aid to help "Third World nations throw off their yoke of colonialism and neo-colonialism."

The AFSC pamphlet criticized the Soviet invasion of Afghanistan as "a brutal, immoral, tragic adventure." However, the pamphlet suggested, it had to be realized that Afghanistan is a territory adjacent to the Soviet Union. The rebellion against the Marxist regime established there in 1977, led by landlords and tribal chieftains opposed to land reform and other programs of social change, received massive outside aid, including aid from the CIA, and threatened to destabilize Soviet authority in Central Russia, with its large Muslim population. Moreover, the pamphlet explained, the Soviet invasion took place precisely at the moment when the U.S. had marshaled a large military presence in the Persian Gulf, including the formation of a NATO-like structure, in response to the hostage-taking in Iran. "From a Soviet perspective," the pamphlet noted, "it may have occurred to them that the US might have been tempted to seize a destabilized Afghanistan and turn it into a new listening post on Russia's southern border."[3]

This fanciful endeavor to prove that the Soviet Union presents no threat to the United States was probably more heavy-handed than most of the AFSC's peace education efforts. The publication took generous liberties with the facts of the Soviet military buildup, and its interpretation of events was strikingly tendentious. Even when the Soviet Union was criticized for actions like the occupation of Eastern Europe and the invasion of Afghanistan, Soviet actions were excused as understandable responses to U.S. aggressive designs. And yet this pamphlet was by no means an isolated instance or aberration, and AFSC staffers like Russell Johnson have many times managed to outdo even this crude piece of propaganda.

When in 1978 the American media gave extensive coverage to new trials against dissidents in the Soviet Union, Johnson complained that these "presumed internal violations of human rights" were being used by the "opinion-moulding business" to "engineer fear and condemnation of the Soviet Union."[4] Johnson argued that from Lenin's decree on peace (which insisted that peaceful co-existence should be the underlying principle of relations between states with different social systems) to Brezhnev's 1981 report to the CPUSSR, the Soviet Union had made it clear that it wanted normal relations with the U.S. "The way to prevent nuclear war is to persuade Americans to stop fearing the Russians," Johnson insisted; that fear was a fraud.[5] Unlike the U.S., the USSR had no lobby to push spending for arms, no private business enterprises making money on the manufacture of weapons, and no unemployment. If the Western powers would cease menacing socialism within the USSR and reduce the threat to Soviet security, Johnson maintained, the Soviet leadership would move in the direction of a more open society. Neither in theory nor in practice did the Soviet Union desire to expand beyond its borders.[6]

During the last few years Johnson led "peace cruises on the Volga," sponsored by the FOR, the WILPF, the Communist-run National Council of American-Soviet Friendship, and other organizations. On these trips American travelers had the opportunity to meet with local Soviet Peace Committees. These committees, Johnson insisted, were not instruments of the state to mislead foreigners about Soviet intentions. He met with them in "a spirit of friendship," and, of course, one could not expect Soviet citizens to think of "political and intellectual democracy in Western terms."[7]

The participants in these cruises returned full of enthusiasm for the warm welcome they received everywhere. They were impressed by the Soviet Union's concern for human welfare and how easy it was to find with their new Soviet friends common priorities for peace such as a mutual nuclear freeze and the prevention of the militarization of space. All were deeply moved by the suffering of the Soviet people during World War II and convinced that, after this dreadful experience and the millions of lives lost, the Soviet Union sincerely wanted peace and would never start a war.[8] Richard Deats, the FOR's executive secretary in 1982, came back convinced that "there *is* much to build on in the relations between our two peoples and that we can indeed live in peace." The widespread negative perceptions about the people of the Soviet Union had been nurtured by years of cold-war propaganda. "Especially since the breakdown of detente, we are fed a constant diet of grim stories about Communist repression and shortages and military intentions."[9] Another participant came back assured that the Soviet Union, a country we were taught to think of as our enemy, was not a threat to the United States. Such misperceptions were due to the fact that Americans suffered from "anti-Soviet hysteria" and "irrational fear and unfounded enmity."[10] Russians and Americans, argued an AFSC staffer, must learn to behave as global citizens, to cooperate and negotiate the different issues that confront us. Americans must stop seeing the Soviet Union as their enemy — "part and parcel of the entanglement of the military-industrial complex which has spread its influence through defense contracts into almost every town and community. We need enemies to justify our continual military build-up."[11]

Jack Powelson, the Colorado Friend who since his clash with the AFSC in 1977 had maintained a discreet silence on the political foibles of some of his fellow Quakers, in November 1984 and February 1985 published a lengthy criticism of one of these euphoric reports on the Soviet Union. There was no unemployment in the Soviet Union, he pointed out, because the government restricted rural-to-urban migration to the number required to fill its labor force and the Russians could declare themselves fully employed even when the farms had a surplus of people. Schools and health care had been cited as evidence that the government cared for its people. Yet the Soviet educational system not only provided education but also sought to promote military strength. The health system provided universal care but also included psychiatric hospitals for dissidents. Moreover, social benefits were unequally distributed and were provided primarily in areas where the state wanted its workers for purposes of industrialization and defense.

On a recent visit to South Africa, Powelson related, he had heard very similar rhetoric about how the state cared for "its Bantus." "In both the Soviet Union and South Africa, it becomes difficult to distinguish between a government caring for its people and a government providing them with goodies so they will do what the state wants them [to do] and be where it wants them to be." Both "the Soviet Union and South Africa have . . . starved and tortured their people, and no part of either system can be separated from that fact." Americans had to make an effort to understand the characteristics of Soviet life, shaped by that country's unique historical development, but, Powelson insisted, "the morality of the system must still be judged both in universal terms and by concrete policies and their effects on many social groups." He was saddened by the fact that Friends referred admiringly to a totalitarian system because some parts of it achieved things perceived as good. It was important to overcome bias and promote mutual understanding, but "the perception we finally come to should recognize injustices where they do indeed exist."[12]

The well-meaning Quakers participating in Russell Johnson's "peace cruises on the Volga" not only have come back with a distorted view of life in the Soviet Union but also serve as unwitting tools of Soviet propaganda that tries to assure the world of the Soviet Union's peaceful intentions. It is no doubt true that the Soviet Union does not want war and would prefer to achieve its goals without having to fight for them. But this country, from Lenin's time on, has never made a secret of its intent to promote the worldwide victory of communism and of its conviction that "peace cannot be lasting until a just political and economic order has been secured for the world's peoples."[13] Consequently, Soviet foreign policy, in the words of an official spokesman, is aimed at "consolidating the positions of world socialism, supporting the struggles of peoples for national liberation and social progress."[14] A war fought for these aims is held to be most just. The Soviet people, who indeed suffered horrendously during World War II, are undoubtedly sincere when they tell Americans of their desire for peace, but, in the absence of democratic institutions, their wishes are, of course, strictly irrelevant. Soviet leadership does not have to justify its military budget before representatives who, as in the American Congress, would rather spend money on social programs that help their re-election. Neither does it have to worry about a press that is free to criticize toughness toward the country's opponent and urge reductions in defense spending.

In recent years the AFSC has rarely been concerned about these kinds of imbalances and has not hesitated to ask the United States to make unilateral moves toward disarmament. Indeed, the AFSC paints such a rosy picture of the Soviet Union in large measure in order to convince itself and others that a more relaxed policy toward the Soviets is possible. An acknowledgment of the expansionism inherent in the Communist worldview would call into question the basic pacifist premise that a peaceful world can be achieved if only enough people want it.

The Nuclear Freeze Movement

In order to maximize their influence, the AFSC and other pacifist groups will often participate in broad-based movements that seek multilateral agreements on arms control. However, this participation is purely tactical and does not mean that pacifists give up their ultimate aim of complete disarmament, to be achieved, if necessary, by unilateral initiatives. A summary of programming, adopted by the FOR staff in June 1978, added to this strategic goal some tactical advice: "We may, however, temper the winds of our language to the shivering sheep of our wider community."[15] In cases where these multilateral efforts fail, pacifists will continue the endeavor anyway and will press for American unilateral concessions. The AFSC's role in the formation of the Committee for a Sane Nuclear Policy and the achievement of a ban on nuclear testing in the early 1960s is a case in point; another example is the more recent drive for a freeze in nuclear weapons.

The idea of a nuclear freeze apparently was the brainchild of Terry Provance, director of the AFSC's disarmament program. At his suggestion the AFSC in the summer of 1979 proposed a "nuclear moratorium" that called on the United States to halt unilaterally the production and deployment of nuclear weapons. Meanwhile, Randall Forsberg, a young M.I.T.-trained arms-control specialist, had started thinking along similar lines, although Forsberg's scheme was bilateral. Soon Provance and Forsberg teamed up, and by March 1980 Forsberg had completed the "Call to Halt the Nuclear Arms Race," the founding document of the nuclear freeze movement. This proposal urged the U.S. and the Soviet Union to adopt a mutual freeze on the testing, production, and deployment of nuclear weapons, missiles, and new aircraft designed primarily to deliver nuclear weapons. Such a freeze was said to be verifiable by existing national means and with the help of the International Atomic Energy Agency.[16] Forsberg's document was quickly endorsed by the AFSC and the FOR; after Forsberg had gone on a speaking tour, talking to peace and antinuclear groups across the country, other personal endorsements and organizational commitments followed in quick order. The AFSC now began petition drives to get the freeze resolution on local ballots in preparation for the November 1980 elections. In March 1981 the first national strategy conference of the new movement was held in Washington.

By 1982 the idea of a nuclear freeze had become a significant public issue. As a result of a skillful organizing effort by AFSC staff and supporters, the freeze resolution was approved by 446 New England town meetings. The resolution was also endorsed by 56 county councils and 11 state legislatures nationwide. More than 2.3 million people signed freeze petitions circulated by a host of organizations and coalitions, including, prominently, Mobilization for Survival, an umbrella group of 49 different peace organizations including the AFSC. The 1983 annual report of the AFSC quoted Forsberg's compliment: "Without the AFSC this campaign would not be where it is today."

On 10 March 1982 Senators Edward M. Kennedy and Mark Hatfield introduced a resolution in the U.S. Senate calling for a bilateral nuclear freeze on the testing, production, and deployment of all nuclear weapons, to be followed later by reductions in nuclear arsenals. A similar resolution was introduced in the House by Representative Edward J. Markey of Massachusetts. These resolutions obtained the endorsement of twenty senators and over 120 representatives. In addition, a large number of well-known public figures and national organizations now flocked to the freeze banner. The nuclear freeze idea, with its simplicity of approach that promised with one stroke to stop the arms race in its tracks, clearly had wide appeal.

Meanwhile, however, the opposition to the freeze was getting organized as well. Critics pointed out that a freeze on the deployment of nuclear weapons would leave the Soviet Union with a monopoly on intermediate-range missiles in Europe, the SS-20s, which the Soviets had begun deploying in 1977 and which the West belatedly had planned to counter with its own medium-range Pershing II and ground-launched cruise missiles. Not surprisingly, therefore, Chairman Brezhnev had given the freeze his enthusiastic support in his address to the 26th Congress of the CPUSSR on 23 February 1981. At the massive freeze rally held in New York City on 12 June 1982, Communists and their fellow travelers were strongly represented; the call to the rally and the list of speakers gave it a pronounced anti-American slant. Michael Myerson, a member of the national council of the American Communist party and executive secretary of the U.S. Peace Council, served on the freeze campaign's international task force, and he pointed out that "Peace Council members have been active, sometimes in leading capacities, in local freeze campaigns, such as those in West Virginia, Colorado, Michigan, Illinois and the District of Columbia."[17] It was not difficult to figure out who stood to benefit the most from the adoption of a nuclear freeze.

By the time a freeze resolution had passed the House in May 1983, it had been amended and watered down so extensively that it only vaguely resembled the original version. Chances of passage in the Senate were rated as nil. In addition to its obvious one-sidedness, the freeze idea had been hurt by the strong endorsement it had received from the Old and the New Left, who had insisted on linking the freeze idea to all kinds of other demands — all directed against American interests — such as the renunciation of the first use of nuclear weapons, reductions in the overall military budget, and opposition to U.S. intervention in Central America and the Middle East. These same elements had also succeeded in returning the freeze idea to its original unilateral conception.

At the national convention of the freeze campaign held in early 1983 in St. Louis, a motion was passed urging "the U.S. Congress to suspend funding for the testing, production, and deployment of U.S. nuclear weapons" and to "call upon the Soviet Union to exercise corresponding restraint." A motion to make U.S. actions "contingent on" the Soviet response was defeated.[18] This new strategy, while appealing to the radical core of the freeze movement, had, of course, even less of a chance to be successful. When last heard of, the freeze movement was finding its unity threatened by growing tension between those who favored the original nuclear freeze idea and those who had succeeded in converting a broadly based campaign for arms control into yet another organizational tool of the anti-American Left.[19] The AFSC was again leading the pack, much to the satisfaction of men like Russell Johnson, who from the beginning had been displeased by the bilateral emphasis of the freeze campaign and had considered it a diversion from the AFSC's "earlier prophetic role in the disarmament movement."[20]

In the wake of the petering out of the freeze movement, and after the peace movement had failed to prevent the stationing of American Pershing II and cruise missiles in Europe, some segments of the pacifist community adopted a more apocalyptic stance. The antinuclear movement, argued two members of the FOR disarmament program in late 1984, had to overcome its timidity; it "must let radicalism out of the closet and into our daily lives. As long as the government won't stop the arms race, we must learn how to stop the government." The FOR had to mobilize for nonviolent direct action and resistance rather than rely on politicians who shift with political winds.[21] Lobbying and electoral work, the FOR staffers maintained, "do not challenge the real roots of the corporate power structure." There was a need to develop "confrontive and revolutionary approaches" to problems like nuclear weapons that "do not really lend themselves to substantive solutions via reformism."[22]

Pacifists raise the spectre of nuclear war where other arguments fail to convince. The peace movement, argued AFSC staffer Joseph Gerson in 1982, neglected to understand "that Washington's nuclear war policy is part and parcel of its efforts to dominate the material resources, markets, and labor of the Third World. . . . Not until the disarmament movement fully addresses the struggles for justice and survival in the Middle East and other parts of the Third World will we be truly mobilized for survival."[23] Very soon a full-fledged campaign got under way, built around the "Deadly Connection" — a slogan referring to the link between U.S. intervention in various local conflicts in the Third World and the danger of a nuclear war. The use of this slogan served the purpose of bringing together the anti-intervention and antinuclear wings of the peace movement. It also enlisted the fear of nuclear war in the drive against an assertive U.S. policy in such international trouble spots as Central America, the Middle East, and the Persian Gulf by suggesting that this policy was likely to end in a nuclear holocaust.

The felicitous rallying cry of the "Deadly Connection" apparently was concocted by Michael T. Klare, a fellow of the Institute for Policy Studies (IPS) in Washington, which has been called the "Think Tank of the Left." The AFSC soon jumped on the bandwagon. In December 1982 it was one of several organizations to sponsor a "Deadly Connection" conference in Boston. One of the main speakers was Jack O'Dell, a member of the AFSC's national peace education committee. O'Dell is also a foreign-policy advisor to Jesse

Jackson's PUSH, a member of the U.S. Peace Council, and, in the words of the *New Republic,* a man "with a long record of public identification with Stalinism, American style" whose "politics will not bear scrutiny."[24] O'Dell told the conference that the Israeli invasion of Lebanon and a recent South African incursion into Angola were "inspired by the American government in the spirit of Cold War confrontation." One of the purposes of the arms race with nuclear weapons was to maintain the status quo in the Third World, to frustrate the "people's efforts to establish peace with justice."[25] In the fall of 1983 the New England regional office of the AFSC issued a statement against the stationing of U.S. medium-range missiles in Europe that warned against the " 'Deadly Connection' between US nuclear war policy and US intervention policy." The U.S. was asked to cease its "efforts to remake the world in our own image and end our commitment to go to war for the short-term economic interests of multi-national corporations."[26]

The AFSC Is Charged with Serving the Communists

Not surprisingly, such stridently anti-American pronouncements have led to the charge that the AFSC works in the service of the Communists. Such accusations are not new. Documents obtained in 1975-76 by the AFSC from various intelligence agencies under the Freedom of Information Act reveal a long-standing pattern of surveillance and investigations by the FBI, the CIA, and other federal agencies. The results of these investigations were all identical: allegations that the AFSC was a Communist front or otherwise was infiltrated and controlled by subversive elements were found to be without substance, and the AFSC was confirmed to be "a sincere pacifist organization." An analysis by the CIA in 1958 concluded, "Ostensibly, this organization is pacifistic to the point of advocating a policy of friendship and cooperation with everyone — including Communists."[27]

The most recent accusation of ties to the Communists came in 1982 when Terry Provance, director of the AFSC's disarmament program and one of the originators of the nuclear freeze idea, was called by author John Barron "a longtime World Peace Council activist" and one "who in 1979 helped found its American branch, the U.S. Peace Council."[28] Provance promptly denied that he had ever been a member of the World Peace Council, which, he said, had listed him as a member in 1977 without his permission. He had supported the convening of the organizing conference of the

U.S. Peace Council in 1979, but he insisted that his presence for some two hours at that meeting should not be construed as either membership or an endorsement.[29]

Given the Communist party's proclivity toward secrecy and manipulation and its frequently stated intention to work closely with the peace movement, one cannot, of course, be absolutely certain that there are no Communists in the AFSC. However, so far no evidence of Communist infiltration has surfaced, and one can probably agree with the appraisal of Chuck Fager, a Quaker, that the AFSC's mistakes and shortcomings are of its own making and not the KGB's. "Serious as some of AFSC's problems are," Fager has concluded, "I for one am grateful that they so clearly do *not* include being run by Moscow or CIA manipulators. The American Friends Service Committee, for better or for worse, is no one's organization but ours."[30]

And yet one cannot leave it at that. Granted, the AFSC is neither a Communist front nor an organization controlled by the KGB. Nevertheless, since about 1965 the AFSC, as we have seen, has adhered to the New Left's policy of nonexclusion and has worked in numerous coalitions with the Communists. During the time of the Vietnam war, the AFSC cultivated close and friendly ties with the NLF and Communist North Vietnam — partly in order to facilitate its relief efforts in Southeast Asia, but also out of sympathy for the aims of this Asian "liberation movement." When Ho Chi Minh died on 2 September 1969, the AFSC expressed its condolences to the people of North Vietnam "on the occasion of the death of your esteemed President, Ho Chi Minh. Both friends and foes must recognize that this remarkable man selflessly devoted his life to the causes of national independence and social reconstruction. His integrity and commitment have won the admiration and respect of the people of the world."[31] Since the AFSC had always insisted that Ho Chi Minh was primarily a nationalist and that the accounts of Ho's Stalinist rule over North Vietnam, including the brutal elimination of "landlords" in the land reform campaign of 1955, were CIA fabrications, the AFSC's infatuation with "Uncle Ho" was, of course, not surprising.

After his return from the World Assembly for Peace and Independence of the People of Indochina held in Paris in February 1972, the AFSC's executive secretary Bronson Clark related with pleasure and pride that during a large demonstration of solidarity with the cause of the PRG, sponsored and organized primarily by the Communist trade unions, he had marched "arm-in-arm" with Dang

Quang Minh, the PRG ambassador in Moscow.[32] Following the triumph of the North Vietnamese divisions over South Vietnam in the spring of 1975, the AFSC received a card of thanks from Hanoi featuring a picture of Ho Chi Minh. Addressed to Louis Schneider, the AFSC's executive secretary, the message read, "With the most sincere gratitude of the Vietnamese people for your precious support and assistance to our just struggle for a peaceful, reunified, independent, democratic and prosperous Vietnam."[33] No one familiar with the AFSC's record during the Vietnam war can doubt that the AFSC had indeed fully earned this citation from its Communist friends in North Vietnam. On 23 August 1975 Schneider left for Vietnam to attend the National Day Celebrations in Hanoi.

Relations with the Soviet Peace Movement

Until 1965 the AFSC had adhered to a policy of keeping a safe distance from Communist-run peace organizations. One of the objections to attending the gatherings of these groups had been the lack of a clear distinction beween "delegates" and "observers" at such conferences. This enabled the Communists to claim that their efforts for peace, expressed in resolutions that were usually adopted without debate in the final session, were supported by a wide array of non-Communist organizations from all over the world. After the start of the war in Vietnam, however, the AFSC decided to seek allies wherever it could, and that included the Soviet Peace Committee and the World Peace Council (WPC).

In July 1965 Stewart Meacham, head of the AFSC's peace education division, was an observer at the WPC-sponsored meeting in Helsinki, the World Congress for Peace, National Independence and General Disarmament. In his report on the congress, Meacham noted that no attention had been paid "to who was a delegate and who merely an observer in determining the right to vote and otherwise participate." He had interpreted his observer status strictly and had abstained from voting and even from being recorded as abstaining. Still, on balance, he felt that the congress had been worth attending. As to future relations with the WPC, Meacham thought that Friends could "engage in meaningful exchange with them; we can challenge them in the area of values and commitment at the very center of their ideological justification for violent struggle."[34]

As the agitation against the war in Vietnam heated up and Meacham became pronouncedly hostile toward an America he saw drifting toward fascism, he increasingly followed the motto "The enemies of my enemy are my friends." In a letter to a Canadian friend written in October 1968, Meacham expressed the view that the WPC was characterized by a new openness and that one should not be afraid of the Communists. New alliances were now possible.[35] In November of that year, Meacham served as chairman of a delegation of American peace-movement members who visited the Soviet Union at the invitation of the Soviet Peace Committee.

Back in 1962 Meacham had signed a declaration dissociating the independent peace movement in the West from the official peace organizations of the Eastern bloc that espouse the policies of their own governments, "whether those policies happen to be developing greater bombs or calling for disarmament."[36] Six years later and three years into the embittering experience of the Vietnam war, Meacham returned from Moscow with "a deep sense of admiration, affection and respect for the officials and staff of the Soviet Peace Committee" who had met all the needs and wishes of the American delegates and had organized "a fruitful and enlightening schedule, . . . to build an ever stronger basis of understanding and confidence between the peace forces of our two countries." Differences of opinion had emerged regarding the Soviet invasion of Czechoslovakia, and the American delegates had recognized "the Soviet Peace Committee's consistent unwillingness to deviate even in nuances from the views of the Soviet government." Nevertheless, Meacham expressed the hope that there would be future meetings between U.S. and Soviet peace organization representatives "to work together to build support for policies of peace."[37]

If one puts together the AFSC's newly discovered admiration for the official Soviet peace movement and the twenty years of close cooperation with Communist and other organizations of the radical Left, described in an earlier part of this book, one cannot but conclude that the AFSC has by now seriously compromised its own independence and integrity. It bears repeating that there is no evidence that the AFSC is run by the Communists or that it consciously serves the Communist cause. The leftward drift of the AFSC, it would appear, was not the result of Communist infiltration. However, after years of coalition work with the Old and the New Left, the AFSC's own distinct philosophy has become blurred. Such joint actions have provided the Communist party and its fronts with a new legitimacy and have pushed the AFSC into muting its universal critique of militarism. Time and again, the AFSC has condemned the U.S. for defending its national interests in various parts of the world while at the same time it has denied or counseled understanding for the expansionist designs of the Soviet Union. The AFSC's indulgence and support of repressive Communist regimes all over the globe, from Vietnam to Nicaragua, did not develop at the behest of the KGB, but does that fact make it any less reprehensible? In order to sup with the devil, one needs a long spoon, but the AFSC has long since thrown away such an elongated tool.

The relationship of the other pacifist organizations to the official Soviet peace movement has followed a broadly similar pattern. While in the Soviet Union in 1982, several FOR members made contact with the Group for the Establishment of Trust between the USSR and USA, an independent peace organization established in June 1982. The leaders of this small group have been repeatedly jailed. One of its founders, Sergei Batovrin, was held in a psychiatric institution. In an appeal to peace activists in Europe, the Group drew attention to the fact that before the peace marches against the stationing of American missiles in Europe had begun, the Soviet Union had deployed SS-20 missiles, "which are capable of striking any point in Europe with a nuclear blow, and which are aimed not only at your cities and factories, but at your very opportunity to conduct these marches, to express your opinion freely and to take part in important decision making in the democratic way." At the time of impressive peace demonstrations in Western Europe, people in Moscow who simply spoke out in favor of establishing trust between nations were being subjected to the suppressive machinery of a totalitarian state. "You have the opportunity and the right to request disarmament from your government. Here there is no such opportunity. Therefore, include in your peace march programs also request[s] directed to the Soviet government to dismantle all the SS-20s, to stop persecuting peace advocates in the USSR."[38] In a similar vein, Batovrin appealed to a participant in an FOR-sponsored peace cruise, claiming that the nuclear threat would remain a reality "until there is a people's movement in the USSR doing freely their peace work hand in hand with the peace movement" in the West.[39]

In August 1982 the FOR participated in a demonstration in front of the Soviet mission to the UN, protesting the incarceration of Batovrin in a psychiatric hospital and the repression visited upon the Trust Group. At other times, however, the attitude of the FOR toward this independent Soviet peace organization has been far more ambivalent — probably for fear of contributing to "anti-Soviet hysteria" or spoiling relations with the official Soviet Peace Committee. In early 1985 Gene Knudsen-Hoffman, a Quaker who had helped create the FOR's US-USSR reconciliation program, warned the peace movement against turning its back on the established government of the Soviet Union. One had to understand that the Trust Group had broken the law which forbade slandering the government. Knudsen-Hoffman argued that this Soviet law, which the Group had violated by implying that the government was not fully dedicated to the pursuit of peace, was no different from laws in the United States such as the law against the holding of unauthorized prayer meetings on military property or the law against killing.[40]

A few months later, Norman Solomon, director of the FOR's disarmament program, defended the official Soviet Peace Committee as a genuine manifestation of the Soviet Union's desire for peace. The Soviet government sponsored disarmament rallies; the U.S. did not. While Soviet society had economic problems and "elements of repression," it also could take credit for "many impressive achievements," and it was without "enormous discrepancies of income, idolatry of wealth, and unremitting pro-war mass culture." It was wrong to identify the Soviet government as the enemy. The main threat of war came from the United States—"the world's single greatest threat to the future existence of humanity."[41]

The same issues surfaced in an exchange between Solomon and E. P. Thompson of the British Campaign for Nuclear Disarmament. The peace movement, Solomon maintained, had to be careful that it did not "unwittingly reinforce chronic American-Soviet antipathies. . . . We cannot reduce our society's cold war fervor by adding to it."[42] Thompson, on the other hand, argued that it was not honest to remain silent about the suppression of Solidarity, the Polish free trade union, or the persecution of the Moscow Trust Group for fear of "anti-Soviet verbiage." The problems of Western society did not justify "fellow-travelling sentimentalism" about the Soviet Union. "Let us never, for the shadow of one moment, engage in arguments that excuse offenses against life or liberty on one side because similar or worse offenses can be pointed to on the other. These remain two offenses; there is no way in which one cancels out the other. The point is to end them both." The Soviet peace offensive, Thompson insisted, was strictly for export. The Soviet Union made sure "that the infection of the peace movement is halted at its borders." Its peace offensive was directed toward the West, while at the same time the East was being placed under quarantine. With the independent peace movement effectively repressed, public opinion in the Soviet Union could scarcely influence the rulers of the country.[43]

During the last years of his life, WRL leader A. J. Muste had been anxious to develop relations with the official Soviet Peace

Committee and the World Peace Council (WPC). He used these contacts to plead for persecuted Soviet dissidents, but he was also interested in meeting with the Soviets in order to exchange ideas. In May 1966 Muste accepted an invitation from the WPC to attend a session of the International Institute for Peace in Vienna, a creation of the WPC; his flight ticket was to be paid for by the WPC.[44] In December 1966 the Institute inquired whether Muste would agree to be nominated by the WPC Secretariat for the Frederic Joliot-Curie Peace Gold Medal.[45] Muste died before he could give his response, and there is no way of knowing whether he would have accepted this somewhat dubious honor.

During the following years, the WRL from time to time has pursued these same contacts. In December 1982 David McReynolds, joined by other WRL staff members and several other peace activists, sent a letter to Yuri Andropov, the new general secretary of the Soviet Communist party. Copies of this letter went to the Soviet Peace Committee and the Institute for U.S. and Canadian Studies. The letter urged Soviet initiatives in disarmament as well as respect for the Helsinki accords, the release of Andrei Sakharov, and free contacts with the independent Soviet peace movement. "We must tell you that one of the most forceful weapons in the hands of men such as Reagan is the charge that the peace movement exists only on one side of the conflict, that on your side the peace movement is entirely controlled by the government. We can think of few things that would be as effective in political and in human terms as permitting a meeting in Moscow that would involve members of our groups, of the Soviet Peace Committee, and of the Group to Establish Trust between the USA and the USSR."[46]

The vice president of the Soviet Peace Committee, O. Kharkhadin, replied on 15 February 1983. The Soviet official welcomed the concern for peace expressed by McReynolds, but rejected the call for new Soviet unilateral moves. The Soviet Union had repeatedly reduced its armed forces, Kharkhadin claimed, but the U.S. had never reciprocated. "But we do not lose hope. We are waiting for your support for the efforts being made by the East — this support is highly needed now." Kharkhadin also objected to any comparison between Afghanistan and Central America. The Soviet Union was sending assistance "to the people of Afghanistan who have embarked on the road of eliminating the semi-feudal survivals, on the road of constructing a new and free life, the road of social progress [and this aid] cannot be termed intervention." The U.S., on the other hand, was assisting the forces of reaction both in Afghanistan and in Central America, and that was indeed intervention.

The Soviet spokesman also disagreed with the WRL's "assessment of the role the so-called 'independent Moscow group' is playing in the peace movement." This tiny group represented nobody but its ten members, and its activities were limited to meeting with Western press correspondents and supplying them with all kinds of fabrication about life in the Soviet Union. The only fighters for peace in the Soviet Union were the millions of Soviet citizens who belonged to the Soviet Peace Committee. In the Soviet Union there had never been and there never would be individuals persecuted for their participation in the struggle for peace. The members of the Trust Group, however, could not be considered supporters of peace and disarmament. Their activities were the "rudest provocation" and were highly detrimental to the cause of peace. Therefore, Kharkhadin concluded, Soviet peace supporters sincerely deplored the fact "that some prominent figures in antiwar organizations and movements in the West have given credence to this slanderous concoction of anti-Soviet professionals and allow disinformed people to be misled by them and, thereby, [enable] those professionals to achieve their main purpose, that of splitting and weakening the genuine world movement for peace and disarmament."[47]

This rebuff should have taught the WRL once and for all that the official Soviet Peace Committee is simply a mouthpiece and an apologist for Soviet foreign policy, and that the Soviet Union will not tolerate a truly independent peace organization. More important, this means, of course, that a real peace movement exists only on one side of the East-West conflict and that the pressure for a reduction in defense expenditures mounted by the WRL and other like-minded groups has an impact only on the Western democracies. This in turn creates a situation of imbalance and, if the lobbying activities of these Western peace organizations are successful, could have seriously destabilizing consequences for the balance of power in the world.

The WRL does not recognize the reality of this problem. It argues that the world cannot wait until disarmament is mutual, multilateral, and verifiable. The League is committed to unilateralism, it denies the necessity for armed forces, and it urges the members of the military to leave the service and those doing military research to end it. The WRL is aware that unilateralism is not a viable political program, but it insists that survival depends on a fundamental break with the logic of the past.[48]

The effect of this new logic became apparent in Africa in 1976. In December 1975 the WRL and other pacifist groups had picketed the Soviet and U.S. missions to the United Nations in an appeal to the two superpowers to end their intervention in the civil war in Angola. Distributed leaflets argued that the people of Angola, emerging from 493 years of colonial rule, were entitled to peace and independence. "Let the people of Angola, without further foreign intervention, determine their own fate. We urge a withdrawal of *all* foreign troops, military material and 'advisors,' and an end to all arms shipments."[49] Predictably, this agitation had an impact only on American policymakers. It coincided with a deep sense of trauma and fear of new foreign involvements caused by the collapse of Vietnam in the spring of 1975. The U.S. Congress subsequently enacted the Clark Amendment, forbidding American intervention in Angola. This unilateral gesture in turn gave the Soviet Union a free run and enabled it, with the help of thousands of Cuban proxy troops, to install a Marxist-Leninist regime in Angola, its first important ally on the African continent. The old logic of the balance of power, it would seem, refuses to die, and those who are foolish enough to ignore it do so at their peril.

A Double Standard on Human Rights

Pacifist organizations have continued to issue statements of support from time to time for the Moscow Trust Group and other independent East European peace groups, although this has not prevented pacifists from adhering to their generally indulgent view of the Communist world. There has prevailed a reluctance to criticize Communist regimes, in part — supposedly — out of fear of contributing to the cold war. For example, the AFSC is committed to support human rights everywhere, but in practice the organization has concentrated its efforts on the non-Communist allies of the U.S. and anti-Communist regimes generally. Chile, South Africa, Israel, and El Salvador rank high among the violators of human rights to be condemned at every opportunity; the Soviet Union, Vietnam, Syria, Ethiopia, and Nicaragua escape with, at worst, an occasional slap on the wrist. The abandonment of democratic procedures by left-wing regimes is justified and excused; right-wing governments must be like Caesar's wife.

The AFSC's own explanation for this one-eyed view of the world is that the organization feels a special responsibility for violations of human rights in countries aligned with the United States. "The focus of AFSC's work," explained an AFSC pamphlet issued in the spring of 1985, "is on specific international situations where there is a record of gross human rights violations and direct United States involvement."[50] American leverage with such countries is said to promise the best opportunities for successful intervention and the amelioration of abuses.

Even if one were to accept this argument at face value, it presents several problems. First, it seriously overstates U.S. influence and leverage. The authoritarian regime of Thieu in South Vietnam, for example, was usually described as a creation and puppet of the United States, and yet in actuality U.S. ability to get the Saigon government to carry out much-needed reforms was strictly limited. For many years, Thieu's expectation that the U.S. would not let his country go down the drain, even if ultimately proven wrong, converted South Vietnam's weakness into a position of total strength. In many ways we became their prisoners rather than they ours, the classic trap into which great powers have often fallen in their relations with weak allies.

Second, and more important, just as a concentration on reducing the military budget of the United States without an effective corresponding pressure on the Soviet Union undermines the global balance of power, so the focus on human rights violations by regimes friendly to or supported by the U.S. distorts and misrepresents the balance sheet of moral evil in the world. Should anyone have seriously believed that the occasional resort to censorship and the flaws in the electoral processes of South Vietnam during the Thieu regime represented a more serious violation of human rights than the complete absence of political rights and civil liberties and the total suppression of a free press in Communist North Vietnam? Is Israel's use of administrative detention for suspected terrorists in the occupied territories morally worse than the continuing use of slave labor in the Soviet Gulag and the incarceration of dissidents in psychiatric hospitals? The same problem can be looked at historically: Back in the 1930s and 1940s, should the United States — because its influence on Great Britain was far greater than its influence on Hitler's Germany — have concentrated its censure on British violations of human rights in India rather than on the unspeakable barbarities perpetrated by the Nazis?

The double standard on human rights violations also seriously threatens the search for peace. The AFSC correctly stresses the interdependence of peace and the realization of human rights, but fails to apply this insight to those countries where it is most per-

tinent — that is, the Soviet bloc. As members of the persecuted independent peace movement in the East — the Group for the
Establishment of Trust between the USSR and USA, and the Charter
77 group in Czechoslovakia — have often told their Western coun-
terparts, it is the achievement of human rights and political democracy in the Soviet Union which alone will provide a check on
the temptation of Soviet rulers to use their vast military power to
endanger the peace of the world. Or, as Andrei Sakharov has
put it, "As long as a country has no civil liberty, no freedom of
information, and no independent press, there exists no effective
body of opinion to control the conduct of the government and its
functionaries. Such a situation is not just a misfortune for its citizens unprotected against tyranny and lawlessness; it is a menace to
international security."[51]

Third, by concentrating its fire on American allies such as, say,
South Korea, the AFSC undermines American support for these
countries. Why should the American public continue to support
South Korea against its enemy in the North if all it hears is a steady
barrage of criticism directed against human rights violations in authoritarian South Korea but nothing against the infinitely worse
human rights abuses in Communist North Korea? If successful, the
AFSC's focus on human rights violations by America's embattled
allies would lead to a further increase in the number of communist
regimes with a consequent worsening of the global human rights
situation. One of the best ways of protecting human rights in the
world is, after all, to halt the spread of communism. But, of course,
the AFSC is not at all convinced that Communist regimes are all
that bad, and it plays the double-standard card precisely to help its
revolutionary friends. By constantly harping on the repressive fea-
tures of the Thieu regime and ignoring the far worse situation in
the North, the AFSC was successful in reducing aid to South Vietnam and helping the North Vietnamese win the war. As we have
seen, an attempt to repeat this performance, using the same strategy,
is now under way with regard to Central America.

The Pro-Soviet Alignment of the WILPF

Of the four major pacifist organizations, the WILPF has developed
the most pronounced pro-Soviet outlook. Indeed, by the middle
1970s one had to conclude that the League, completing a trend
perhaps begun as early as 1967, had ceased to be part of the New

Left and had adopted the classical stance of Communist fellow travelers.

The differences between the Old and the New Left are sometimes not very pronounced. For example, both the Old and the New Left admire so-called national liberation movements in the Third World, and both regard the United States as the greatest threat to world peace. Nevertheless, important differences distinguish the two groups. Whereas the New Left is generally critical of the bureaucratic character of Soviet communism and sometimes also of the Soviet Union's foreign policy, Communist fellow travelers admire and defend the Soviet Union as a superior kind of democracy and uncritically follow the twists and turns of Soviet foreign policy. Fellow travelers also are active members of Communist front organizations that the Communist party uses to recruit members and to reach out to a wider constituency. Front organizations serve the interests of the party under the guise of some honorable activity such as promoting racial harmony or world peace. Judged by these criteria, the WILPF by 1976 had crossed the Rubicon and had assumed an outright pro-Communist position. The manifestation of this ideological shift can be traced in several areas.

Back in 1961 the WILPF had started a program of exchange visits between small groups of American and Soviet women. At that time the leaders of the League had no illusions about the handpicked character of the Soviet women with whom they were meeting, but they regarded these contacts as worthwhile nevertheless. By the late 1960s the WILPF had established a working relationship with the Soviet Women's Committee, and League members traveling to the Soviet Union were often ideological pilgrims who came back full of praise for life under Soviet communism. One of the members of a 1968 delegation was Kay Camp, who a year later became president of the WILPF. In her report on the trip, published in *Four Lights*, Camp described how the Soviet hosts had overwhelmed the American women "with flowers, gifts, and a packed program of sights and visits. They are proud, hard-working, disciplined — but fun-loving and with a capacity for instant friendship. . . . The accomplishments of Soviet womenpower are impressive. . . . We were impressed by the many social achievements of the Soviet peoples; their progress in the areas of unemployment, crime prevention, education and welfare should inspire other countries struggling with these problems." This visit took place shortly after the Soviet invasion of Czechoslovakia. The American women were told that the Soviet intervention had become necessary because of the strength of counter-revolutionary forces in Czechoslovakia and because of Soviet fears of an increasingly aggressive, heavily armed West Germany. Even though "in the context of Vietnam and Chicago," as Camp related in her article, the Americans "had no place to stand from which to criticize the Soviet military intervention," they did make clear their disapproval of what Camp called a "Soviet blunder."[52]

Another such delegation, which visited the Soviet Union in July 1974, came back with even more enthusiastic news. The American women, a participant reported, "learned much about the functioning of the democratic process in the USSR. From 1500 to 2000 people elect a delegate to the local Soviet, with whom they meet frequently. Delegates continue their regular jobs but take time out for their legislative duties. Serving is a responsibility as well as an honor." Soviet citizens write countless letters to the media and their local government, and "the law requires that every letter be treated seriously and answered within one month." According to this participant, the entire trip was "an unforgettable experience."[53]

Prior to 1965 the WILPF had shared the American peace community's skeptical attitude toward the official Soviet peace movement, which they regarded as an apologist for Soviet foreign policy. By 1968, however, the relations between the WILPF and the Soviet Peace Committee had become cordial. At its October 1968 meeting, the WILPF board discussed an invitation that it had received from the Soviet Peace Committee to send a delegation to a meeting to be held in November in the Soviet Union. The minutes recorded that, after some discussion, the board voted "to go ahead, enthusiastically."[54]

During the 1970s one of the people who worked hardest for a closer relationship between the WILPF and various Soviet-sponsored organizations was Dorothy Steffens, the League's executive director. The political views held by this key WILPF staff person help explain her interest in the building of bridges toward the Communist world. In September 1975 Steffens was one of the sponsors of a newly established U.S. Committee for Friendship with the German Democratic Republic (better known as Communist East Germany), which hailed "the profound anti-fascist and humanist origins of the German Democratic Republic" and proclaimed that the "heritage of the first socialist state on German soil is indeed relevant to the best in our own democratic traditions."[55] In an interview with a correspondent for the Soviet news agency Tass, published in the Soviet Union in April 1976, Steffens praised the Soviet Union's desire for peace. "The League and Committee of Soviet Women are agreed how much peace means to the Soviet nation, and I think the Soviet women and our followers understand that the Soviet nation sincerely wants peace and does not need war."[56] A month later, *New World Review,* a magazine originally sponsored by the Friends of the Soviet Union and at all times dedicated to praising the wonders of Soviet communism, published a special issue on the 25th Congress of the Communist party of the Soviet Union. The brief essay that Steffens contributed and signed with her title — "Executive Director, WILPF" — was a frank celebration of the Communist system.

Steffens noted that the recent congress of the CPUSSR had provided a sharp contrast to the American primary elections held at the same time. It also supplied valuable insights into the meaning of democracy in the two countries. In the United States, she claimed, "our capitalist economic system . . . has subverted and distorted the Constitutional guarantees and turned our government into a government of the military-industrial complex, serving the insatiable maw of the military machine and the faceless owners of the multinational corporations who reap profit from it." The Communist party congress, on the other hand, demonstrated what "socialist democracy" is all about. The congress, "with its sober evaluation of past successes and weaknesses, serious consideration of grassroots programs and proposals, and realistic, yet forward-looking establishment of future goals was an exercise in participatory democracy." Tens of millions of people had been involved in the process of debating these proposals. Seventy-seven percent of the delegates had been from the working class; 25 percent were women. "The people at the 25th Party Congress defined their major concerns as increasing worker participation in the management of production and extending the powers of the Soviets (national, regional and local government bodies)."

The WILPF, Steffens wrote, had had meetings with Soviet women since 1961 in order to breach the cold-war curtain. "These 15 years of 'detente' with our Soviet sisters have enabled us to ask questions, probe answers, and witness first-hand during our visits to their country what grassroots democracy means and how it works to improve the quality of people's lives. The juxtaposition of the US primary elections and the USSR Party Congress made the differences very clear indeed."[57]

The editor of *New World Review* was Jessica Smith. She was honored on her eightieth birthday — 1 February 1976 — at a luncheon sponsored by Communist party notables Gus Hall and Angela

Davis and assorted party sympathizers. At the luncheon Smith received the "Order of Friendship of the Peoples of the USSR" as well as a citation from the WILPF "in recognition of a lifetime of distinguished service." The fact that the WILPF had bestowed a citation upon Smith came to light only several months later. Dorothy Detzer, who had known Smith as a secret Communist for many years, wrote two letters to Mildred Scott Olmsted in which she expressed her surprise that the WILPF would honor an agent of the Soviet Union and an apologist for Soviet terror. Such a thing, Detzer wrote, could not have happened during the earlier years of the League and marked a "drastic change in W.I.L. policy."[58]

In the spring of 1973, the WILPF was invited to serve on the international preparatory committee for the World Congress of Peace Forces, planned by the World Peace Council for October of that year in Moscow. Steffens was one of the WILPF delegates attending this preparatory meeting, and in a letter to Marii Hasegawa, president of the American section, she reported that the meeting had been characterized by flexibility and a willingness to consider suggestions. "Whether anything actually does happen in October depends partly on the world situation but also very much on how much we non-communist international peace groups are willing to put into it."[59] One of the WILPF delegates to the congress wrote after her return from Moscow that the meeting, attended by 3,500 delegates from 144 countries, had been "the biggest assembly of peace forces ever" and that Soviet hospitality had been "generous." Highlights of this "productive conference" included a major policy address by chairman Leonid Brezhnev and a midnight meeting with the delegation from North Vietnam. The WILPF, the delegate related with pride, had been prominently involved in the work of the congress. The international chairwoman of the WILPF had been one of only two women to preside at the plenary session; international vice president Kay Camp had "the honor of presiding over the meeting of women delegates."[60]

In 1974 the WILPF was designated to function as the U.S. "activating group" for the World Congress of Women to be held in October 1975 and organized by the Women's International Democratic Federation.[61] This group—like the World Peace Council, with which it closely cooperates—is one of several international Communist front organizations in existence today and has been under Soviet control since its inception in 1945. The WILPF also served on the international executive committee preparing the East

Berlin Congress, another example of the close integration into Soviet-sponsored activities which the League had achieved by that time.

The question of the WILPF's relationship with the World Peace Council (WPC) was the subject of a discussion at a meeting of the League's advisory committee in March 1978. Several members had objected to the fact that the WILPF delegates to WPC-sponsored meetings in Europe had had their transportation expenses paid by the WPC. Mildred Scott Olmsted, who had played a prominent role in the League for more than forty years and held the title "executive director emerita," indicated that "when she was leading WILPF we did not take WPC's money." Others objected to the acceptance of such financial support on more prudential grounds, arguing that it called into question the independent status of the WILPF. Kay Camp pointed out that since the WPC was in the process of establishing a U.S. Peace Council, such independence was more important than ever. Echoing the same sentiment, another member argued that "it is important for us to maintain our image in Washington as a separate, independent organization." After this exchange of views, it was decided to refer the matter to the national board.[62]

WILPF president Marjorie Boehm was unhappy about the prospect of the board's having such a discussion. The issue of the WILPF's relationship with the WPC, she wrote the regional vice presidents, would very likely be divisive. Many members had supported the work of the WPC for many years; the WILPF had no right to expect that its rank-and-file and board members wear only the hat of the League. "A [red-]baiting discussion in our board meeting would seriously affect the coalition work of our San Francisco branch. This same situation probably exists in many of our branches."[63] Naomi Marcus, in a memo addressed to WILPF officers and marked "Eyes Only," agreed that the issue of the WPC should not be discussed by the board, and she too stressed the tactical importance of the WILPF's independent image. The League had to reach and educate the large segment of the American public that was not already on the Left. To accomplish this task, the WILPF had to maintain its credibility. "It is one thing for us to be critical of our government's anti-Soviet positions for our own reasons. But I think it is quite another for us to make that position credible if we are closely allied with organizations that reflect the Soviet viewpoint."[64]

Concern for the WILPF's image came to the fore also in the League's relationship with a domestic Communist front. In February 1976 WILPF president Naomi Marcus proposed that in order to move on toward disarmament and peace, the women's movement should focus on "the need to release money that now goes for military spending, and use it instead for programs for child care, health needs, continuing education, and jobs." Women had to work with other groups, similarly exploited by the military-industrial-governmental axis, to demand cuts in the military budget and release funds for social programs. They also had to insist on "a restructuring of the economic system so that people's needs come before profit."[65] In line with this proposal, the WILPF in September 1976 decided to start a major program thrust in favor of reordering national priorities, using the slogan "Feed the Cities . . . Not the Pentagon." In preparation for this campaign, executive director Steffens got in touch with Joseph Harris, research director of the Labor Research Association, requesting his help in preparing a fact sheet to be used in this new WILPF activity. The League could pay only two hundred dollars for this work, Steffens wrote Harris, but we "hope you will wish to do it in order to help this important program."[66]

Steffens and Harris apparently were well acquainted with each other. Steffens began her letter with "Dear Joe." She also seems to have known that the Labor Research Association could be counted on to contribute its work for the sake of a common cause. The Labor Research Association had been founded in 1927 by the American Communist party to render research services to trade unions and other workers' organizations; its ostensibly non-Communist head, Robert F. Dunn, was a secret party member who upon his death in February 1977 was eulogized by the *Daily Worker* as "part of us for virtually all his adult life."[67] When Harris sent Steffens the final draft of the fact sheet, he explained that implicit in his approach in preparing it had been "the idea that the stronger the USSR is, the better off the workers of the world are. This runs counter to the liberal approach which opposes military might from all angles." Harris contended that such thinking was wrong because "Soviet military might is the guarantee of Cuba, Angola, and many other nations' independence." He had focused on "the issue of anti-Sovietism," he wrote Steffens, "more than has been done before by an organization such as WILPF. But at some point a frontal attack is necessary. And why not now??? I don't know if you could get WILPF to undertake it, but I think you should try."[68]

Steffens did not think that the WILPF was ripe for such a "frontal attack." The correspondence between her and Harris bears annotations such as "speak with him about WILPF" and, next to Harris's suggestions for an outright pro-Soviet approach, "Not asked for!" Ultimately, the literature produced by the WILPF for its "Feed the

Cities ... Not the Pentagon" campaign used sources such as the Coalition for a New Foreign and Military Policy, the successor organization to the Coalition to Stop Funding the [Vietnam] War, and the writings of Seymour Melman, SANE's disarmament expert.

Some West Coast members of the WILPF objected to this more moderate approach. Millie Livingston, an officer of the San Francisco branch, teamed up with members of the Communist Labor party, a Maoist splinter group, and tried to take control of the local "Feed the Cities" campaign. Livingston called branch meetings at her house without notifying Vivian Hallinan, another branch officer and the national coordinator of the "Feed the Cities" campaign. Hallinan, disturbed, informed the national office that people who had never turned out for branch meetings before turned out for those meetings now. Hallinan also inquired whether the Communist Labor party "is a part of the authentic American Communist party," but Steffens, who was knowledgeable in such matters, responded that she was "quite sure it was not the Communist Party." Eventually Marjorie Boehm managed to make peace in the San Francisco branch, and the "Feed the Cities" program was able to proceed on track.[69]

The turmoil in the San Francisco branch was not the only crisis facing the WILPF at that time. In late 1968, in the midst of the agitation against the Vietnam war, the WILPF had had a membership of over 11,000. By 1976 the League was down to 5,300 members, and of 119 officially accredited branches, only 66 were actually functioning. The sharpest decline in membership had occurred between 1969 and 1972, coinciding with the gradual weakening and eventual demise of the antiwar movement, but dissatisfaction with the increasingly strident pro-Soviet course of the WILPF may also have played a role. Some Jewish members in particular were unhappy with the League's pro-Palestinian stance and resented the WILPF's failure to speak up for the plight of Soviet Jewry. In a letter published in the February 1972 issue of *Peace and Freedom*, Irma Weinstein, an officer of the Baltimore branch, asked why WILPF delegates visiting the Soviet Union did not meet with dissidents as well as government officials, as the League had done during missions to South Vietnam. "I have noticed a tendency on the part of peace and freedom organizations to be more accepting of suppression and oppression in socialist or Third World countries than in capitalist or Western countries," Weinstein stated. "If we are truly devoted to human rights and social justice, we must condemn repression and discrimination wherever they occur."

Naomi Marcus, editor of *Peace and Freedom*, took care to have

Weinstein's letter countered by no less than three rebuttals. One of the respondents argued that "most of the unfavorable stories we hear about the USSR are false" and that there was probably more anti-Semitism in the United States than in the USSR. Another defender of the Soviet Union's Jewish record was national board member Greta Lynch, who in the thirties had been one of the founders of the American League Against War and Fascism. She criticized the inadequate support available in America for poor, old Jews and noted that "people living in glass houses shouldn't throw stones."[70]

Disagreement also surfaced on how to react to the Soviet-Chinese split. The WILPF at first tried to ignore the conflict and stay on good terms with both the Soviet Union and Communist China. In the early seventies several WILPF members visited the People's Republic of China and came back with enthusiastic stories. Ruth Gage-Colby, the League's UN representative and, like Lynch, an old-time leftist, reported in November 1971 that the Cultural Revolution had been a success and that she had found in China "a freeing of the human spirit, a pride in being human."[71] Evelyn Alloy, an active member of the Philadelphia branch, wrote in *Peace and Freedom* in April 1975 that the program of the Chinese Communist party aimed at the liberation of both men and women, and that "the Chinese people are reaping the benefits of their new and advanced socialist way of life."[72]

The Chinese attack upon Vietnam in early 1979, in the wake of the Vietnamese invasion of Cambodia, caused great consternation because the WILPF now finally had to choose between these two Communist regimes. Not surprisingly, the League came down on the side of Vietnam and its ally, the Soviet Union. The WILPF, together with other peace organizations such as the AFSC, SANE, and Women Strike for Peace, signed a statement on the crisis in Southeast Asia that condemned "the concept of punishment advanced by the Chinese to justify their actions in Vietnam" and urged an "immediate Chinese withdrawal from Vietnam" as a precondition for achieving a peaceful solution to the problem of Cambodia.[73] In March the WILPF was represented at an emergency session of the World Peace Council in Helsinki that condemned the "Chinese aggression" and "called upon all peace-loving forces to intensify the solidarity movement with Vietnam." A WILPF delegate reported with obvious approval that most speakers "reaffirmed their allegiance to the Soviet Union as the leader of the socialist world, as opposed to the betrayal of Marxism by the Chinese leaders. The Soviet Union was lauded for its statesman-like restraint in this crisis and for its support for peace and the independence and sovereignty of nations."[74]

A few WILPF members took exception to the new pro-Soviet alignment. In a letter to *Peace and Freedom,* Evelyn Alloy protested the failure of the League to give the Chinese point of view a fair hearing. Instead there prevailed a "well entrenched sentimentalization toward the Soviet Union as the 'first socialist country,' particularly strong among older WILPF members, backed up by associations through the years with the Soviet Women's Committee (government controlled), and our remembrance of our anti-war struggle that is clouding WILPF's official vision and position."[75] Alloy also wrote to the national board, saying, "I believe that some very peculiar changes are occurring in WILPF that are a reflection of pro-Soviet allegiances on the part of some members who are now in position to dominate WILPF policy."[76] In a letter to Mildred Scott Olmsted, Alloy told her friend of a meeting in Philadelphia that featured the Vietnamese ambassador to the UN, a meeting which she had attended and which had been characterized by the same anti-Chinese bias. This meeting had been organized by the Delaware Valley Peace Council and co-sponsored by the AFSC and the WILPF, but actually, Alloy claimed, it "was *led* and *controlled* by members of the Communist party." Alloy related that the question-and-answer period was tightly controlled, that the atmosphere was that of a lynching, and that when she was recognized for a question, she was shouted down. "How did WILPF come to endorse such a meeting?" she asked.[77]

These kinds of criticisms have failed to change the pro-Soviet orientation of the WILPF. Complaints about pro-Soviet bias receive the standard reply that the WILPF has no specific policy toward the Soviet Union and that the organization is host to a wide diversity of political viewpoints—the same formula used by the Communists in fending off charges of pro-Soviet bias made against front organizations like the U.S. Peace Council.[78] The few members who made unsuccessful challenges to the leadership eventually became discouraged and have withdrawn from the League, and these withdrawals have further strengthened the elements who brought about the ideological realignment in the first place. Accordingly, during the last few years the WILPF's identification with the Soviet Union and Communist Vietnam has become quite blatant.

The WILPF proved helpful in putting a good face on the politically awkward Soviet invasion of Afghanistan. "While military intervention is always regrettable," wrote Kay Camp, WILPF international president, "the Soviet interest in having close relations with a neighboring country with which it shares a 2,000 mile border is understandable." The Soviet Union had had reason to worry about various hostile U.S. policies of confrontation and the possibility that the U.S. would play the "China card." The most important thing now was to oppose any aid to the Afghan guerillas and to redouble efforts for a freeze on all weapons production and deployment.[79]

The "myth of the Soviet threat" and the affirmation of the peaceful intentions of the Soviet Union have been constant themes of WILPF publicity. Soviet military efforts, *Peace and Freedom* told its readers in April 1979, "are and always will be directed only at assuring their defense capacity." The Warsaw Pact was prepared to disband as soon as NATO was willing to do likewise, although, of course, the socialist bloc was "not ready to give up support for the oppressed people."[80] In 1980 Ruth Sillman, the WILPF representative to the UN, explained that the false stories of the "Soviet threat" were promoted by powerful interests in the United States. In the USSR, on the other hand, according to the country's constitution, war propaganda was prohibited by law.[81]

In 1983 the Palo Alto branch of the WILPF published a short book of essays, *Give Peace a Chance: Soviet Peace Proposals and U.S. Responses.* According to this publication, the Soviet Union had consistently taken the initiative for disarmament while the U.S. had been the instigator of and leader in the arms race. The United States, its government dominated by the military-industrial complex, had a lopsided, bloated war economy, and the large corporations would lose money if peace ever broke out. "This is the source of 'our' prosperity, such as it is," the book lamented. Conversely, since 1917 the Soviet Union had made 129 proposals to strengthen international security and bring about cuts in military budgets, to outlaw weapons of mass destruction and forbid the first use of nuclear weapons.[82] The essays in this book included notes listing the sources relied upon and a bibliography. However, the reader was not told that much of the information in this WILPF publication, including the figure of 129 Soviet proposals for disarmament, came from a book on the same subject—*Swords into Plowshares: Soviet Initiatives for Peace, Security and Disarmament, 1917-1982*—that had been issued a year earlier by the National Council of American-Soviet Friendship, a well-known Communist front founded in 1942.[83]

Despite the WILPF's concern not to be too closely linked in the public eye to organizations clearly reflecting the Soviet viewpoint, the League continues to maintain an intimate relationship with the World Peace Council (WPC) and actively participates in its propaganda offensives. A WILPF delegate, Pauline Rosen, attended the International Forum to Stop the Neutron Bomb, organized on 18 March 1978 in Amsterdam by the Dutch Communist party and the WPC. The forum ended the next day with a reception that, Rosen reported, brought the two hundred delegates together "in a spirit of warmth and solidarity," a fitting conclusion to an "inspiring weekend."[84]

A year later, WILPF representatives participated in a special session of the WPC held on 2-5 February 1979 in East Berlin. Edith Ballantyne, WILPF international secretary-general, addressed a plenary session on disarmament and détente, stressing "the need in the West to show that detente is not inconsistent with national liberation struggles and to clarify the genuine threats to world peace." She also expressed concern about "a Chinese axis with Japan and other countries directed against the Soviet Union." The WILPF delegates participated in founding a Women's Commission of the WPC.[85] In September 1980 a WILPF delegation — including Carol Pendell, the new American international president — attended the World Parliament of the Peoples for Peace, convened by the WPC in Sofia, Bulgaria. The parliament passed resolutions against the nuclear strategy of the United States, which "rests on the monstrous doctrine of 'limited nuclear war' " and in "support of all movements for liberation and peace in Africa, Asia, Latin America, the Middle East, and against racism and all other forms of discrimination."[86]

In 1980 the WPC began to make preparations for a massive campaign against NATO's plans to counter the Soviet SS-20 missiles with its own medium-range rockets and cruise missiles. The WILPF quickly fell into step and agreed to make the prevention of the stationing of Pershing II and cruise missiles in Europe a program priority. Greta Lynch, WILPF vice president for the southern region, attended the International Conference against the Arms Race and for Disarmament convened by the WPC in Stockholm during 6-8 June 1981. In an address to the conference, Lynch expressed the League's "deep concern about the excesses of the Pentagon at the expense of human services to the people of the United States." She also voiced hope for "worldwide unity in the peace movement and the wish that 36 years after the end of World War II, the occupation of Europe by our troops will come to an end and our boys will come home."[87] In testimony before Congress in the fall of 1982, the WILPF opposed the funding of Pershing II rockets and cruise missiles and instead urged a freeze on the production and deployment of nuclear weapons.[88] Randall Forsberg, one of the initiators of the nuclear freeze idea, was a member of the WILPF and a former chairperson of the League's Boston branch. The WILPF joined the nuclear freeze movement early on, and in 1984 endorsed the Soviet proposal of a "No First Use" pledge of nuclear weapons as an appropriate companion to the freeze concept.[89] In the fall of 1984, the WILPF launched a campaign for a comprehensive test ban, and in 1985 the League denounced "Star Wars" as "a U.S. effort to regain nuclear superiority."[90]

The WILPF, together with the WPC, was part of the international preparatory committee for the International Conference on Nicaragua and Peace in Central America held in Lisbon on 3-6 May 1984. Three WILPF delegates attended this conference, which called on all those working for peace and progress "to support vigorously the struggle of the people of El Salvador and Guatemala for their national liberation" and to oppose the violent intervention of the U.S. in the internal affairs of these countries. The same resolution recognized "the right of Nicaragua to request and receive all forms of assistance" in order to protect its political independence and revolution. The conference praised "the Nicaraguan government's humanitarian policy and democratic solutions to the economic, social and cultural problems." The United States was condemned for the military invasion of Grenada and for its policy of political destabilization and terrorism against Nicaragua and the other Latin American countries.[91] Early in 1985, the WILPF joined the same peace and justice network organizations previously mentioned in a "Call to Action"—a program of demonstrations, sit-ins, and civil disobedience held in Washington during 15-22 April. "The call" demanded an end to U.S. military intervention in Central America, the Middle East, and Europe.[92]

The WILPF has also maintained close ties with the American affiliate of the WPC, the U.S. Peace Council, which is headed by Michael Myerson, a longtime Communist functionary. The U.S. Peace Council did not hold its first formal convention until November 1979, but its activities started already two years earlier. Kay Camp, then international president of the WILPF, together with the U.S. Peace Council, was among the sponsors of a meeting called "Dialogue on Disarmament and Detente" with a WPC delegation in Washington from 25 January to 27 January 1978. When the League was asked to help promote an American tour of the WPC delegates, the executive director replied that the League would be glad to provide an audience for them in the Philadelphia area. "We are excited at the opportunities offered by both the Washington conference and the area visit and will do everything we can to make the most of these opportunities. Needless to say, we hope our efforts will be rewarded with visibility for our organization."[93]

In January 1979 the U.S. Peace Council invited the WILPF to endorse a conference on Nicaragua. The invitation was extended by the Council's solidarity coordinator, Sandy Pollack, a member of the national council of the Communist party. She appears to have been well acquainted with the League's president, Marjorie Boehm, whom she addressed as "Dear Marge." The WILPF accepted the invitation, and thus began a long string of cooperative ventures that has continued to the present day. The League's president co-sponsored "the call" to the first national conference of the Peace Council in November 1979, which stressed the importance of organizing the country's peace majority in its entire spectrum. In his address to the conference, WPC president Romesh Chandra emphasized the link between the struggle for peace and support for national liberation movements. "People ask me, 'You are a peace movement. Why do you support the armed struggles in Nicaragua, Palestine, Vietnam?' And I reply, 'The armed struggle in these countries *is* the peace movement.' "[94]

The WILPF, as we have seen, holds the same position; the League, too, untroubled by pacifist sentimentalism, supports the struggle of the oppressed except when the struggling takes place in Communist-ruled countries like Afghanistan, Angola, or Kampuchea. The British peace activist E. P. Thompson has repeatedly warned against collusion with the far-flung operations of the WPC. He has argued that they would make the Western peace movement in effect a movement opposing NATO militarism only—a sure recipe for its political isolation and ultimate defeat. American socialist Ronald Radosh, too, has told the American peace movement that "there is no good reason to collaborate with Communists, and plenty of reason not to.... There is a difference between Red-baiting which must be rejected, and anti-Communism which is a moral and political necessity."[95] The WILPF has shown itself to be unimpressed by such arguments.

In June 1981 one of the largest peace action coalitions, Mobilization for Survival, made yet another attempt to capitalize on the American public's well-known desire to hold down defense expenditures by organizing a nationwide program called "Jobs with Peace."

The WILPF and the rest of the pacifist community quickly jumped on the bandwagon, and so did the U.S. Peace Council, which devoted considerable time at its second convention in November to the unfolding "Jobs with Peace" campaign. This campaign came at a time when the new Reagan administration had set its sights on a sharp increase in the defense budget and when unemployment was rising, and the Council greeted it as a way of creating grass-roots pressure in the opposite direction — "to put an end to Reagan's confrontation and 'bombs instead of jobs' policies."[96] In view of the interlocking membership in the peace and justice network, it is possible that the Peace Council and WILPF members also had a direct share in the formation of "Jobs with Peace." The strong emphasis of the campaign on issues of foreign policy certainly suggests that whoever dreamed up this program had a lot more in mind than the creation of jobs.

The "Jobs with Peace" campaign statement of purpose called upon Congress to reduce significantly "the amount of tax dollars spent on nuclear weapons, foreign military intervention and wasteful military programs" and instead to make more money available for jobs and social programs in order to "promote a healthy economy, true national security and jobs with peace." The campaign also supported a freeze of nuclear weapons and an end to military intervention in the affairs of other countries. "American firepower should not be used to prevent internal change that is primarily a result of poverty and inequality," the statement declared.[97]

A pamphlet issued in April 1983 by the Massachusetts affiliate of the "Jobs with Peace" campaign argued that the United States led the arms race and that Pershing II and cruise missiles were weapons designed to initiate a nuclear war, not to retaliate. "The current administration uses military power as its main foreign policy instrument to solve the problems of economic and democratic development." According to the pamphlet, the massive expansion of the Navy and the Rapid Deployment Force had been undertaken not for defending against the Soviets but "for policing the Persian Gulf and for intervening against small countries like Nicaragua and El Salvador. On the pretext of fighting communism, we are propping up dictators that brutally suppress independence movements and labor organizing."[98]

This tendentious program was endorsed not only by the AFSC, CISPES, and the National Lawyers Guild, but — indicative of the gullibility of many well-meaning people — by the Massachusetts Council of Churches, the Massachusetts Federation of Teachers, and

Governor Michael S. Dukakis. A newsletter issued in February 1985 noted that "Central America is a critical area of concern for the Jobs with Peace Campaign" and called upon supporters to attend workshops sponsored by the Boston Area Network on Central America, of which the "Jobs with Peace" campaign was a part.[99] The connection of all this to the issue of jobs was rather remote.

The WILPF has also continued its close relationship with the Soviet Women's Committee and the Soviet Peace Committee. In late November 1983 six WILPF leaders flew to Moscow to meet once again with leaders of the Soviet Women's Committee. The members of this delegation also met with leaders of the Soviet Peace Fund, founded by the Soviet Peace Committee. The American women were impressed when told that eighty million Soviet citizens voluntarily contributed to this fund, which is used to support the work of peace organizations both inside and outside the Soviet Union. When the delegation told their hosts that some people in the Western peace movement had suggested the desirability of a Soviet unilateral peace initiative such as the dismantling of some SS-20 rockets, the delegation was informed that the Soviet Union had already put forth numerous disarmament initiatives and that this matter was not only a concern of the peace movement but "rather a national security need of the Soviet Union and the Soviet people."[100]

In the summer of 1984, twenty-four WILPF members took part in a "peace cruise on the Volga," during which they heard lectures by members of local Soviet Peace Committees. One of the cruise participants, the president of the Cleveland branch of the WILPF, was most impressed by the amount of building that had taken place since the terrible destruction of World War II. The rebuilt and newly built cities, she reported in *Peace and Freedom* after her return, told of the desire of the Soviet people "to continue building their country on the pattern of Soviet Marxism where basic needs are provided for all." The Soviet system of government was different from that of the United States, but so were the history, topography, and climate of the country. "One must thoughtfully take all these things into consideration before passing judgment."[101]

Back in 1961 the official WILPF handbook had listed among the League's basic principles the belief in democracy and the day-to-day practice of the democratic method "to achieve for everyone freedom, justice and peace. Communism and all totalitarian systems are opposed to this process, therefore we do not believe they can produce the most enlightened form of government." Americans had to inform themselves of other ideologies, but it was important to distinguish between the loyal, nonconforming citizen who expressed his "dissent from commonly held thinking, and an individual who actually gives his loyalty to another country, adhering to a party line dictated by that country."[102] By 1969 this entire section opposing communism and totalitarianism had been omitted from the list of the basic beliefs of the WILPF.[103] As we have seen, the political orientation of the League by then had begun its steady drift toward a clearly pro-Communist position. In July 1982 the U.S. State Department, in a publication that described various Soviet activities designed to promote Soviet foreign policy goals, included the WILPF among "well-known international fronts," nominally independent organizations that were actually controlled by the Soviets.[104]

The WILPF called this characterization a smear and, invoking the Freedom of Information Act, requested all the documents used by the State Department in making this assessment. According to the WILPF's account of this affair, when nine months had passed without a reply, the League, with the help of the ACLU, brought suit. The State Department then released eight documents that showed the WILPF's ties to the World Peace Council and the Women's International Democratic Federation. In the eyes of the WILPF, these facts did not support their characterization as a "front organization." Evidently, wrote Libby Frank, the League's executive director, "the aspect of WILPF that scares the Administration the most is the aspect of which we are most proud: our international contacts and our sisterhood with women all over the world, including the Soviet Union. . . . Not only do we have a right to this free association, we have the obligation."[105]

The WILPF's reply is, of course, largely beside the point. The issue is not the right of a private organization like the WILPF to associate with Soviet-dominated groups — they undoubtedly have this right — but the inferences that can legitimately be drawn from such an association. Common sense has always recognized that a person's reputation is affected by the company he keeps. Americans have not hesitated to repudiate public officials whose habitual cronies are gangsters or racketeers. There is no reason to treat organizations any differently from individuals.

Indeed, a strong argument can be made that the government has a positive duty to publicize information it has about links between American political organizations and the underworld of Soviet machinations and subversion. When an organization conceals its true purposes or sources of support, the people have no fair way of judging the merit of the ideas propounded. For example, the public ought to know whether an organization that lobbies for the legalization of marijuana is financed by drug dealers. Similarly, when an American organization supports all of the foreign policy objectives of another country, it is relevant to know whether that organization is in effect an agent of that foreign nation. Only thus can people judge the true motives of those who try to sway them, and only with this kind of information out in the open can the competition of ideas be conducted honestly and fairly.

Congress has long recognized the importance of disclosures and has required public statements of ownership from radio stations and other media of mass communication as well as from lobbyists, foreign and domestic, who seek to influence the legislative process. Back in 1947 the President's Committee on Civil Rights in its report *To Secure These Rights* criticized the "totalitarians of both left and right" who "have in common ... a reluctance to come before the people honestly and say who they are, what they work for, and who supports them."[106] The Committee suggested that disclosure, not outlawry, was the appropriate way of dealing with those who sought to subvert the free marketplace of ideas, and this recommendation is as valid today as it was forty years ago. The WILPF and the rest of the American Left have a perfect right to peddle their merchandise, but the public is entitled to the proper labeling of the package.

The real question is whether the WILPF's close ties to the World Peace Council and other Communist front organizations justify the conclusion that the League is itself a Soviet front, operating under the control of Communists, or whether we are dealing here simply with unfailing fellow travelers of the Communist movement. The available public record, including the internal papers of the WILPF that can be consulted at its repository at the Swarthmore College Peace Collection, does not permit a conclusive answer to this question. Communist front organizations typically harbor a few strategically placed members of the party whose task it is to make sure that the organization toes the line and supports unwaveringly the positions desired by the party and/or the Soviet Union. In the case of the WILPF, no such individuals have been identified among the leadership of the organization, although, obviously, this does not mean or prove that there are no Communists among them. Some of these leaders appear to be old-time fellow travelers with a sentimental attachment to the Soviet Union as the world's first socialist country. Others are graduates of the New Left who have embraced the motto "My enemy's enemies are my friends." From 1965 on, an alliance of these two elements apparently gradually took control of the WILPF, until by 1976 or so the League had become a firm supporter of Soviet policies and positions. By then the WILPF had also established close ties with the World Peace Council and the various Communist women's organizations. It is safe to conclude that at that point the League had become, at the very least, a "front of fronts" — it functions in close cooperation and coordination with actual Communist front organizations without clear evidence that it is itself a front.[107]

An independent mind can very well come to the same conclusions as the Soviets on such issues as nuclear testing, recognition of the PLO, "Star Wars," and the necessity for re-education camps in the Socialist Republic of Vietnam. However, when an individual or organization is in systematic agreement with *all* positions supported by the Soviets and changes them whenever the Soviets do, one can no longer dismiss this phenomenon as coincidental. The only question that remains open is whether the WILPF reached its present status as a Soviet auxiliary as a result of Communist manipulation, carried out by cadres specifically assigned to this task, or whether the League slid into it without such central direction. In the final analysis the difference is probably rather inconsequential. It is the corruption of the WILPF's original pacifist ideals that looms large and overshadows everything else in this tragic story.

Anti — Anti-Communism

Alongside their benevolent view of communism, all the four major pacifist groups today espouse the philosophy of anti–anti-communism — a reflexive reaction to what they regard as the irrational fear of communism on the part of a majority of Americans. In 1969 the AFSC published a book-length study, *Anatomy of Anti-Communism,* in which anti-communism was described as a political strategy "that fights not only Communism, but neutralism and democratic revolution as well. It is based on antipathy to social change and a defense of the status quo." The dread of communism was said to have led to more and more government control in the area of civil liberties and the creation of secret police forces. Writing in the midst of an unheard-of wave of political dissent — the antiwar movement with its mass demonstrations all over the country — the AFSC contended that America had become a repressive "garrison state" that stifled political criticism. The legacy of anti-communism, the study argued, was the alienation of American youth and the subversion of the revolutionary aspirations of exploited underdeveloped nations. "These consequences of a blind, emotional anti-Communism pose the most critical problem that American society presently confronts."[108]

In the years since then the AFSC has continued to maintain that America is a repressive society, nourished by the inane and unfounded fear of communism. The charges of widespread espionage made by congressional committees in the 1940s and 1950s were said to be unproven; an effective Communist spy ring had allegedly never been able to operate in the United States. In a statement approved by its board in April 1976, the AFSC called for the abolition of the CIA and the Internal Security Division of the FBI.[109] Because of the fear of communism, declared the AFSC board statement on Central America issued in 1984, the U.S. government failed to realize that Third World movements for social justice were due not to Soviet subversion but to local stirrings of nationalism and a desire for fuller participation in society. Such fears were also said to lead to the curtailment of open discussion of policy, to secrecy, and to national chauvinism. In short, as the AFSC sees it, if the people of this country could only get over their phobia of anti-communism, both America and the world would be better places to live in. There is no recognition of the possibility that the unrest and armed conflict in international trouble spots like Central America might be due to both social deprivation *and* the machinations of the Soviet Union, or that America may have legitimate security interests in that area.

Given the strong hold of the Left entrenched in the government of the AFSC and the weakness of its critics, there is little likelihood that the AFSC will change this warped view of the world any time soon. In 1984 the AFSC spent 28.9 percent of its program budget on "seeking peace, reconciliation and disarmament" — the work of the peace education division. However, this figure does not indicate the true scope of the AFSC's effort to propagate its particular political philosophy. The money earmarked for overseas programs supports not only traditional relief programs such as providing food, clothing, medicines, rehabilitation services, and development projects, but also literacy courses and training programs to foster leadership and raise the consciousness of Third World people. Support is also provided for local human rights organizations of the Left. What this means is that an organization that achieved a lofty reputation for feeding the hungry and helping the unfortunate of this world is now a multimillion dollar international pressure group for a "progressive" world order.

There is nothing subversive about any of that except that many people who contribute to the work of the AFSC probably have little understanding of what the world of "peace and justice" sought by the organization really is and who benefits from the funds they provide. There is nothing wrong with a pacifist organization seeking to create an informed public on issues of war and peace, yet there is a problem of moral integrity when that same organization qualifies its adherence to the principles of love and nonviolence with the idea of the "just revolution" and the legitimate "violence of the oppressed."

Like any other organization in a free society, the AFSC has a perfect right to seek supporters wherever it can find them, to ally itself with whomever it wishes, and to support whatever political causes it desires, yet a bit more candor about its political goals and activities might not be amiss. The use of Marxist categories of analysis can be criticized as simplistic, but it is not reprehensible; to hide one's sympathies for communism behind the facades of Marxism or "radical social change" or the code word "progressive" represents calculated deceit. How many people during the days of the Vietnam war knew that the AFSC was not just an organization in favor of peace in Indochina but part of a network of support for the NLF and Communist North Vietnam? How many people today know about the links between CISPES, the AFSC's ally, and the Salvadorean Communist party, or about the AFSC's close ties to the New Jewel movement of Grenada, a Marxist-Leninist party in all but name?

It will not do to deny the significance of these links by protesting against "guilt by association" or "red-baiting." Ever since the 1930s the Left has attempted to shield itself behind these slogans and has claimed an immunity from criticism that no other political organization is allowed to enjoy. The currently fashionable anti–anti-communism notwithstanding, the principled rejection of Communist theory and practice remains a litmus test of political and moral integrity. Unless American pacifists face up to these issues, they will continue to remain isolated from the mainspring of American public life and deserve to be seen as simply another faction of the radical Left.

PART IV

The Future of American Pacifism

CHAPTER 11

The Impotence of Dissent

The American pacifist community is a closely knit group, and there are few dissenters from the prevailing orthodoxies. As in any other political or religious organization, there have been rank-and-file members who have quietly dropped out for one reason or another, but hardly any leading figure has publicly criticized the leftward drift of American pacifism during the last twenty years. Those few individuals who have tried to challenge the governing New Left ideology from within have taken care not to reveal these differences of views to outsiders. Some of those most critical of pacifist policies during the Vietnam war years today look back on these disagreements as part of a past that has been overcome. There is little awareness of the fact that the ideological assumptions which led American pacifists to become closely enmeshed with the radical antiwar movement and to support revolutionary violence still govern the political thinking of the major pacifist organizations.

The Waning Influence of Quakers in the AFSC

The internal records of all four pacifist groups show the existence of dissenters. Several members of the AFSC board, for example, have criticized the new acceptance of "the violence of the oppressed" and the large number of non-Quakers on the staff of the organization. In March 1977 Kale Williams, executive secretary of the AFSC regional office in San Francisco, wrote a letter to Lou Schneider, the AFSC's national executive secretary. In it Williams raised the question of whether the AFSC had abandoned its traditional nonpolitical stance and now judged socialist governments and movements by a different standard than those on the right.

It seems to me there is a great deal of evidence that we have and do, and I am deeply troubled by that. I would cite our primary

225

identification with the PRG rather than the Third Force in Vietnam, the discussion (and failed attempt to state a position) in respect to Angola, the recent book on Puerto Rico, the Latin American paper, much of the material on the New Economic Order. If I were alone in these views, I would suspect my own observations or judgment even more than I do, but I know that these perceptions are shared by others, including others on the Board. When I have spoken on these issues, or others have, I often sense a resonant response, but seldom do I feel that anything changes.[1]

Other board members have brought up the question of staff commitment to nonviolence. In May 1977 board member Dick Taylor wrote to Schneider, explaining how, some years ago at a meeting with a new social-change organization, he had heard two representatives of that group take the position that nonviolence was a purely tactical matter. "One of them spoke strongly for the idea that we should not even talk about nonviolence very much, since to do so would make people less prepared to use the violent methods that will at some point be required in the social change struggle. Both of these people were subsequently hired by AFSC and have since taken rather prominent roles in national AFSC programs." From brief conversations with them, Taylor had concluded that "they have continued to take the above-stated view of nonviolence." Taylor wanted not to remove these people from the staff but to raise the broader question of hiring policy. "I think it's reasonable of us — and essential to our integrity as a Quaker organization — to ask that staff have a serious commitment to nonviolence and nonviolent methods of social change."[2]

Marge Nelson, another board member, drew attention to the low percentage of Quakers on the AFSC staff. This was a serious problem, she wrote Schneider, and not only because staff has the dominant influence on the life and direction of a large organization; there was also the question of the values held by the staff. She had the sense that "many non-quaker staff/committee people not only don't share or even understand many basic Quaker values but are at times impatient [with] or intolerant [of] them." She then proceeded to give some examples that had caused her "pain and disquiet." One regional staff member had voiced the view that the AFSC was not a Quaker organization but only founded on Quaker principles; others had complained about the need to reach decisions by consensus and had disparaged the need to keep up a dialogue with both sides in a conflict. There was also the "almost total lack of reference in many documents that come to the Board [to] any spiritual or religious dimension [in] our decisions." Nelson expressed the hope that the AFSC would make a conscious determination to return to a more intimate relationship with the Religious Society of Friends.[3]

Back in 1949 William W. Comfort, president emeritus of Haverford College, had praised the AFSC for drawing together in a common cause all sorts of Friends in America, and he had called AFSC "the greatest development in the Society during this century."[4] Today it would be difficult to find anyone who would make such a complimentary appraisal of the organization. The divisions that opened up between many Friends and the AFSC during the time of the Vietnam war, described earlier, have deepened. On several occasions Yearly Meetings that had been faithful supporters of the AFSC for many decades retargeted their annual contributions away from the national organization in Philadelphia. Evangelical Friends in particular have criticized the AFSC for its lack of an explicit Christian identification, its trendy support of abortion and gay rights, and the politically tendentious and often blatantly partisan publications put out by the national organization and most of the regional offices.[5]

The critics of the organization have pointed out that the influence of Quakers in the governance of the AFSC has weakened, while the role of non-Quakers and "progressives" has increased. In the Corporation, the AFSC's legal entity, Yearly Meeting delegates are outnumbered by "at large" members selected by the Philadelphia-based nominating committee. More important, the Yearly Meeting members are all but unrepresented on the board of directors, the AFSC's official governing body. In 1981 only three out of forty board members were Yearly Meeting members of the Corporation. With three quarters of the board members chosen by that same nominating committee for three-year terms, control of the board by the Philadelphia national office is assured. The AFSC's national administrative staff itself is increasingly made up of non-Quakers. Whereas 56 percent of that staff were Quakers in 1962, by 1981 a mere 36 percent were members of the Society of Friends. At that time all three major program divisions were headed by non-Quakers, and there were no Quakers at all among the AFSC's overseas staff in Latin America, the Middle East, and Africa. In short, as the critics saw it, an informal "power structure" had taken control of the AFSC and had moved the organization away from its traditional Quaker concerns and values. In the words of one Quaker critic, the

227

AFSC had "become probably the most divisive internal force in American Quakerism."[6]

The few critics of these trends within the AFSC appear discouraged and limit themselves to occasional mildly worded statements of disagreement. In March 1978 Daniel Seeger, the maverick executive secretary of the New York metropolitan office of the AFSC, and Kenneth Boulding, the dissenter from Colorado, met in order to exchange views on an appropriate Quaker witness in contemporary affairs. Both men agreed that their attempts to address issues from within the AFSC had been futile. "Kenneth Boulding had the impression that his intervention with AFSC leadership in Philadelphia had not made any kind of a dent." Seeger felt that the views of the New York office, the only one of ten regional offices to take a somewhat independent stand, "were respected, but for all practical purposes ignored, and they were misconstrued as being conservative." He saw no possibility of establishing an organizational alternative that could compete with the AFSC's $10-million-a-year operation. The real malady, as Seeger saw it, was the lack of a compelling vision, "a grasp of animating values which provide the basis for illuminating difficult contemporary issues. In the vacuum, various 'imported' ideologies are adopted by AFSCers seeking some way to address complex concerns." He felt, therefore, that what was needed was the definition, articulation, and projection of a positive set of goals that would be more constructive than the past habit of reactive critiquing. Such a vision, rooted in Quakerism and developed through a network of like-minded Friends, might have a chance to compete successfully with the trendy ideologies presently imported into the AFSC from the larger peace movement.

Seeger also suggested developing a capacity for independent action in such areas as South Africa, where the AFSC seemed effectively to have cut itself off from contact with Quakers and other nonviolent elements. At a recent meeting of the national peace education committee, it had been "implied that undue concern for non-violence in Southern Africa is an expression of racism and of insensitivity to the plight of the oppressed there." However, Seeger pointed out, with the help of the British Friends Service Council and the International Fellowship of Reconciliation, it should be possible to hold consultations with nonviolent South African leaders independent of the AFSC bureaucracy and to promote nonviolent ideas. Boulding and Seeger agreed to use the upcoming Friends General Conference to be held in Ithaca, New York, to convene a meeting of Friends to discuss future strategy.[7]

Thus, in early July 1978, a group of fifteen Friends — including Seeger and Boulding and other critics of past AFSC policies like Marjorie Nelson and Kale Williams — met at Ithaca for a three-session workshop. In a report on this meeting to the national board, the participants stressed that they had gathered "under a deep sense of love for the AFSC and a profound concern for its witness and service." The group made three recommendations. First, the board should subject one major program area to a thorough deliberative process that would enlist the best resources of the Society of Friends, involve consultations with the various perspectives that exist among AFSC constituents, and through focus on the basic philosophy of Quakerism provide more complete and unified work in that program area. The program in South Africa was suggested because it would most likely be a continuing concern for the AFSC and because the board had not undertaken such a review of AFSC work in that country. Second, for the fiscal year beginning in October 1980, the normal budgeting process should be suspended and replaced by a board-initiated process in which the size and variety of and the priorities among AFSC activities would be examined. This process, too, should involve the Corporation, Friends meetings, and contributors as well as staff. Third, Friends with special expertise on the various AFSC programs should be consulted on a regular basis, and staff committees with responsibility for these programs should seek advice and comments from Quaker experts.[8]

In an article published in May 1979 in the Quaker magazine *Friends Journal*, Seeger discussed the difficult dilemmas raised for pacifists by the liberation struggles of the Third World. The resolution of these dilemmas, he argued, was "not advanced by an exaggerated sense of guilt or of complicity in the evils of the status quo." Pacifists had not created the racist, sexist, and colonialist structures that enmesh the culture in which they live; "exploitation, war, and violence are not exclusive inventions of our own time and culture, but have existed in practically all times and cultures." They certainly were to be found in the Russian, Chinese, and Cuban revolutions, which had plenty of skeletons in their closets.

Seeger noted that one of the ironies of the discussions going on at the time was that while many pacifists hesitated to preach non-violence to oppressed people, they had no compunction about lending tacit or overt support to military struggles that might well lead to disaster and that in any event were not likely to achieve true liberation. "The fact that there may be a vocal leadership in a situation, and perhaps even a credible majority of those whom we identify as oppressed who seem ready to opt for violent solutions, does not absolve us from the responsibility entailed in encouraging them along a disastrous path." The fact that nonviolent elements were small and seemingly irrelevant should not deter pacifists from supporting them in every possible way. During the Vietnam war the peace movement had been predominantly sympathetic to the NLF and North Vietnam and had largely ignored the pacifist Unified Buddhist Church. Seeger argued that the same mistake was now being repeated in South Africa. American involvement with oppression in other countries had to be challenged through nonviolent direct action, but a consistent perspective was essential here. "It would not be credible to sympathize with violent revolutionaries while urging nonviolent responses on 'oppressors,' as it is sometimes suggested we do."[9]

We do not know how the AFSC board responded to the suggestions made by the Seeger-led group. The record of AFSC pronouncements suggests that the concerns of Seeger and his colleagues about South Africa have been ignored as completely as were those voiced by these same critics during the days of the Vietnam war. A lengthy AFSC study, *South Africa: Challenge and Hope,* published in 1982, once again repeated the tired cliché that it was fruitless to advise people suffering from oppression to choose only nonviolent means of liberation. The study mentioned the existence of nonviolent black groups, opposed to the African National Congress and its commitment to revolutionary struggle, but it did not disavow violence. In the face of the violence of the status quo, the study insisted, it was impossible to remain neutral. One could hope for alternatives to a violent, chaotic revolution in South Africa, "but the decision on tactics remains with those struggling for freedom."[10]

In 1986 the A. Philip Randolph Educational Fund, headed by the veteran civil rights leader and pacifist Bayard Rustin, started "Project South Africa." The purpose of this project was to provide links between South African individuals and groups waging a peaceful struggle to end apartheid and replace it with democracy and American organizations and individuals who could furnish financial and moral support for these South African democrats. In Rustin's eyes nothing was to be gained from pushing the people of South Africa into substituting a new form of political servitude for the distasteful and despicable system of apartheid. The AFSC was among the organizations from which Rustin sought support for "Project South Africa." Daniel Seeger responded enthusiastically, but the national AFSC, after some hesitation, declined to be associated with this effort to encourage peaceful change.[11] In regard to both South Africa and Central America, the AFSC has adhered to its strategy, proven during the Vietnam war, of helping the revolutionary elements by getting the U.S. out of the way and by halting U.S. aid to the governments under attack. Seeger's warning that pacifists have undermined their moral and political credibility by sympathizing with violent revolutionaries while simultaneously urging governments to respond nonviolently to revolutionary violence has been disregarded.

The efforts of other groups of Friends to get the AFSC to return to more Quaker-like ways have fared no better. In July 1979 Chuck Fager, a Quaker journalist and writer, organized a discussion on the AFSC at the Friends General Conference held at Earlham College in Indiana. Interest in this discussion was so great that the one session planned had to be extended to three; a summary of concerns was signed by more than 130 Friends. It spoke of the insufficient religious basis of AFSC activities and pronouncements, expressed regret that the great majority of staff members were neither Quakers nor pacifists, and criticized the partisan positions taken in conflict situations without regard to nonviolent principles.[12] A committee of the board studied the concerns expressed, and a special committee of the Corporation was appointed to improve communications between Friends and the AFSC, but otherwise things continued as before. In a widely distributed communication to Friends, AFSC officers attributed the disagreements and divisions that exist to "profoundly different perceptions among Friends as to what our Christian commitment in today's world calls for."[13] The number of Quakers on the AFSC's staff continues to decline and in 1985 stood at 18.6 percent; back in 1962 it had been 36 percent.[14] Unease with AFSC policies among Friends remains pronounced.

A Catholic Pacifist Opposes Liberation Theology

One of the few leading members of the FOR to express in print his unease over the new indulgence of revolutionary violence is the Catholic pacifist Gordon Zahn. In June 1977 *Fellowship* published his article entitled "The Bondage of Liberation: A Pacifist Reflection," which was accompanied by two responses. Zahn's essay was longer than those of his critics. Nevertheless, the fact that his position, sharply condemnatory of the acceptance of revolutionary violence by many pacifists, had been subjected to criticism by two authors not only was indicative of the political preferences of the journal's editor but also reflected the strength and support that these rival positions had achieved in the FOR.

The long-awaited end of hostilities in Indochina, Zahn observed, had left most of the active opponents of the war in a state of near total exhaustion. Therefore, prudence seemed to counsel that it was time to stress the positive and avoid risking any kind of split among the relative few who had not succumbed to the temptations of a retreat to normalcy and apathy. On the other hand, it could be argued that in this time of weakness it would be disastrous not to confront the challenge of an unresolved controversy that involved the very core of pacifism — "the compatibility of a thorough commitment to pacifist ideals with support for national liberation movements."

Zahn related how as an active member of the Catholic peace organization Pax Christi he had watched the spread of liberation theology among religious pacifists. This new set of theological precepts had restored the respectability of the morality of the "just war." Worse still, it had "opened the way to virtually uncritical support not only for wars of national liberation but for the full range of guerilla tactics, not excluding indiscriminate acts of terrorism." Many supporters of liberation theology contended that the violence of the guerilla warrior should not be thought of as violence "but, rather, as *counter*violence, a forced response to the violence perpetrated by the status quo." This easy play on words, Zahn argued, diverted attention from the fact that guerilla and terrorist actions were reprisals not only directed against officials responsible for repressive policies but extended to include anyone guilty of "supporting the system," no matter how indirect that support might be. Sooner or later, even those members of the oppressed classes not ready or sufficiently eager to join the forces of liberation became targets as well. Convinced Christians could not approve or participate in such warfare.

Zahn charged that the consciousness-raising undertaken by those promoting violent opposition to repressive regimes all too often became an activity that imposed "elitist definitions and aspirations upon 'the common man' without giving due consideration to the additional burden and sacrifices he might have to bear as a result." Outsiders were denied the right to speak to the victims of oppression about nonviolent alternatives. "The thoroughly justifiable effort to arouse an awareness of deprivation where such awareness was lacking need not become the occasion for deliberately inciting a spirit of animosity and hatred." Instead, victims and oppressors alike should come to recognize and respect the humanity of the other side.

Justice gained at the cost of wholesale death and destruction, Zahn argued, was not likely to be of long duration. Costly struggles to overthrow imperialist or rightist oppression in Cuba, Vietnam, and Cambodia had produced new oppressions from the other extreme of the political spectrum. All those interested in peace and liberation should develop truly objective standards of protest so that brutality and torture at the hands of would-be liberators would be condemned as much as the same kinds of excesses carried out by military juntas in Chile and Thailand. "Such standards would inspire the same measure of protest against restrictive policies of post-liberation Vietnam that drive Buddhist monks to self-immolation as once marked the protest in response to similar acts directed against Diem and his successors." The idea that inequities of wealth and opportunity could be remedied through building a collective society where all individuality was either suppressed or restricted to whatever limits might be permitted by some dictatorial authority, Zahn maintained, was incompatible with the Christian vision of a just society. Similarly, the notion that liberation could come only through violent conflict was inspired by false prophets. "Christ the Liberator is not likely to be found behind the guerilla's rifle or planting the terrorist's bomb in some crowded marketplace."[15]

The two critics of Zahn's essay insisted that pacifists had to be on the side of the oppressed even when the latter resorted to violence. One of them accused Zahn of "a paranoid reaction to the creative theological searching coming from Latin America" and of using in his arguments "the brutal strategy of overkill."[16] Not surprisingly, in recent years Zahn has withdrawn from any active role in the FOR.

Over the years the FOR has encouraged the development of peace fellowships in various religious traditions, and there now exist Catholic, Lutheran, Buddhist, Unitarian-Universalist, and Jewish peace fellowships that are affiliated with the FOR. Occasionally, tensions have emerged between these groups and the parent organization. In 1979 Naomi Goodman, the president of the Jewish Peace Fellowship, criticized an article in *Fellowship* on "the Palestinian question" which had accepted at face value statements from PLO sources that the PLO wanted a peaceful settlement. "The terrorist attacks and the avowed aims of ending Israeli existence make it difficult to place all the blame for the difficulties on the Israeli side, as is done in this article."[17] But on the whole, FOR members appear to be a docile lot who share their leadership's political views. At the end of the sixties, the FOR had more than eighteen thousand members. In 1986 it is said that there were about twenty-four thousand active members.

The Silent Minority

The leftward drift of the WILPF has drawn the concern of some prestigious, old-time leaders of the organization. In a letter she sent to several leading League figures in 1971, Mercedes Randall, author of several well-known works dealing with the history of the WILPF and the lives of its founders, deplored the fact that some pacifists "are beginning to succumb to the persuasiveness of violence."[18] Dorothy Detzer, for twenty-four years (1924-47) the League's executive director, wrote Randall the same year that she, too, "and not with such tolerance as you," had noticed the basic shift in WILPF policy. "Those running the show now have lost the WIL's central function." In September 1974 Detzer informed Randall that she was no longer a paying member of the WILPF. Whether she was a member or not, Detzer wrote her friend, was really not all that important. "But it's tragic that Jane Addams, and the principles on which she founded the organization are dead letters. I resent that to the bottom of my toes."[19] In late 1975 Dorothy Hutchinson communicated to Randall her sense that the WILPF had undergone "an insidious and basic change" in both manner and methods.[20]

Similar sentiments have been expressed by some foreign observers who have noticed the political shift in the American section of the WILPF in particular. Johanne Reutz Gjermoe, a member of the governing board of the Norwegian WILPF, noted in a letter to Mercedes Randall that members of the U.S. section, without much historical experience, had come to admire political extremists "and look to Soviet and Chinese socialism, which we were looking forward to 40 years ago, and have seen through long ago."[21] Nelly Weiss, a British member of the WILPF, wrote Randall that she was depressed over developments in the organization — "impetus and drive was taken over by those who do not adhere to the WILPF principles of non-violence."[22]

Significantly, none of these women voiced their criticism publicly, nor did most of them even press it within the WILPF. No doubt this is partly explained by the fact that these critics by then were in their seventies, and many were in frail health. But there also prevailed a strong sense of "Right or Wrong, my WILPF" — the organization with which they had identified over a lifetime had to be protected against the outside world even after it had strayed from its original principles. Dorothy Hutchinson was the only one who attempted to take a stand for her beliefs, and even she did not persist after she had been rebuffed by the national board in 1973.

In his 1967 letter of resignation as vice chairman of the WRL, Charles Bloomstein had noted that in "the best of all possible worlds, pacifist activity would be both pure and politically relevant. Failing such a world, a pacifist can decide on maintaining his purity at the cost of relevance, or exposing himself to impurity in the hope of becoming relevant."[23] When A. J. Muste said at a Quaker service in 1940, "If I can't love Hitler, I can't love at all,"[24] he chose purity of pacifist principle over relevance. On the other hand, from about 1965 on, the pacifist community has opted for relevance at the expense of moral principle. Pacifists allied themselves with anyone, including Rennie Davis's violent crazies and Communists of all sorts, in order to bring about an end to the Vietnam war. The few opponents of this course for the most part sought hard to avoid intramovement strife and refused to attack these policies publicly for fear of strengthening the position of the Johnson and Nixon administrations, who regularly accused the peace movement of being made up largely of supporters of the Vietnamese Communists.

Since the end of the war, American pacifists have followed the same coalition politics, culminating in the WRL's acceptance of Colonel Qaddafi into the club of liberation movements. Such a course would seem to signal the choice of both impurity *and* irrelevance, yet the voices who might challenge this descent into the ghetto of the radical Left are no longer heard.

CHAPTER 12

Pacifism and Peace

The American pacifist community is numerically small, but its political influence reaches well beyond its own membership. The four pacifist organizations of this country play a prominent role in the larger peace movement. In recent years pacifist ideas have become influential in the political thinking of the mainline Christian churches. The Roman Catholic bishops of the United States have questioned the moral acceptability of the doctrine of nuclear deterrence, the cornerstone of the West's defense posture; the United Methodist Council of Bishops has rejected it completely.

Today the so-called religious Left, to which most pacifist groups belong, has considerable leverage with Congress in regard to our Central American policy in particular. Since 1979 an estimated 40,000 Americans have visited Nicaragua to learn about the "progress" made by the Sandinista regime. Hundreds of thousands have been persuaded by the "peace and justice" network to send food, medicine, and money to the Sandinistas and their Marxist-Leninist allies in Central America. It is one thing to question the prudence of aiding the Contras; it is quite another thing to become cheerleaders for as well as financial supporters of the various leftist guerillas and to help them bring down the struggling democracies of Central America.

In a democratic system, of course, all political voices have a right to be heard. At the same time, it is essential that we know the true agenda of those who try to sway us. That is why the ideology of contemporary American pacifism must command our attention.

Pacifism as One of the Casualties of the Vietnam War

During the last twenty years, American pacifism has undergone a series of far-reaching ideological changes that have brought all four major pacifist organizations into the camp of the political Left. The

American Friends Service Committee, the Fellowship of Reconciliation, and the War Resisters League today are an integral part of the New Left — an amorphous collection of political groups who regard the United States as an imperialist nation responsible for the poverty of the Third World and who blame America for starting and maintaining a dangerous arms race that threatens nuclear catastrophe. Members of the Women's International League for Peace and Freedom have assumed the posture of Communist fellow travelers who laud the peaceful intentions of the Soviet Union and defend its foreign policy at every step. All of these organizations now affirm their solidarity with Marxist-controlled guerillas in various parts of the world, and they defend the violence carried out by these guerillas as the inevitable struggle of the oppressed exonerated by the violence of an unjust status quo. While American pacifists continue to affirm the moral superiority of nonviolence, they support these so-called liberation movements by actively pleading the justice of their cause before the American people and by seeking to prevent American military aid to the governments under attack.

After such liberation movements succeed in seizing power, pacifist organizations praise the new societies that are being created and deny their totalitarian character. Whether in Cuba, Vietnam, or Nicaragua, the socialism of these regimes is seen as indigenous and unique and often is held to be superior to the capitalist way of life prevailing in the West. Double standards abound. It is permissible for leftist guerillas to use violence in the pursuit of their goals but impermissible for lawfully elected governments to defend themselves against foreign-sponsored subversion. Pacifist organizations endorse the sanctuary movement for politically motivated refugees from El Salvador and Guatemala; they ignore the almost 200,000 Nicaraguans who in recent years have fled to Honduras and Costa Rica. Pacifist groups decry the imperfect human rights record of American allies like Israel and South Korea but find few words of condemnation for the far worse record of Communist-ruled states like North Korea and Ethiopia. The pacifist community is concerned with the oppressed people of this world, but by its definition there are no truly oppressed people in socialist countries, and little if any sympathy is shown for their plight. Indeed, the appellation "socialist" suffices to legitimate every revolutionary cause and regime, no matter how brutal and repressive.

It was not always so. Until the early 1960s American pacifists identified with the democratic values of the United States, and they opposed totalitarianism of every kind. Pacifists refused to make common cause with Communist-led peace movements, which they criticized as political instruments of the Soviet Union. While personally unwilling to bear arms, American pacifists respected the democratic process and did not attempt to prevent their fellow citizens from fulfilling their patriotic duties.

All this changed as a result of the American war in Vietnam. From the beginning the sending of American troops to a faraway land ruled by a clique of generals was not particularly popular. As the war dragged on with rising American casualties and little light at the end of the tunnel, Americans of all political persuasions increasingly began to question the prudence and wisdom of the American involvement in Southeast Asia. Many of these people became the foot soldiers of a burgeoning antiwar movement that from the beginning was led by the Left. The leadership of this movement exploited the growing desire of the American people for an end to the killing; their primary goal, however, was not peace but a victory of the NLF and the North Vietnamese Communists. After it was all over, Fred Halstead, one of the leading figures in the antiwar movement and a member of the Trotskyite Socialist Workers party, revealed that slogans like "Victory to the Vietnamese Revolution" were ineffective from the point of view of mobilizing the mass of Americans; "our central task . . . was to put maximum pressure on the U.S. to get out of Vietnam. That would help the Vietnamese revolution more than anything else we could possibly do."[1]

American pacifists who saw an opportunity to break out of their political isolation quickly assumed a prominent role in the leadership of the antiwar movement. Many of them undoubtedly believed the claims of the NLF to be a broadly based movement of national and social liberation. The pacifist movement had always been attracted to socialist ideas; sympathy for the underdog now facilitated identification with these courageous Asian revolutionaries who had taken on the world's leading capitalist and military power. As the American involvement deepened and the antiwar movement failed to convince a majority of the American people to accept its demand for an immediate and unconditional American withdrawal from Vietnam, antiwar activists became increasingly disillusioned with the struggle for votes and took their protest to the streets. Convinced of the supreme rightness of their cause, the mood of the protesters soon turned ugly. Demonstrations conducted under the principle of nonexclusion attracted all kinds of militant fringe groups and often turned violent. At times pacifists were able to restrain their more impatient allies and impose a nonviolent discipline. In many other instances, however, they failed to prevent provocations and clashes with the forces of law and order. Voices were beginning to be heard from within the pacifist camp that called into question the very principle and binding obligation of nonviolence — for the guerillas fighting a just war in Southeast Asia as well as for their supporters in the war at home.

Frustrated by their inability to end the war on their terms, pacifist groups became radicalized and began to use the vocabulary of the extreme Left. The war in Vietnam was seen not only as a mistake of American foreign policy but as a necessary result of a corrupt and decadent system that had to be fundamentally changed if not destroyed. Allegations that American troops intentionally killed Vietnamese civilians and engaged in other atrocities and war crimes fell upon fertile soil and became the staple of antiwar propaganda. As the war dragged on without showing signs of a successful con- clusion, elite groups like the media, the churches, business and professional leaders, and Congress became more and more disen- chanted with a war that did not work. At the same time, public opinion polls indicated that if there was anything even more un- popular than the war, it was the antiwar movement. The antiwar movement's hostility toward American society and its militant tac- tics of disruption antagonized middle America, and as a result be- leaguered pacifists moved ever closer to their extremist allies. By the time the American role in the war in Vietnam had ended in early 1973, organized American pacifism had become a major compo- nent of what was known as "the Movement" — a conglomerate of leftist groups united by their alienation from American society, their infatuation with Marxist-led liberation movements, and the search for "communism with a human face."

As we have seen, a few American pacifists unsuccessfully fought the drift to the Left. Alfred Hassler, Charles Bloomstein, and Robert Pickus strongly opposed what they saw as an unacceptable com- promising of pacifist principles. In 1975 Hassler concluded regret- fully that as a result of the prevailing tendency of pacifists to justify the killing violence of liberation movements, pacifism itself had be- come "one of the casualties of Vietnam."[2] On account of their resistance to the abandonment of nonviolence, these men were eased out of or left voluntarily the leadership positions in the pacifist community they had occupied for many years.

Other dissenters like Daniel Seeger and James Forest have re- mained in their respective organizations but are unable to exert any real influence. There is also the tiny Catholic Worker movement, founded in the 1930s by Dorothy Day and Peter Maurin, which has resisted the temptation to glorify revolutionary violence. The major pacifist organizations, however, have continued on the political course charted during the time of the Vietnam war. Individual pacifists who disagree with the prevailing leftist orthodoxy have either dropped their membership in these groups or resignedly retain it out of a reluctance to break associational bonds of a lifetime. Dissent has disappeared; for the most part, the voice of principled pacifism is no longer heard.

The armed conflicts in Central America have given organized pacifism another opportunity to line up with Communist-led revolutions. Pacifist groups today are in the forefront of those who support the Sandinista regime in Nicaragua and seek to end U.S. aid for the centrist Duarte government of El Salvador, which is battling an insurrection supported and sustained by the Soviet bloc. Once again the pacifists' strategy consists in trying to get America off the backs of their revolutionary friends.

There is, of course, a moral case that can be made for armed rebellion and revolution. In some situations no peaceful recourse is available against tyranny and oppression, and resort to violent struggle, if successful, may actually save lives and reduce human suffering in the long run. But such a pragmatic calculus is forbidden to the true pacifist, who must uphold the principle of nonviolence and oppose the use of force for any and all purposes. Still less can a real pacifist adhere to a "just war" or "just revolution" philosophy and pick and choose the rebels he will support — Marxist guerillas in Southeast Asia and Central America but not the Afghan mujaheddins or Angola's Unita, who fight against Communist rule over their countries. A pacifist's principles preclude his having favorite wars or revolutions.

The Moral Dilemmas of Statecraft

There have been pacifists who have opted for an ethic of consequences and who have conceded that in the imperfect world in which we live it may be possible or even necessary to defend values by using force. Bertram Pickard, a British Friend, has observed that, as long as the modern state is composed of citizens who in their majority do not share the pacifist gospel of altruistic love, "coercive force not only will but must be used in the creation and maintenance of order. The fact that we ourselves feel unable, because of a special contribution we feel called upon to make, to cooperate in the application of such force, is not affected by our admission. In fact our position will be better appreciated on account of our frankness."[3] According to another leading British pacifist, Cecil John Cadoux, a founding member of the British Fellowship of Reconciliation, a pacifist can even approve of certain wars waged for good causes without contradicting "his own refusal to participate in any such war himself."[4]

This kind of "realistic pacifism" bears some resemblance to the position of contemporary American pacifists who endorse the violence of the oppressed without themselves participating in hostilities. In both cases armed conflict is no longer seen as the supreme evil. On the other hand, British pacifists like Pickard and Cadoux were convinced democrats who had no sympathy for the totalitarian Left supported by today's American pacifists. They also were fully aware that the pacifist, qua pacifist, has no program for the political world of power and states that now exists, and that his main function consists in bearing witness to the values of nonviolence and reconciliation. According to the American Quaker theologian David Elton Trueblood, the pacifist, by his extreme position, "is helping the state to avoid settling back into a mood in which war and the preparation for war are taken for granted. He is the gadfly of his civilization, somewhat as Socrates was the gadfly of the Athenian civilization."[5]

In the final analysis, then, there is no such thing as a political position that is truly pacifist. The pacifist is committed, in the words of Max Weber, to an "ethic of ultimate ends" that affirms the sanctity of human life. He feels responsible not so much for the political consequences of his actions but primarily for seeing that the flame of pure intentions is not squelched. This is the purpose of his exemplary acts, his protest against violence, his refusal to kill. The possibility that good intent may lead to bad results is essentially irrelevant.

Pacifists, committed to the supreme value of nonviolence, remind the rest of us who are not pacifists of the link between means and ends. Their personal "No" to killing carries an important ethical message. The pacifist vision of a world free of the threat of war can help build support for the development of an ordered political community at the international level able to resolve conflicts peacefully and justly. However, at the moment that pacifists enter the political arena to seek to influence the policies of their nation, they cease to speak as pacifists and become subject to what Weber called the "ethic of responsibility," which takes account of the realities of power and the likely consequences of political decisions. The personal "No" of pacifists, representing an act of conscience, is morally unassailable if this act of refusal does not jeopardize the survival and well-being of others. In view of the fact that pacifists are usually a small minority of a country's population, this condition will be met in most cases. On the other hand, the national policies proposed by pacifists must, like all policies, be judged in terms of foreseeable results. As the Catholic theologian George Weigel has correctly pointed out, "the morality of political judgment must include a consequential criterion. To argue, for example, that unilateral disarmament is the sole moral option, even if its results would be to make war more likely, is not an act of prophetic witness, but a moral absurdity."[6]

The pacifist is entitled to participate in the political process and to propose policies like any other citizen. He should recognize, however, that when entering the policy arena he must adopt standards of judgment distinct from those he applies in his personal life. He should not urge a course of action that, if implemented, would leave his country undefended or would tip the balance of power in the world in favor of expansionist and aggressor nations. As Reinhold Niebuhr argued during World War II, it may be noble for an individual to sacrifice his life rather than participate in the defense of order and justice, but one cannot ignore the "distinction between an individual act of self-abnegation and a policy of submission to injustice, whereby lives and interests other than our own are defrauded or destroyed."[7] Individual perfection is not a basis on which to build a political platform. Pacifists have every right to avoid the moral dilemmas posed by the world of statesmanship and statecraft and seek individual salvation through ethical absolutism and purity, but they have no right to sacrifice others for the attainment of this vocation.

American pacifist organizations today do not adhere to these principles. Worse still, they are less than candid about the muddled Marxist ideology that they have embraced and that they clothe in innocent-sounding humanitarian slogans. Pacifist groups counsel policies that are couched in the language of peace and justice but that in fact support and promote some of the most brutal and ruthless forces in the world. Instead of openly acknowledging that they have become partisans of Communist revolution in the Third World, they call themselves "progressives" and speak of working for the establishment of a new economic world order. Instead of admitting that they seek the unilateral disarmament of the United

States, they criticize the use of money for defense rather than social welfare. Seeking to convince themselves and others that national defense is no longer possible, they paint hysterical scenarios of total war in which every recourse to force is seen leading to nuclear Armageddon. In order to soothe the country's concern about the military might of the Soviet Union and its messianic drive for world revolution, the spokesmen for American pacifism attack what they call "the myth of the Soviet threat." In 1940 Niebuhr criticized the American churches and their periodicals for not telling the true story of Japanese aggression and of German tyranny in Europe for fear of arousing the "war spirit." Similarly, American pacifist organizations today decry talk about Soviet expansionism and its evil empire on the grounds that it may stimulate a new cold war.

Since pacifists do not want to use force in the defense of the society in which they live, they argue that American democracy is not worth defending. American society is described as militaristic, unjust, and repressive, and the root cause of evil in the world. During World War II Niebuhr forcefully argued against the pacifists' perfectionism, which he criticized as "unable to make significant distinctions between tyranny and freedom because it can find no democracy pure enough to deserve its devotion. . . . If it is not possible to express a moral preference for the justice achieved in democratic societies, no historical preference has any meaning."[8] Today's generation of pacifists is even more alienated from American democracy, and instead of simply counseling surrender to tyranny denies that our Communist antagonists represent morally evil principles. Our own society is measured by utopian standards of perfection; socialist states are judged by promises and postdated checks rather than by their record. There exists no recognition of the fact that societies that call themselves socialist have, according to all available empirical evidence, consistently performed more poorly than the liberal democracies — both in providing economic well-being and in protecting human freedoms.

While the major American pacifist organizations today accept the use of force in the struggle against pro-American authoritarian regimes, they at the same time continue to adhere to pacifist principles with regard to wars between nations. In order to solve the conflict between the United States and the Soviet Union, pacifists counsel disarmament — unilateral disarmament if necessary — and a less assertive foreign policy generally. Peace at any price is their demand. It therefore may not be amiss to point out that world peace is not necessarily promoted by the refusal to threaten or use force.

Some Common Fallacies

We should remember that, once before, pacifists who badly wanted peace sowed the seeds of war. During the 1930s most American and British churchmen adhered to pacifist ideas, denounced the arms race, predicted that it would lead to war, and pressured their governments for a reduction in armaments. Early in 1934 FOR leader Kirby Page sent a questionnaire dealing with attitudes toward war and peace to 100,490 American Protestant ministers. Of the 20,870 who replied, 67 percent expressed the view that the churches should not sanction or support any future wars, and 77 percent were in favor of arms reductions by the United States — unilateral reductions if necessary.[9] Predictably, since Hitler and Mussolini were not under similar pressure to disarm, this kind of agitation weakened the Western democracies, encouraged the aggressive designs of the Fascist axis, and eventually brought on another disastrous world war. In a symposium on pacifism in 1955, the Socialist leader Norman Thomas, a lifelong pacifist, acknowledged, "I am now convinced (as I was not in 1935) that the willingness of Britain and France to use force to prevent Hitler's effective rearmament of Germany and the stationing of troops on the Rhine would have checked the Nazi drive for conquest and might have prevented World War II."[10] It would seem that those who sneer at or ignore the Roman proverb "If you wish peace, prepare for war" do so at their peril.

Organized American pacifism has not learned these lessons, as a review of their principal assertions shows.

For example, these groups maintain that the continuation of the arms race will necessarily lead sooner or later to war with the Soviet Union. In fact, of course, wars are caused not by arms but by men who direct arms. In 1939 the world was thrown into a murderous conflict not because the Germans had a huge arsenal of tanks and planes but because they had Hitler. As Prime Minister Margaret Thatcher put it so well in her address to a joint session of Congress on 20 February 1985, "Wars are not caused by the building of weapons. They are caused when an aggressor believes he can achieve his objectives at an acceptable price. The war of 1939 was not caused by an arms race. It sprang from a tyrant's belief that other countries lacked the means and the will to resist him."[11] Armaments, we must remember, are a symptom, not the cause, of international conflict. Nations do not distrust each other because they are armed; they are armed because they mistrust each other's intentions. Therefore, disarmament cannot proceed faster than the development of international legal and political instruments able to resolve conflicts peaceably between the nations of the world.

American pacifist groups consider the cold war with the Soviet Union to be the result of irrational fears and misunderstandings. People-to-people contacts, they assert, will enable us to see the Soviet people as human beings who have suffered immeasurably during World War II and who sincerely want peace. Unfortunately, this belief, too, is largely erroneous and based on wishful thinking.

In fact, the true core of our persistent conflict with the Soviet Union is not mutual distrust, though mistrust does of course exist, but the hard reality that the two political systems have diametrically opposed values and interests. The rulers of the Soviet Union believe that socialism will inevitably succeed capitalism and that it is their historical mission to help this process along by rendering all possible assistance to so-called liberation movements. This can be put more crudely but more clearly: Since they are Marxist-Leninists, the Soviet leaders are convinced that communism should rule the world, and they act on this belief system because it is their sole source of legitimacy. The United States, on the other hand, is committed to defending the basic ideals of a free society. It opposes Soviet expansionism and seeks to nurture democracy worldwide as the best guarantee of international stability.

Better and more frequent contacts with the Soviet people will not eliminate the root cause of this conflict for two reasons. First, because the Soviet people, unlike the people in Western democracies, have no discernable influence on the foreign policy of their dictatorially governed country. Second, because in the foreseeable future, no amount of good will on the part of the West will cause Soviet leaders to abandon their objective of doing away with capitalism. The Soviets do not want war; they want victory. They hope to win this worldwide struggle without war by intimidating the West with their military might and playing on the strong desire of people everywhere for peace. As Carl von Clausewitz observed in his classic *On War*, "The aggressor is always peace-loving . . . ; he would prefer to take over a country unopposed. To prevent his doing so, one must be willing to make war."[12]

American pacifists urge that the United States negotiate its differences with other countries rather than resort to force or the threat of force. In fact, power and diplomacy are not contradictory alternatives but complementary and reinforcing components of foreign policy. Diplomacy that is not backed up by power can never lead to desirable results; military power is essential when negotiating with adversaries who themselves rely upon the power of their arms. Recent history provides an example. After Hitler had broken the Munich agreement and in March 1939 had occupied all of Czechoslovakia, Neville Chamberlain told the British parliament that he meant to stay with his policy of substituting "the method of discussion for the method of force in the settlement of differences."[13] Within six months, despite Chamberlain's renewed show of good will, Hitler had attacked Poland, and World War II had broken out. Reliance on military power, it should be remembered, is not an evil. All depends upon the ends for which such power is enlisted.

American pacifists believe that wars never settle anything. They mean only mass killings and misery, and out of so much evil no good can ever come. Actually, history provides us with numerous instances in which the cause of human freedom and dignity has been advanced, or at least protected, by a successful appeal to arms. A few of the better-known examples can be cited: the liberation of the Netherlands from Spanish rule, the American War of Independence, and the defeat of Hitler in World War II. The pacifist argument that these wars did not solve all problems and indeed often created new ones is correct but also beside the point. The question is not whether war is able to usher in a utopian world of eternal peace but whether the results of going to war are better than those that can be achieved by inaction.

The invention of nuclear weapons has introduced important new dimensions into the moral calculus of resort to armed force. Pacifists, therefore, are correct in reminding us that the prevention of nuclear war must be the number-one priority for all statesmen. At the same time, it is not obvious that all armed conflicts must lead to catastrophic all-out nuclear war. Even in the nuclear age, it is possible to use force to defend important human values — whether it be deterring or responding to terrorist attacks or defending the independence of a small nation. More important, the notion that peace must be bought at any price is both morally degrading and self-defeating. In the words of the philosopher Sidney Hook, "It is better to be a live jackal than a dead lion — for jackals, not men. Men who have the moral courage to fight intelligently for freedom have the best prospects of avoiding the fate of both live jackals and dead lions. Survival is not the be-all and end-all of a life worthy of man. Sometimes the worst thing we can know about a man is that he has survived. Those who say life is worth living at any price have already written for themselves an epitaph of infamy, for there is no cause and no person they will not betray to stay alive. Man's vocation should be the use of the arts of intelligence in behalf of human freedom."[14]

The Role of Pacifists in a Democratic Society

It is due to the fact that most men are willing to die for their freedom that pacifists are able to propagate their ideas freely. They enjoy the benefits of order and security, the advantages of citizenship, without assuming all of the obligations that are entailed by citizenship. Still, their position can be considered morally justified if by their act of moral witness they make war less likely. This means that we should judge the role played by pacifists in our society not in terms of the intentions they proclaim, honorable and sincere as these may be at times, but in terms of results and consequences. "Sincerity is not itself a virtue," Albert Camus correctly pointed out in a provocative essay he composed in 1946. "Some kinds are so confused that they are worse than lies. Not the language of the heart but merely that of clear thinking is what we need today."[15]

If American pacifists today were to practice clear thinking, they would acknowledge, first of all, Max Weber's earlier-mentioned distinction between the ethic of ultimate ends and the ethic of responsibility. Each has its place, but they should not be confused. In the best of all possible worlds, pacifist activity could be both morally pure and politically relevant. In the real world, that is usually not possible. When pacifists present their language of the heart as a political alternative to the pressures and compromises of the political order, they, as Niebuhr noted, "invariably betray themselves into a preference for tyranny." For the moral ambiguities of history and the world of politics, Niebuhr insisted, ambiguous methods and answers are required. "Let those who are revolted by such ambiguities have the decency and courtesy to retire to the monastery where medieval perfectionists found their asylum."[16]

Of course, more than clear thinking is needed if American pacifism is to regain the high moral ground it once occupied as one of the keepers of the humanitarian conscience. American pacifists would have to return to the democratic values that they espoused until the early 1960s. They would have to abandon their routine resort to civil disobedience and other tactics of resistance to democratically enacted law whenever they found themselves outvoted. What would happen to the stability of our democratic society if every minority that considers its cause just were to opt out of the democratic process and seek to coerce consent to its demands? American pacifists would have to cease blaming America for all the ills of the world and end their coalition with the totalitarian Left. The American Communist party today may no longer pursue as aggressively as it did in the 1930s its policy of infiltrating and seeking to take over other organizations. However, the party's role as an apologist for the Soviet Union continues unchanged, and cooperation with the Communists therefore remains devoid of political or moral justification.

Nobody will expect pacifists to be active supporters of nuclear deterrence, of the use of force against terrorists, or even of military aid to weak regimes facing the threat of foreign-sponsored subversion. But neither should they obstruct all such policies that the democratically elected government of the United States pursues in order to assure the country's survival as a free society. When the pacifist's conscience does not allow him to support policies that utilize force or the threat of force, the proper course for him is to remain silent. A historical precedent for such a stance is the withdrawal of Quaker politicians from the government of the province of Pennsylvania in 1756 because they wanted to be neither an interference in nor a party to the waging of war against the Indians.

Back in 1941 Percy Hartill, the chairman of the Anglican Pacifist Fellowship, criticized nonpacifist English Christians for harping unduly upon the evils of the Nazi system and the crimes of Hitler and his henchmen. Anyone studying the pronouncements of the leaders of the English churches, he complained, will find plenty said about the "duty of saving the victims or potential victims of Nazi sins; he will find even more about the need for crushing or restraining the Nazis. But he will find very little indeed about saving the Nazis from their sins; very rarely will he find these leaders urging their flocks to pray for the conversion of Herr Hitler; most rarely of all will he find them suggesting that the right way (because it is God's way) of meeting sin is by forgiveness, even onto seventy times seven."[17] By ignoring this utopian perfectionism, the people of Britain assured their survival as free men and women.

American pacifists today rarely invoke God or the Sermon on the Mount, and few of them pray for the conversion of Soviet leader Gorbachev. Their flight from reality, however, is no less pronounced than Hartill's; their abandonment of the fundamental values of

Western civilization is one of the great moral tragedies of our age. Our free society can afford to tolerate those who seek to undermine our will to resist our current adversaries. But, like the people of Britain during World War II, we must recognize that the successful defense of our freedom will depend upon the repudiation of advice that, if followed, would indeed guarantee the triumph of tyranny.

NOTES

In the notes that follow, these abbreviations have been used in referring to archival sources:

AFSC   Archive of the American Friends Service Committee, Philadelphia, Pennsylvania
DG   Document Group
PED   Peace Education Division
SCPC   Swarthmore College Peace Collection, Swarthmore, Pennsylvania
SSC   Sophia Smith Collection, Smith College, Northampton, Massachusetts

Notes to Chapter 1

1. On the origins of American pacifism generally, see Merle Curti, *Peace or War: The American Struggle, 1636-1936* (New York, 1936).

2. Devere Allen, *The Fight for Peace* (New York, 1930), p. 665.

3. Peter Brock, *Twentieth-Century Pacifism* (New York, 1970), p. 143; and Lawrence S. Wittner, *Rebels against War: The American Peace Movement, 1933-1983* (Philadelphia, 1984), pp. 8-9.

4. Muste, "Pacifism and Class War," *The World Tomorrow*, Sept. 1938, reprinted in *The Essays of A. J. Muste*, ed. Nat Hentoff (Indianapolis, 1967), p. 181.

5. Niebuhr, "The Religion of Communism," *Atlantic*, Apr. 1931, p. 466.

6. Niebuhr, "Is Peace or Justice the Goal?" *The World Tomorrow*, 21 Sept. 1932, p. 277.

7. Matthews, "The Cross and the Sword," *Christian Century*, 6 Dec. 1933, p. 1541.

8. Matthews, quoted in the *Daily Worker*, 7 Apr. 1933, p. 4, cited by Harvey Klehr, *The Heyday of American Communism: The Depression Decade* (New York, 1984), p. 101.

9. Charles Chatfield, *For Peace and Justice: Pacifism in America, 1914-1941* (Knoxville, 1971), p. 259.

10. Quoted in Charles Daniel Brodhead, "F.O.R. Holds Tense Session," *Christian Century*, 1 Nov. 1933, pp. 1383-84.

11. The text of the questionnaire can be found in John Bennett, "That Fellowship Questionnaire," *The World Tomorrow*, 21 Dec. 1933, pp. 690-91.

12. Niebuhr, "Why I Leave the F.O.R.," *Christian Century*, 3 Jan. 1934, pp. 17-19.

13. "Communists and the United Front," *The World Tomorrow*, 1 Mar. 1934, p. 100.

14. Page, "A Christian Revolution," *Christian Century,* 20 Feb. 1935, p. 236.

15. Chatfield, *For Peace and Justice,* pp. 258-59.

16. "Fellowship and United Front," *Fellowship,* Apr. 1940, p. 59.

17. "The Way to Peace with Russia," *Fellowship,* Apr. 1946, p. 60.

18. FOR national council statement of May 1948, published in *Fellowship,* Sept. 1948, p. 11.

19. Milgram, "Beware the Common Front!" *Fellowship,* Sept. 1948, pp. 9-10, 12.

20. Letter to the editor and editorial statement, *Fellowship,* Feb. 1949, p. 31.

21. Cited by Wittner, *Rebels against War,* p. 205.

22. The full text of the declaration and its background can be found in a memo of Alfred Hassler, SCPC, DG 125, Acc. 81A-93, Box 9.

23. Hassler, "The World's Newest Peace Group," *Fellowship,* 1 Mar. 1963, p. 26.

24. Cited in Gertrude Bussey and Margaret Tims, *Women's International League for Peace and Freedom, 1915-1965: A Record of Fifty Years' Work* (London, 1965), p. 39.

25. Cited in Bussey and Tims, *Women's International League for Peace and Freedom, 1915-1965,* p. 122.

26. Cited from *Peace and Bread in Time of War,* in *Beyond Nationalism: The Social Thought of Emily Greene Balch,* ed. Mercedes M. Randall (New York, 1972), p. xvi.

27. Detzer, *Appointment on the Hill* (New York, 1948), pp. 192, 193.

28. SCPC, DG 43, Reference Material, Folder 45.

29. Hutchinson, "Living within a Plan," unpublished autobiographical manuscript, SCPC, D. Hutchinson, Acc. 81A-96, Box 17.

30. Rough draft of minutes of the Peace Section Rancocas retreat, 21-22 Oct. 1933, AFSC, Peace Section 1933, General Files, AFSC Peace Retreat (Rancocas), 1933.

31. AFSC, Peace Section, Emergency Peace Campaign, Correspondence and Programs and Reactions, 1936-41.

32. Clarence Pickett to Willard Uphaus, 23 Oct. 1951, quoted in Ralph Lord Roy, *Communism and the Churches* (New York, 1960), p. 217.

33. Muste, "Thawing but Unsettled: Report on What's Happened to the Cold War," *Fellowship,* July 1949, p. 23.

34. Muste, "Communism and Civil Liberties," *Fellowship,* Oct. 1949, p. 10.

35. Muste, quoted in Nat Hentoff, *Peace Agitator: The Story of A. J. Muste* (New York, 1963), p. 162.

36. Thomas, quoted in Hentoff, *Peace Agitator,* p. 166.

37. Finch, "An Observer Reports on the Communist Convention," *Liberation,* Mar. 1957, p. 5.

38. Mygatt, quoted in Jo Ann Ooiman Robinson, *Abraham Went Out: A Biography of A. J. Muste* (Philadelphia, 1981), p. 104.

39. Page, *How to Keep America Out of War* (Philadelphia, 1939), pp. 3-4, 56.

40. Muste, *Non-Violence in an Aggressive World* (New York, 1940), pp. 45, 139.

41. Muste, *The World Task of Pacifism,* Pendle Hill Pamphlet no. 13 (Walling-ford, Pa., 1941), p. 27.

42. FOR executive board, "Our Way in the Midst of War," cited by Glen Zeitzer, "The Fellowship of Reconciliation on the Eve of the Second World War: A Peace Organization Prepares," *Peace and Change,* Summer-Fall 1975, p. 50.

43. Detzer, *Appointment on the Hill,* p. 239.

44. Hutchinson, *A Call to Peace Now: Message to the Society of Friends* (Phil-adelphia, 1943), p. 33.

45. Lens, "China's Leap: The Human Cost," *Fellowship,* Mar. 1959, p. 10.

46. Lens, "Cuba: A Second Look," *Fellowship,* 1 Nov. 1961, pp. 6, 16.

Notes to Chapter 2

1. *Peacework,* July-Aug. 1979, p. 2.

2. Johnson, "The Tangled American Web," *Liberation,* 1 Nov. 1965, p. 5.

3. AFSC, PED Administration Vietnam, 1966, Box 1, General Administration: Roundup Peace Secretaries.

4. Meacham, "Justice and Social Revolution," *Liberation,* Mar. 1967, pp. 28-29.

5. *Peace in Vietnam: A New Approach in Southeast Asia,* report prepared for the AFSC (New York, 1966), p. 25.

6. Memo, "Those Interested in U.S. Policy toward Vietnam," AFSC, PED Administration Vietnam, 1965, Box 2, Vietnam Correspondence.

7. "Peace with Honor in Vietnam," AFSC, PED Administration Vietnam, 1968, Box 1, General Papers by S. Meacham.

8. AFSC staff memo prepared for the U.S. Department of State, "Contacts with the National Liberation Front of South Vietnam: 1965-68," May 1968, pp. 7-8.

9. Stewart Meacham to Paul L. Noble, 22 May 1969, AFSC, PED Administra-tion Vietnam, 1969, Box 1, Correspondence, Individuals A-Z.

10. Stewart Meacham to peace education secretaries, 19 Sept. 1966, AFSC, PED Administration Vietnam, Box 2, Vietnam Projects.

11. Ben Seaver to Stewart Meacham, 13 Sept. 1966, AFSC, *ibid.*

12. Seeger, "Trends in the Anti-War Movement," 22 Dec. 1967. Copies of this and several other memos written by Seeger were made available to me by a member of the New York Friends Group.

13. Seeger, "More about Trends in the Anti-War Movement," 22 Feb. 1963, memo made available by a member of the New York Friends Group.

14. "Report of meeting to assess direction and relevance of the nonviolent movement," Pendle Hill, 1 Oct. 1968, AFSC, PED Administration Vietnam, 1968, Box 1, National Action Group.

15. National Action Group meeting, 22 Oct. 1968, *ibid.*

16. Minutes of peace education committee meeting, 11 June 1969, AFSC, PED Administration Vietnam, 1969, Box 1, Chicago Conspiracy.

17. Bronson Clark to Stewart Meacham, *ibid.*

18. Draft of opening talk, *ibid.*, Papers and speeches of Stewart Meacham.

19. Letter of participant, *ibid.*, Executive Committee.

20. Stewart Meacham to peace education secretaries, 25 Sept. 1969, *ibid.*, Box 2, AFSC Relationship to the New Mobilization.

21. Joseph and Mary Kovner to Stewart Meacham, 24 Oct. 1969, *ibid.*, New Mobe Correspondence.

22. Levering's memo is filed in *ibid.*, New Mobe Correspondence. See also the minutes of the board meeting in *ibid.*, BD 1970 Minutes, Board of Directors.

23. Lens, *Unrepentant Radical: An American Activist's Account of Five Turbulent Decades* (Boston, 1980), pp. 318, 290.

24. Stewart Meacham, "The AFSC's Relationship to Coalition Activities: Spring 1971," AFSC, PED Administration Vietnam, 1971, Box: Conferences through Regional Offices, Spring Offensive.

25. For a description of the divisions within the PCPJ and of the Washington May Days, see Nancy Zaroulis and Gerald Sullivan, *Who Spoke Up? American Protest against the War in Vietnam: 1963-1975* (Garden City, N.Y., 1984), pp. 345-64.

26. "Excerpts from Regional Responses," AFSC, PED Administration Vietnam, 1971, Box: Conferences through Regional Offices, People's Peace Treaty.

27. Charles Bloomstein to Bronson Clark, 21 July 1971, *ibid.*

28. American Friends Service Committee, *Indochina 1971: Requirements for Peace in South Asia* (Philadelphia, 1970).

29. SCPC, DG 80, Box 3, Misc.

30. Minute adopted 27 Apr. 1972, AFSC, PED D/C 1972, Indochina Program, Vigil in Washington, D.C. — 3 May.

31. Ed Doty to peace education secretaries, 8 May 1972, *ibid.*, Regional Offices: New York Metropolitan.

32. Bronson Clark to Ed Doty, 11 May 1972, *ibid.*

33. Bristol, *Nonviolence not First for Export* (Philadelphia, n.d.).

34. Dung, "Great Spring Victory," published originally in the official North Vietnamese Communist party newspaper *Nhan Dang* in Apr.-May 1976 and brought out in an English translation by Monthly Review Press in 1977. See Guenter Lewy, *America in Vietnam* (New York, 1978), pp. 205-8.

35. American Friends Service Committee, *Indochina 1972: Perpetual War* (Philadelphia, 1972).

36. News release, 24 Jan. 1973, AFSC, PED Indochina Program 1973, Statement on Ceasefire.

37. John McAuliff to Steve Cary, 20 Sept. 1973, *ibid.*, Interoffice Correspondence.

38. Earle Edwards to Lou Schneider, 6 July 1973, *ibid.*, North/South Fund.

39. Cf. Lewy, *America in Vietnam*, pp. 294-97.

40. AFSC/NARMIC, "Questions on U.S. Military Aid to South Vietnam," 10 May 1974.

41. "Peace in Indochina: The Final Phase," AFSC, PED Indochina Program 1974 (Administration: Conferences and Seminars), Program Development.

42. Ruth Dodd to Lou Schneider, 19 Aug. 1971, SCPC, DG 13, Hassler files, Collegium.

43. "Third Force in Vietnam," *Common Sense,* 15 Sept. 1974, distributed by the AFSC Indochina program.

44. Arlene Eisen, *Women and Revolution in Vietnam* (Totowa, N.J., 1984), p. 125. On PKG infiltration of the Third Force, see Paul Quinn-Judge, "Inside Saigon: Eye Witness Report," *Commonweal,* 26 Sept. 1975, p. 430.

45. Ron Young to Phan Thi Minh, 14 Jan. 1975, AFSC, PED Indochina Program 1975, Trips, Paris — Ron Young.

Notes to Chapter 3

1. "Vietnam," *Fellowship,* July 1964, p. 2.

2. Cf. Harrington, *Fragments of the Century* (New York, 1973), p. 158.

3. SCPC, DG 50, Reel 89.29.

4. Ronald Young to members of the national council, 6 Apr. 1966, SCPC, DG 13, Box 4a, FOR Reports 1966.

5. Minutes of the national council meeting, 19 Apr. 1967, pp. 9, 15, *ibid.,* FOR Minutes 1967.

6. Hassler, "Memo to the National Council," 15 Mar. 1968, *ibid.,* FOR Reports 1968.

7. Minutes of the national council meeting, 17-19 Apr. 1968, *ibid.,* FOR Minutes 1968.

8. Minutes of the executive committee meeting, 12 June 1968, *ibid.*

9. See Nhat Hanh, *Vietnam: Lotus in a Sea of Fire* (New York, 1967), p. 84.

10. Hassler, letter to the editor, *New Politics,* Summer 1967, p. 97.

11. Cf. Sidney Lens, "The Stockholm Conference and 'Realism' in the Vietnam War," *Fellowship,* Sept. 1967, pp. 9-12. For a more realistic appraisal, see Dorothy Hutchinson, "Requiem for the Third Force?" *Fellowship,* Jan. 1968, pp. 13-15.

12. Hassler, "Vietnam" and "On Revolution," *Fellowship,* July 1968, pp. 2-3.

13. Minutes of the executive committee meeting, 2 Sept. 1969, SCPC, DG 13, Box 4b, FOR Minutes 1969.

14. "Violence and the United States," statement adopted by the national council, 20 May 1970, *ibid.,* FOR Minutes 1970.

15. The resolutions on Vietnam and on violence can also be found in *Fellowship,* July 1970, pp. 24-25.

16. Brick, "T.D.A.: The Day After," July 1970, SCPC, DG 13, Hassler Correspondence.

17. Hassler, "Pacifism and the Problems of the '70s," *ibid.*

18. Cf. Chap. 2, p. 44.

19. Minutes of the executive committee meeting, 19 Jan. 1971, SCPC, DG 13, Box 4b, Minutes 1971.

20. Alfred Hassler to W. H. Ferry, 11 Feb. 1971, *ibid.,* Hassler Correspondence.

21. Alfred Hassler to John Trostle, 8 Mar. 1971, *ibid.*

22. Minutes of the national council meeting, 19-21 May 1971, *ibid.*, FOR Minutes 1971.

23. Alfred Hassler to personnel committee, 11 Apr. 1972, *ibid.*, Hassler Correspondence.

24. "FOR policy statement on Vietnam," 11 May 1972, *ibid.*, FOR Minutes 1972.

25. Hassler, "Watergate and the Peace Movement," *Fellowship*, Aug. 1973, p. 2.

26. Forest, "Solzhenitsyn and American Pacifists," *Fellowship*, Oct. 1973, p. 2.

27. Daniel and Philip Berrigan, "On the Torture of Prisoners," *Fellowship*, Sept. 1973, p. 4. For the full text of the Berrigans' letter and Hanoi's reply, see *WIN*, 6 Sept. 1973, p. 16.

Notes to Chapter 4

1. Minutes of annual meeting, 17 Oct. 1965, SCPC, DG 43, Box 20, Folder 3.
2. *Ibid.*
3. Orlie Pell to Elizabeth Polster, 19 Oct. 1965, *ibid.*, Folder 2.
4. Hutchinson, "Background of WILPF Policy regarding Representation at International Congresses," *ibid.*, Folder 6.
5. "Report of the Executive Director" to annual meeting, 10-13 Jan. 1966, *ibid.*
6. Elise Boulding, "International Roundup," *Four Lights,* July 1966, p. 2.
7. Dorothy Hutchinson et al. to Russell Stetler, 21 Sept. 1966, SCPC, DG 125, Acc. 81A-93, Box 9, WIL International Chairman 1965-68.
8. *Four Lights,* Oct. 1966, p. 1.
9. Graham, "In Focus," *Four Lights,* Feb. 1967, p. 2.
10. Minutes of the national board meeting, 10-12 Feb. 1967, SCPC, DG 43, Box 20, Folder 7.
11. Resolution on Vietnam, minutes of the annual meeting, 19-24 June 1967, *ibid.*, Folder 11.
12. Graham, "In Focus," *Four Lights,* Oct. 1967, p. 2.
13. Jo Graham to the national board and branch chairmen, 5 Dec. 1967, SCPC, DG 13, Hassler Correspondence, WILPF.
14. Corrected minutes of the national executive committee meeting, 6-7 Dec. 1967, SCPC, DG 43, Box 20, Folder 8.
15. Policy committee memo, Feb. 1968, *ibid.*, Folder 10.
16. Minutes of the national board meeting, 10 Feb. 1968, *ibid.*, Folder 12.
17. Minutes of the annual meeting, 28 June – 2 July 1968, *ibid.*, Folder 14.
18. Minutes of the annual meeting, 26-30 June 1969, *ibid.*, Box 20a, Folder 18.
19. *Peace and Freedom,* May 1970, p. 3. In 1970 the WILPF magazine *Four Lights* was renamed *Peace and Freedom.*
20. Camp, "President's Message," SCPC, DG 43, Box 20b, Annual Meeting 1970.

21. "Group Meets at Annual Meeting to Discuss Radical Economic Change," *Peace and Freedom,* July 1970, p. 4.

22. Minutes of the annual meeting, 10-14 June 1970, SCPC, DG 43, Box 20b, Annual Meeting 1970.

23. Draft statement on "World Revolution," SCPC, DG 125, Acc. 81A-93, Box 11, Congress 1971.

24. Norwegian section to 18th WILPF Congress, 28 Dec. 1970 – 3 Jan. 1971, SCPC, DG 110, Box 1, International Correspondence.

25. "18th International Congress in India," *Peace and Freedom,* Feb. 1971, p. 1.

Notes to Chapter 5

1. Dellinger, "The March on Washington and Its Critics," *Liberation,* May 1965, p. 31.

2. Pickus, "Political Integrity and Its Critics," *Liberation,* June-July 1965, pp. 36-40, 46.

3. Muste, "Crisis in the World and in the Peace Movement," *Liberation,* June-July 1965, pp. 30-35.

4. Dellinger, "Vietnam and the International Liberation Front," *Liberation,* Aug. 1965, pp. 14-16.

5. Bloomstein, memo, n.d., made available by Bloomstein.

6. Muste, "Mobilize for Peace," *Liberation,* Dec. 1966, p. 25.

7. Muste in an interview with James Finn published in the latter's *Protest: Pacifism and Politics* (New York, 1967), pp. 198, 200-201.

8. McReynolds in an interview with James Finn published in Finn's *Protest: Pacifism and Politics,* pp. 210-15. See also McReynolds's letter in the Dec. 1966 issue of *Liberation,* p. 37.

9. "Statement on WRL Principles," Nov. 1966, copy made available by Charles Bloomstein.

10. Charles Bloomstein to the WRL executive committee, 11 June 1967, copy made available by Bloomstein.

11. Charles Bloomstein to the editorial board of *Liberation,* 27 June 1967, copy made available by Bloomstein.

12. Charles Bloomstein to the WRL executive committee, 6 Oct. 1967, copy made available by Bloomstein.

13. Scott, "Harmony of Ends and Means," 26 Oct. 1967, copy made available by Bloomstein.

14. Lyttle, "Why I Am Working for the Coalition," *WIN,* 12 May 1967, pp. 9-10.

15. McReynolds, "Withdrawal Now?" *Fellowship,* Mar. 1968, pp. 6-8.

16. Pickus, "Withdrawal Again," *Fellowship,* May 1968, pp. 28-29.

17. "On Wars of Liberation: A W.R.I. Statement," *WIN,* 15 Oct. 1968, p. 7.

18. Nancy Zaroulis and Gerald Sullivan, *Who Spoke Up? American Protest against the War in Vietnam, 1963-1975* (Garden City, N.Y., 1984), p. 176.

19. U.S. House, Committee on Un-American Activities, *Subversive Involvement in Disruption of 1968 Democratic Party National Convention,* Hearings, 90th Cong., 2nd sess., Oct.-Dec. 1968, Part 3, pp. 2712-13, 2731, 2774-78.

20. Dellinger, "Communists in the Antiwar Movement," in *Revolutionary Nonviolence: Essays* (Indianapolis, 1970), p. 200.

21. Marty Jezer, "WRL: The First 50 Years," *WIN,* 26 July 1973, p. 8.

22. Dave Dellinger to Charles Bloomstein, 21 Apr. 1969, copy provided by Bloomstein.

23. Dellinger, "A Time to Look at Ourselves," *Liberation,* Aug./Sept./Oct. 1970, pp. 7-8.

24. McReynolds, "After the May Days," *WRL News,* May-June 1971, no pagination.

25. Marx, "The Peace Movement: Alive but Not Well," *Christian Century,* 3 Dec. 1975, pp. 1106-7.

Notes to Chapter 6

1. John McAuliff to the Indochina task force and national peace education committee, 15 May 1975, AFSC, PED Indochina Program 1975, Administration Indochina Task Force.

2. *Indochina Program Newsletter,* 5 May 1975, p. 1.

3. AFSC, PED Indochina Program 1975, Coalition to Stop Funding the War.

4. *WIN,* 1 May 1975, pp. 5, 8, 13.

5. Lazar, "Military Victories Are Not Cause for Celebration," *Peacework,* May 1975, p. 3.

6. Letter to the editor, *Peacework,* June 1975, p. 11.

7. Swann, "The Agonizing Dilemma of a Pacifist," *Peacework,* June 1975, pp. 7-8.

8. *Peacework,* July-Aug. 1975, pp. 4-5.

9. *WIN,* 1 May 1975, p. 13.

10. James H. Forest, *The Unified Buddhist Church of Vietnam: Fifteen Years of Reconciliation* (Hof van Sonoy, Holland, 1978), pp. 12-13, 20-21; James Sterba, "Ordeal of a Famed Buddhist in Ho Chi Minh City Related," *New York Times,* 14 July 1979; and Stephen Denney, "The Religious Policy of the Socialist Republic of Vietnam," *Indochina Journal,* Jan.-Feb. 1983, pp. 11-13.

11. John McAuliff, memo to "People coming to Roundup," 21 July 1975, AFSC, PED Indochina Program 1975, PED Roundup.

12. Editorial, *Peacework,* June 1975, p. 1.

13. Johnson, "The Lessons of Vietnam," *Peacework,* June 1975, p. 1.

14. *Peacework,* Jan. 1976, p. 1.

15. *Peacework,* Oct. 1976, p. 14.

16. Minutes of the summer 1975 roundup of peace education secretaries, AFSC, PED Indochina Program 1975, PED Roundup.

17. *Peacework,* Apr. 1976, p. 3.

18. Forest, "Vietnam: Unification without Reconciliation," *Fellowship,* Oct. 1976, pp. 20-21.

19. Jim Forest to Paul Quinn-Judge, 3 Nov. 1976, AFSC, PED Indochina Program 1976-77, Box 2, Human Rights in Vietnam—Forest Controversy.

20. "Report on a Discussion regarding AFSC's Response to the Jim Forest Mailing," 13 Oct. 1976, AFSC, PED Indochina Program 1976-77, Box 2, Human Rights in Vietnam—Forest Controversy.

21. John McAuliff to peace education committee, 15 Oct. 1976, *ibid.*

22. Ian Lind to Ron Young, 26 Oct. 1976, *ibid.*

23. Ed Lazar to Lou Schneider, 14 Oct. 1976, *ibid.*

24. Bob Vogel to Lou Schneider, 20 Oct. 1976, *ibid.*

25. Charles Bloomstein to Lou Schneider, 3 Dec. 1976, *ibid.*

26. Alfred Hassler to John McAuliff, 11 Nov. 1976, AFSC, PED Indochina Program 1976-77, Box 2, Human Rights Projects—Vietnam.

27. Louis Schneider, letter to "Dear Friend," 17 Dec. 1976, AFSC, PED Indochina Program 1976-77, Box 1, AFSC Relationship with Friends.

28. Stewart Meacham letter, no addressee, 6 Jan. 1977, *ibid.*, Box 2, Human Rights in Vietnam—Forest Controversy.

29. *New York Times*, 30 Jan. 1977.

30. Memo of staff agreement regarding the ad hoc committee's Vietnam statement, 12 Nov. 1976, SCPC, DG 13, Box 4b, Vietnam Post-war Government.

31. Alfred Hassler to Barton Hunter, 29 Nov. 1976, *ibid.*

32. Minutes of the executive committee meeting, 6 Dec. 1976, *ibid.*, Box 4c, FOR Minutes 1976.

33. "Commentary on Jim Forest's Vietnam statement" by David McReynolds, 13 Dec. 1976, *ibid.*, Box 4b, Vietnam Post-war Government.

34. Jim Forest to "Dear Friends in the WRL," 17 Dec. 1976, *ibid.*

35. Minutes of the executive committee meeting, 7 Feb. 1977, *ibid.*, Box 4c, FOR Minutes 1977.

36. "An Open Letter on Vietnam," *Fellowship*, Mar.-Apr. 1977, p. 24.

37. *WIN*, 1 May 1975, p. 15.

38. SCPC, DG 13, Box II/4b, Vietnam Post-war Government.

39. "A Discussion of Human Rights in Post-War Vietnam," 1 Feb. 1977, edited transcript, AFSC, PED Indochina Program 1976-77, Box 2, Vietnam Delegation 1977.

40. Interview with Wallace Collett, 6 Feb. 1977, *ibid.*, Collett Interview.

41. Minutes, NPED Committee, 18-20 Feb. 1977, *ibid.*, NPED Committee Discussions 1977.

42. Tjossem, "Vietnamese Extend Warm Welcome: AFSC Group Tours Vietnam," *Quaker Service Bulletin*, Spring 1977, pp. 1, 4.

43. Bragg, "Vietnam Today and the Issue of Human Rights," Part One, *Peacework*, Nov. 1977, pp. 11-14.

44. Bragg, "Vietnam Today and the Issue of Human Rights," Part Two, *Peacework*, Jan. 1978, pp. 1-4.

45. Kenneth Boulding to Louis Schneider and Stewart Meacham, 25 Jan. 1977, AFSC, PED Indochina Program 1976-77, Box 1, AFSC Relationship with Friends: Boulding Concern.

46. Kenneth Boulding to AFSC board and concerned staff, 31 Jan. 1977, *ibid.*

47. Jack Powelson to "Dear Friends of Colorado General Meeting," 17 Mar. 1977, and "What Happened, and How," 14 Mar. 1977, *ibid.*, Box 3, Jack Powelson.

48. Lou Schneider to Colorado General Meeting, 13 Apr. 1977, *ibid.*

49. Boulding, "A Friendly Clarification," AFSC, General Administration 1977, Office of the Executive Secretary, Correspondence and Criticism—Friends. The phrase "half-baked Marxism" was used by Boulding in his discussion with Schneider on 11 Mar. 1977 and was reported to the AFSC board by Schneider in a memo dated 17 Mar. 1977, *ibid.*

50. Judy Danielson to Lou Schneider, 18 Feb. and 1 May 1977, *ibid.*, Relationship with Friends: Boulding Concern, and Box 3, Jack Powelson.

51. AFSC, PED Indochina Program 1977, Administration, Consultation on Indochina Work and AFSC.

52. *Ibid.*, PED Committee Discussions.

53. SoRelle, "Some Views of a Quaker Socialist," AFSC, General Administration 1978, Office of the Executive Secretary, Correspondence and Criticism—Friends, Communist/Socialist Theory and AFSC.

54. Excerpts from a Hassler letter circulated by Richard Deats, director of FOR interfaith activities, 21 July 1977, SCPC, DG 13, Box 4b, Vietnam Post-war Government.

55. Alfred Hassler letter to "Dear Friends," *Fellowship*, Sept. 1977, pp. 2, 23.

56. Minutes of the executive committee meeting, 19 Sept. 1977, SCPC, DG 13, Box 4c, FOR Minutes 1977.

57. Geoffrey Pope to Richard Chartier, 9 Aug. 1977, *ibid.*, Box 4b, Vietnam Post-war Government.

58. Jim Forest to Richard Deats, 12 Aug. 1977, *ibid.*

59. John Sullivan to Dave Elder/Julie Forsythe, 25 Aug. 1977, AFSC, PED Indochina Program 1976-77, Forest Article.

60. Elder, "Another View on Human Rights in Vietnam," *Fellowship*, Oct. 1977, p. 16.

61. Minutes of the executive committee meeting, 5 Dec. 1977, SCPC, DG 13, Box 4c, FOR Minutes 1977.

62. "Proposal for F.O.R. Programming," *ibid.*, FOR Reports 1978.

63. Minutes of the executive committee meeting, 20 Feb. 1978, *ibid.*, FOR Minutes 1978.

64. Minutes of the national council meeting, 16-19 Aug. 1978, *ibid.*

65. *Fellowship*, Sept. 1973, pp. 2, 23.

66. McAuliff, "Vietnam: The Words Have Not Yet Healed," *Peace and Freedom*, Nov. 1978, p. 9.

67. Charles Bloomstein to Lou Schneider, 9 Aug. 1978, and John A. Sullivan to Charles Bloomstein, 22 Sept. 1978, AFSC, General Administration 1978, Office of the Executive Secretary, Correspondence and Criticism, New York Friends Group.

68. Joan Baez, quoted by Robert Lindsay, "Peace Activists Attack Vietnam on Rights," *New York Times*, 1 June 1979.

69. Dellinger, "American Roulette: In War or Peace, It's Always the Vietnamese Who Get Shot At," *Seven Days,* 29 June 1979, p. 29.

70. Joan Baez to "pacifist friends," 28 Feb. 1980, AFSC, PED Indochina Program 1976-77, Box 1, Vietnam: Baez Appeal.

71. David McReynolds to Joan Baez, 14 Mar. 1980, *ibid.*

72. Eric Weinberger, "Report from Bratislava," *WIN,* 16 Oct. 1967, p. 7.

73. McReynolds, "On Pacifism and Nonviolence," *Peace and Freedom,* Jan. 1972, p. 4. This article had first been published in the Sept.-Oct. 1971 issue of *WRL News.*

74. "Commentary on Jim Forest's Vietnam Statement by David McReynolds," 13 Dec. 1976, SCPC, DG 13, Box 4b, Vietnam Post-war Government.

75. Ruth Cadwallader, "Appeal from Vietnam's Women's Union," *Peace and Freedom,* Oct. 1979, p. 8.

76. Ruth Cadwallader, "WILPF Women Tour Vietnam and Kampuchea," *Peace and Freedom,* Apr. 1980, pp. 5-6.

77. Johnson, "Cambodia — What Next?" *Peacework,* Apr. 1975, p. 9.

78. McAuliff, "Anniversary Thoughts," *Indochina Program Newsletter,* 16 Apr. 1976, p. 2.

79. Larry Erickson to Indochina Program, 20 Apr. 1976, AFSC, PED Indochina Program 1976-77, Correspondence — Criticism.

80. Russell Johnson, letter to the editor, *Peacework,* May 1976, p. 11.

81. *Peacework,* Mar. 1977, p. 13, and *Peacework,* Apr. 1977, p. 15.

82. *Matchbox,* Autumn 1978, p. 5.

83. Snyder, "Kampuchea: Challenge to the World's Conscience," *FCNL Washington Newsletter,* Nov. 1979, p. 1.

84. Jerry Elmer and Carol Bragg, "The Vietnam-Cambodia Conflict: An Analysis," *Peacework,* Feb. 1979, n.p.

85. "Statement on the Crisis in Southeast Asia," *Peace and Freedom,* Apr. 1979, p. 3.

86. Johnson, "The Meaning of the Cambodia Tragedy," *Peacework,* Feb. 1980, n.p.

87. *Peacework,* Oct. 1980.

88. Amnesty International, *Report of an Amnesty International Mission to the Socialist Republic of Vietnam: 10-21 December 1979* (London, 1981), p. 7.

89. Truong Nhu Tang, "The Myth of a Liberation," *New York Review of Books,* 21 Oct. 1982, p. 35.

90. Abrams, quoted in Barbara Crossette, "Hanoi Linked to Cambodia Torture," *New York Times,* 15 Nov. 1984.

91. Marvine Howe, "Prisoners Abused, Rights Group Says," *New York Times,* 3 June 1987.

92. Mike Jendrzejczyk, "Political Prisoners in Kampuchea," *Fellowship,* July-Aug. 1987, pp. 24-25.

Notes to Chapter 7

1. American Friends Service Committee, *Cuba Ten Years After: A Quaker Team's Report on a Visit to the Revolution* (Philadelphia, 1970).

2. AFSC, PED Administration 1969, Box 1, Mission to Cuba.

3. Dorothy Hutchinson to Lyndon Johnson, 9 Oct. 1962, SCPC, DG 43, Box Reference Material, Policy Material.

4. Camp, "Cuba: Survival and Significance," *Four Lights,* Oct. 1969, p. 2.

5. Minutes of the national board meeting, 26-28 Oct. 1973, SCPC, DG 43, Box 20b, National Board Minutes 1971-75.

6. Telegram to the FMC, 30 Dec. 1975, *ibid.,* Temp. Box 1975-77, Folder 3.

7. Meeting of the national board, 12-14 Mar. 1976, *ibid.*

8. The FMC to the WILPF, 22 Mar. 1977, *ibid.*

9. The FMC to the WILPF, 20 Apr. 1977, *ibid.*

10. Lacefield, "The Cuban Revolution," *Fellowship,* Sept. 1978, pp. 3-7; letter to the editor, *Fellowship,* Nov. 1978, p. 19.

11. Paul and Ruth Deats, "Reflections on a Visit to Cuba: Summer 1980," *Peacework,* Oct. 1980, n.p.

12. Dossar, "Cuba of Today," AFSC, *Third World Coalition News,* Aug. 1981, p. 4.

13. Johnson, "US Foreign Policy Contradictions," *Peacework,* Apr. 1976, pp. 1-2.

14. Cf. U.S. House, Committee on Foreign Affairs, Subcommittee on Human Rights and International Organizations, *Human Rights in Cuba,* Hearing, 98th Cong., 2nd sess., 27 June 1984.

15. Nick Eberstadt, "Literacy and Health: The Cuban Model," *Wall Street Journal,* 10 Dec. 1984.

16. Mark Falkoff, "Cuba as a Marxist-Leninist State," *Cuban Update,* Summer 1986, p. 2. See also Laurence H. Theriot, "Revolutionary Balance Sheet," in U.S. Congress, Joint Economic Committee, *Cuba Faces the Economic Realities of the 1980s* (Washington, D.C., 1982).

17. Valladares, cited in Humberto Belli, *Christians under Fire* (Garden City, Mich., 1984), p. 8. See also the testimony of Valladares before the House Subcommittee on Human Rights, *Human Rights in Cuba,* Hearing, 98th Cong., 2nd sess., 27 June 1984; and his book *Against All Hope,* trans. Andrew Hurley (New York, 1986).

18. Antal, "Report on U.S. Religious Delegation to Cuba – November 3-11, 1985," mimeographed and available from the FOR.

19. AFSC, *Third World Coalition News,* Fall/Winter 1983, pp. 6-7.

20. AFSC, *ID Bulletin,* Mar. 1984, p. 1.

21. See Maurice Bishop's "Line of March" speech, 13 Sept. 1982, and his speech at a leadership meeting, 25 Sept. 1983, printed in *The Grenada Papers,* ed. Paul Seabury and Walter A. McDougall (San Francisco, 1984), pp. 63, 315.

22. Jacobs, cited in *The Grenada Papers,* pp. 37, 207-8.

23. Bishop, cited in *The Grenada Papers,* p. 69.

24. Jacobs, cited in *The Grenada Papers,* pp. 163-69.

25. Brown, "Grenada Follow-Up . . . Part II," AFSC, *Third World Coalition News,* no. 8, n.d.

26. Martin, "Caribbean Theory of Domination and Liberation," *Third World Coalition News,* Fall/Winter 1983, pp. 31-32.

27. Marshall Ogarkov in a meeting with top Soviet and Grenadian military personnel, 10 Mar. 1983, cited in *The Grenada Papers,* p. 190.

Notes to Chapter 8

1. Young, "U.S. Aid Imperils Human Rights in El Salvador," *Peace and Freedom,* June-July 1980, pp. 8-9.

2. Dossar, "No More Martyrs—No More Vietnams," SCPC, DG 2, Series II, Box: Recent Materials.

3. Cf. *Fellowship,* Apr.-May 1981, p. 18.

4. AFSC/NARMIC, "Militarizing Central America: The U.S. in Guatemala and Honduras," Oct. 1981.

5. R. Bruce McColm, *El Salvador: Peaceful Revolution or Armed Struggle?* (New York, 1982), p. 39. See also the U.S. Department of State 1981 release on the trip of Farid Handal, brother of the head of the Communist party of El Salvador, to the United States in February 1980 in order to lay the groundwork for CISPES.

6. Garment, *Wall Street Journal,* 3 Dec. 1982, p. 22.

7. Elmer, "Vietnam and Central America: Six Lessons for America," *Peacework,* May 1982, n.p.

8. "Stop U.S. Intervention: A Call for Peace and Justice in Central America," *Peacework,* Jan. 1983, n.p.

9. Richard Chartier, "U.S. Resumes Military Aid to El Salvador," *Fellowship,* Jan.-Feb. 1981, p. 21.

10. Camp, report on the northeast regional biennial, 8-10 June 1984, *Peace and Freedom,* Sept. 1984, p. 15.

11. See, most recently, Richard E. Welch, Jr., *Response to Revolution: The United States and the Cuban Revolution, 1959-1961* (Chapel Hill, N.C., 1985).

12. Szulc, *Fidel: A Critical Portrait* (New York, 1986). The quotation is from an excerpt in the *New York Times Magazine,* 19 Oct. 1986, p. 47.

13. The speech, also printed in a pamphlet, is cited by Humberto Belli in *Christians under Fire* (San José, Costa Rica, 1984), p. 13, and by Douglas W. Payne in *The Democratic Mask: The Consolidation of the Sandinista Revolution* (New York, 1985), p. 33.

14. Phillip Berryman, *What's Wrong in Central America and What to Do about It* (Philadelphia, 1983), pp. 14, 27, 34-35.

15. Berryman, *The Religious Roots of Rebellion: Christians in Central American Revolutions* (Maryknoll, N.Y., 1984), p. 329.

16. Berryman, *The Religious Roots of Rebellion,* p. 354.

17. Dan R. Ebener, "Is There a Future for Nonviolence in Central America?" *Fellowship,* Oct.-Nov. 1983, p. 28.

18. Mano Barreno, "A Latin American Response," *Fellowship*, Oct.-Nov. 1983, p. 7.

19. Lens, "The Fallacy of U.S. Policy in Nicaragua," *Fellowship*, Jan. 1984, pp. 4-8.

20. Minutes of the national council meeting, 7-11 May 1983, SCPC, DG 13, Temp. Box, FOR Minutes 1983.

21. "A Call to Action," call to demonstrate in Washington, D.C., during 19-22 Apr. 1985, *Fellowship*, Jan.-Feb. 1985, p. 12.

22. "Fort Bragg Project," *Fellowship*, Jan.-Feb. 1985, p. 20.

23. Capps, "Report from Nicaragua," *WRL News*, Mar.-Apr. 1983, pp. 7-8.

24. The text of this letter can be found in *War Resister*, May-June 1984, p. 4.

25. "Document on National Dialogue of the Nicaraguan Resistance," signed in Costa Rica on 8 Mar. 1985.

26. Galan, cited by Douglas W. Payne, "Sandinistas Bid 'Farewell to the West,'" *Freedom at Issue*, Nov.-Dec. 1985, p. 12.

27. Cited by Stephen Kinzer, "U.S. Indians Enlist in the Miskito Cause," *New York Times*, 11 Nov. 1985.

28. *Quaker Service Bulletin*, Fall 1985, p. 3.

29. Stephen Kinzer, "Nicaragua Said to Order Censorship of Rights Unit," *New York Times*, 22 Nov. 1985; Edward Cody, "Sandinistas Interrogate Opponents," *Washington Post*, 15 Dec. 1985.

30. *Quaker Service Bulletin*, Fall 1985, p. 2.

31. Phillip Berryman, *Talking Sense about Nicaragua* (Philadelphia, 1985), p. 6.

32. See, for example, Julia Preston, "What Duarte Won," *New York Review of Books*, 15 Aug. 1985, p. 33.

33. Lindsey Gruson, "Land for Salvador's Poor: To Many, Bitter Victory," *New York Times*, 28 Sept. 1987.

34. AFSC/NARMIC, *The U.S. Pacification Program in El Salvador: A Report on the Central American War* (Philadelphia, 1984).

35. AFSC, "A War by Any Other Name," Sept. 1984.

36. Mill, "A Few Words on Non-Intervention," *Fraser's Magazine*, Dec. 1859, reprinted in *The Vietnam War and International Law*, vol. 1, ed. Richard A. Falk (Princeton, N.J., 1968), p. 38.

37. Tim Lambert, "A Pledge of Resistance to U.S. Agression in Central America," *Catholic Worker*, Dec. 1986, p. 2.

Notes to Chapter 9

1. Report of Dorothy Steffens to biennial meeting, 14-18 June 1973, SSC, Box 16, Folder 10.

2. "Florence Luscomb Addresses WILPF Biennial 1973," *Peace and Freedom*, Oct. 1973, p. 8.

3. Memo from Dorothy Hutchinson, "WILPF's Evening with Gene Sharp at Biennial 1973," SCPC, DG 43, Box 20b, National Board Minutes 1971-75.

4. Dorothy Hutchinson to Dorothy Steffens, 25 Aug. 1973, SCPC, DG 125, Acc. 81A-96, Box 11, WILPF—U.S. Section.

5. Dorothy Hutchinson to Mildred Olmsted, n.d., SCPC, DG 82, Box 3, Series II, Letters 1973.

6. Hutchinson, "Statement on Liberation Struggles or Statement on Nonviolence," 3 Oct. 1973, SCPC, DG 43, Box 20b, National Board Minutes 1971-75.

7. Minutes of the national board meeting, 26-28 Oct. 1973, *ibid.*

8. *Peace and Freedom,* Dec. 1973, pp. 4-5.

9. Draft statement, "Justice, 'Liberation,' and Nonviolence," 20 Mar. 1979. This statement is missing from the FOR records at the SCPC. It was made available to me by Jim Antal, FOR executive secretary.

10. AFSC Latin America Program, "All-Staff Conference Statement on the AFSC Commitment to Nonviolence in Latin America." A copy of this statement was made available to me by a member of the Society of Friends.

11. "AFSC Perspectives on Nonviolence in Relation to Groups Struggling for Social Justice," 24 Jan. 1981 (Philadelphia, n.d.).

12. American Friends Service Committee, *A Compassionate Peace: A Future for the Middle East* (New York, 1982), p. 65.

13. *A Compassionate Peace,* p. 189.

14. *A Compassionate Peace,* p. 52.

15. Ihsan A. Hijazi, "P.L.O. Decides to Shift Priority to Armed Struggle," *New York Times,* 2 Nov. 1986.

16. Gerson, "Middle East Conflict: US Deeply Involved Again," *Peacework,* Dec. 1976, p. 13.

17. Gerson, "Peace Movements in the Middle East," *WRL News,* July-Aug. 1984.

18. Peretz, "Terrorists and Pacifists," *New Republic,* 18 Nov. 1985, inside back cover.

19. *Liberation,* Jan. 1975, p. 4.

20. "Why the Nonviolent Activist," *The Nonviolent Activist,* Dec. 1984, pp. 2-4.

21. McReynolds, "Four Days in Malta — Peace and Liberation," *WRL News,* May-June 1984, p. 2. See also the report on this conference in the *International Journal on World Peace,* Autumn 1984, pp. 84-85.

22. Farrakhan, cited in "Qaddafi Urges Blacks to Revolt," *New York Times,* 26 Feb. 1985.

23. Kinnock, cited in Barnaby J. Feder, "British Mine Union Says It Talked with Qaddafi," *New York Times,* 29 Oct. 1984.

24. AFSC, "Perspectives and Guidelines on Civil Disobedience," Apr. 1984 (available from AFSC national office).

Notes to Chapter 10

1. "AFSC/Coalitions Guideline," 27 Sept. 1979 (available from AFSC national office).

2. *New York Times,* 6 Nov. 1983.

3. AFSC Disarmament Program, *Questions and Answers on the Soviet Threat and National Security* (Philadelphia, 1981), pp. 18, 11-12, 14.

4. Johnson, "Some Questions about the Anti-Soviet Hysteria," *Peacework,* July-Aug. 1978, n.p.

5. Johnson, "Stop Fearing the Russians," *Peacework,* July-Aug. 1981, n.p.

6. Johnson, "Refuting Incorrect Assumptions about the USSR," *Peacework,* Dec. 1982, n.p.

7. *Ibid.*

8. Cf. Andrea Ayvazian, "Helping Americans See the Soviets as People," *Peacework,* Dec. 1984, n.p.; and David McCauley, "The USSR: Seeing for Ourselves," *Friends Journal,* 1 Feb. 1985, pp. 10-12.

9. Deats, "Seeing the Soviets as People: Reflections on a Journey for Peace," *Fellowship,* Oct./Nov. 1982, p. 4.

10. Deborah Lubar, "Establishing Trust," *Fellowship,* Oct.-Nov. 1984, p. 13.

11. Letter to the editor by Laurama Pixton, *Friends Journal,* Jan. 1985, p. 18.

12. Jack and Ken Powelson, "The Soviet Union, South Africa and Us," *Friends Journal,* Nov. 1984, pp. 15-17; and a letter to the editor by Jack Powelson, *Friends Journal,* Feb. 1985, p. 19.

13. Marilyn Bechtel, *The Soviet Peace Movement: From the Grass Roots* (New York, 1984), p. 59.

14. Y. Nalin, *Detente and Anti-Communism,* trans. Barry Costello-Jones (Moscow, 1978), p. 23.

15. "Summary of Basic Agreements and Presuppositions regarding Programming," 23 June 1978, SCPC, DG 13, Box 4c, FOR Reports 1978.

16. For the full text, see Adam M. Garfinkle, *The Politics of the Nuclear Freeze* (Philadelphia, 1984), pp. 227-28.

17. Michael Myerson in a letter to the editor, *New Republic,* 7 Mar. 1983, p. 6.

18. Cf. Charles Krauthammer, "A Turn toward Unilateralism: Half a Freeze," *New Republic,* 7 Mar. 1983, p. 13.

19. Cf. *Peacework,* Jan. 1985.

20. Johnson, "AFSC's Peace Work from the '50s to the '80s," *Peacework,* Sept. 1983, n.p.

21. Ada Sanchez and Norman Solomon, "How to Get the Peace Movement Going Again," *Guardian,* 21 Nov. 1984, p. 19.

22. Ada Sanchez and Norman Solomon, "Direct Action May Be What It Takes to Save Humanity," *Guardian,* 16 Jan. 1985, p. 19.

23. Gerson, "Middle East: A Nuclear Trigger," *The Mobilizer,* Sept. 1982, p. 14.

24. *New Republic,* 28 Nov. 1983, p. 10.

25. *Peacework,* Apr. 1983. The talks given at the 1982 conference have been published by the New England regional office of the AFSC under the title *The Deadly Connection: Nuclear War and U.S. Intervention,* ed. Joseph Gerson (Philadelphia, 1986).

26. *Peacework,* Nov. 1983, n.p.

27. Quoted in Margaret H. Bacon, "The Friends and the Feds," *The Progressive,* Nov. 1976, p. 41.

28. Barron, "The K.G.B.'s Magical War for Peace," *Reader's Digest,* Oct. 1982. The article was a condensation of Barron's *KGB Today: The Hidden Hand* (New York, 1983). The quote in question appears on p. 233.

29. Frank Donner, "But Will They Come? The Campaign to Smear the Nuclear Freeze Movement," *The Nation,* 6 Nov. 1982, p. 461. See also Provance's letter to the *Reader's Digest* of 30 Sept. 1982.

30. Fager, "The AFSC, the Freeze and the Communists," *A Friendly Letter,* Oct. 1982, n.p.

31. *Four Lights,* Oct. 1969, p. 4.

32. Clark, "Report on the Paris World Assembly for Peace and Independence of the People of Indochina," n.d., AFSC, PED, Box D/C, 1972 Indochina Program, Paris World Assembly.

33. AFSC, PED Indochina Program 1975, Correspondence—Ho Chi Minh.

34. Meacham, "Report on World Congress for Peace, National Independence and General Disarmament," August 1965, SCPC, DG 125, Box 6, ACLU.

35. Stewart Meacham to Dimitrios Roussopoulo, 28 Oct. 1968, AFSC, PED Administration 1968, Box 1, Conferences Misc. A-Z.

36. The full text of the declaration and its background can be found in a memo of Alfred Hassler, SCPC, DG 125, Acc. 81A-93, Box 9.

37. "Report on the American Peace Delegation's Visit to the Soviet Union and Czechoslovakia, November 6-21, 1968," SCPC, DG 2, Series II, Box 6.

38. The full text of the undated appeal is reprinted in *Return Address Moscow,* Sept. 1984, p. 8. This magazine is published by Sergei Batovrin, now living in New York City.

39. Sergei Batovrin to Deborah Lubar, quoted in her article in *Fellowship,* Oct.-Nov. 1984, p. 15.

40. Knudsen-Hoffman, "Planting Seeds of Hope," *Friends Journal,* 1 Feb. 1985, p. 16.

41. Solomon, "Soviet Peace Groups: The Real Thing," *Guardian,* 23 Oct. 1985, p. 19.

42. Solomon, "Letter to E. P. Thompson," *The Nation,* 11 June 1983, p. 720.

43. Thompson, "Sleepwalking into a Trap: END and the Soviet Peace Offensive," *The Nation,* 23 Feb. 1983, pp. 232-36; and "Peace Is a Third Way Street," *The Nation,* 16 Apr. 1983, pp. 473-81.

44. A. J. Muste to the International Institute for Peace, 17 May 1966, SCPC, DG 50, Reel 89.31. Muste later canceled this trip because of other pressing business.

45. International Institute for Peace to A. J. Muste, 28 Dec. 1966, *ibid.*

46. David McReynolds to Yuri Andropov, 14 Dec. 1982, copy provided by the WRL.

47. O. Kharkhadin to David McReynolds, 15 Feb. 1983, copy provided by the WRL.

48. Cf. David McReynolds, "Star Wars: An Analysis," WRL pamphlet, Dec. 1985.

49. "For Life in Angola," *Fellowship,* Jan.-Feb. 1976, p. 23.

50. American Friends Service Commitee, "Upholding a Vision of a Peaceful World: AFSC Efforts for Justice and Peace," Spring 1985.

51. Sakharov, quoted by Secretary of State George Shultz in a speech before the Commonwealth Club of San Francisco, 31 Oct. 1986, U.S. Department of State Current Policy #883.

52. Camp, "U.S. Visitors Hear U.S.S.R. Views on Invasion of Czechoslovakia," *Four Lights,* Oct. 1968, pp. 1-3.

53. "U.S., Soviet Women Meet; Share Desire for Peace," *Peace and Freedom,* Aug.-Sept. 1974, p. 8.

54. Minutes of the national board meeting, 19-21 Oct. 1968, SCPC, DG 43, Box 20, Folder 12.

55. List of initial sponsors, *ibid.,* Temp. Box 1975-77, Folder 8.

56. Interview of Dorothy Steffens with Vladislav Legantsov, *ibid.,* Folder 4.

57. Steffens, *New World Review,* May-June 1976, pp. 26-27.

58. Dorothy Steffens to Mildred Olmsted, 11 Nov. 1977 and 2 Jan. 1978, SCPC, DG 82, Box 4, Series II, Correspondence July-December 1977; DG 86, Temp. Box 5, Randall et al.

59. Dorothy Steffens to Marii Hasegawa, 31 July 1973, SCPC, DG 125, Acc. 81A-96, Box 11, WILPF U.S. Section.

60. Rachel Tilsen, "World-Wide Peace Forces Meet," *Peace and Freedom,* Nov. 1973, p. 5.

61. *Peace and Freedom,* Nov. 1974, p. 1.

62. Minutes of the advisory committee, 15 Mar. 1978, SCPC, DG 43, Temp. Box 1975-77, Folder 2.

63. Marjorie Boehm to vice presidents and executive director, 28 Mar. 1978, *ibid.*

64. Naomi Marcus to Ruth Sillman et al., 29 Mar. 1978, *ibid.*

65. Marcus, "Arms and the Women," *Peace and Freedom,* Feb. 1976, pp. 4-5.

66. Dorothy Steffens to Joseph Harris, 24 Sept. 1976, SCPC, DG 43, Temp. Box 1975-77, Folder 4.

67. Cf. Harvey Klehr, *The Heyday of American Communism: The Depression Decade* (New York, 1984), pp. 373, 476, n. 20. Among the directors of the Labor Research Association was Victor Perlo, another secret Communist, identified by Whittaker Chambers and Elizabeth Bentley as well as Perlo's former wife as a member of a Soviet spy ring in Washington. See Allen Weinstein, *Perjury: The Hiss-Chambers Case* (New York, 1978), p. 22.

68. Joe Harris to Dorothy Steffens, 22 Mar. 1977, SCPC, DG 43, Temp. Box 1975-77, Folder 4.

69. Unsigned memo, "House Plans," 15 Oct. 1976; Naomi Marcus to Dorothy Steffens, 29 Oct. 1976, *ibid.,* Folder 9.

70. Weinstein, "Anti-Semitism — U.S. and U.S.S.R.," *Peace and Freedom,* Feb. 1972, p. 3.

71. *Peace and Freedom,* Nov. 1971, p. 1.

72. Alloy, "Women in China: Yesterday and Today," *Peace and Freedom,* Apr. 1975, pp. 8-9.

73. "Statement on the Crisis in Southeast Asia," *Peace and Freedom,* Apr. 1979, p. 3.

74. Madeline Duckles, "World Meeting on Indochina," *Peace and Freedom,* May 1979, p. 12.

75. Evelyn Alloy to *Peace and Freedom,* 31 May 1979, SCPC, DG 82, Box 5, Correspondence April-June 1979.

76. Evelyn Alloy to members of the national board, 19 June 1979, *ibid.*

77. Evelyn Alloy to Mildred Scott Olmsted, 19 June 1979, *ibid.*

78. Cf. *Peace Courier,* Apr. 1984, p. 2.

79. Camp, "On Afghanistan and the New Cold War," *Peace and Freedom,* Mar. 1980, pp. 4, 7. See also Camp's letter to the *New York Times* reprinted in *Fellowship,* Mar.-Apr. 1980, p. 18.

80. Leonore Veltfort, "Peace Proposals from the Other Side," *Peace and Freedom,* Apr. 1979, pp. 6-7.

81. Sillman, "Soviet Peace Initiatives at the U.N.," *Peace and Freedom,* Jan.-Feb. 1980, p. 18.

82. Peninsula Branch, WILPF, *Give Peace a Chance: Soviet Peace Proposals and U.S. Responses* (Palo Alto, Cal., 1983), pp. 16, 36.

83. *Swords into Plowshares: Soviet Initiatives for Peace, Security and Disarmament, 1917-1982,* compiled by Daniel Rosenberg (New York, 1982). On the Communist origins of the National Council of American-Soviet Friendship, see Maurice Isserman, *Which Side Were You On? The American Communist Party during the Second World War* (Middletown, Conn., 1982), pp. 111-12.

84. Report by Pauline Rosen on the International Forum to Stop the Neutron Bomb, 17-19 Mar. 1978, SCPC, DG 43, Temp. Box 6/77 – 6/79, Folder 4. On the Communist sponsorship of the forum, see J. A. Emerson Vermaat, "Moscow and the European Peace Movement," *Problems of Communism,* Nov.-Dec. 1982, p. 47.

85. Doris Grieser Marquit, "WILPF Joins in Call to Cut World Military Budget," *Peace and Freedom,* Apr. 1979, p. 17.

86. Report on the World Parliament of the Peoples for Peace, 23-27 Sept. 1980, *Peace and Freedom,* Dec. 1980, p. 15.

87. Lynch, "International Conference against the Arms Race in Europe," *Peace and Freedom,* Aug.-Sept. 1981, p. 22.

88. See *Peace and Freedom,* Oct. 1982, pp. 6-7.

89. Pat Birnie, "No First Use Campaign," *Peace and Freedom,* Apr.-May 1984, p. 4.

90. Christie Balka, "Star Wars," *Peace and Freedom,* July-Aug. 1985, p. 7.

91. "WILPF Attends International Conference on Nicaragua," *Peace and Freedom,* Oct. 1984, pp. 3, 21. See also the World Peace Council magazine, *Peace Courier,* May 1984, p. 8.

92. "A Call to Action," *Fellowship,* Jan.-Feb. 1985, p. 12; see also *Peace and Freedom,* May 1985, p. 13.

93. Melva L. Mueller to Carlton Goodlett and Abe Feinglass, 10 Jan. 1978, SCPC, DG 43, Temp. Box 1975-77, Folder 4.

94. Chandra, cited by Rael Jean Isaac and Erich Isaac, "The Counterfeit Peace-makers: Atomic Freeze," *American Spectator,* June 1982, p. 12.

95. Radosh, "The 'Peace Council' and Peace," *New Republic,* 31 Jan. 1983, p. 18.

96. "U.S. Peace Council Holds Second Conference," *Peace Courier,* Dec. 1981, p. 3.

97. "Jobs with Peace: You Can't Have One without the Other," n.d.

98. "Massachusetts Jobs with Peace Budget," Apr. 1983.

99. "Campaign News Update," Feb. 1985.

100. Anne Nelson, "Mission in Moscow, Part II," *Peace and Freedom,* Mar. 1984, pp. 4-5.

101. Louise Lawler, "Peace Cruise up the Volga," *Peace and Freedom,* Oct. 1984, pp. 4-5, 24.

102. "Handbook," May 1961, SCPC, DG 43, Box 20, Folder 12.

103. Cf. the "Leader's Manual," n.d., SCPC, DG 43, Box 20a, Folder 16. The material in the folder is from the year 1969.

104. U.S. Department of State, Bureau of Public Affairs, *Soviet Active Measures: An Update,* July 1982, p. 3.

105. Frank, "WILPF Is Target in Anti-Freeze Campaign," *Peace and Freedom,* Dec. 1982, pp. 2-3. See also "Why Did the U.S. State Department Smear WILPF?" *Peace and Freedom,* Mar. 1984, pp. 6-7.

106. President's Committee on Civil Rights, *To Secure These Rights* (Washington, D.C., 1947), p. 51.

107. The use of "fronts of fronts" by the CPUSA is discussed in a publication of the U.S. Department of State, *Soviet Influence Activities: A Report on Active Measures and Propaganda, 1986-87* (Washington, D.C., 1987), pp. 81, 84.

108. American Friends Service Committee, *Anatomy of Anti-Communism* (New York, 1969), pp. xv, 61, 58.

109. American Friends Service Committee, *The Police Threat to Political Liberty* (Philadelphia, 1979), p. 144.

Notes to Chapter 11

1. Kale Williams to Lou Schneider, 6 March 1977, AFSC, General Administration 1977, Office of Exec. Sec., Correspondence and Criticism — Friends.

2. Dick Taylor to Lou Schneider, 2 May 1977, *ibid.,* Box ID 1976, Southeast Asia Programs, Jack Powelson.

3. Marge Nelson to Lou Schneider, 25 May 1977, *ibid.*

4. Comfort, *Quakers in the Modern World* (New York, 1952), p. 200.

5. See Chuck Fager, "AFSC and Its Friendly Critics," *A Friendly Letter,* Oct. 1981, n.p., and the special issue dated 21 Dec. 1981, which took into account a reply received from the AFSC national office.

6. *Ibid.*

7. Memo by Daniel Seeger, "Conference with Kenneth Boulding," 28 Mar. 1978, AFSC, General Administration 1978, Office of Exec. Sec., Friends Corre-

spondence and Criticism, Box 1, AFSC Relationship with Friends General Conference.

8. Memo by Kenneth Boulding et al. to Wallace Collett, Louis Schneider, and members of the board of directors, 1 Sept. 1978, *ibid*.

9. Seeger, "U.S. Pacifists and Third World Liberation Movements," *Friends Journal*, May 1979, pp. 5, 7.

10. American Friends Service Committee, *South Africa: Challenge and Hope* (Philadelphia, 1982), pp. 8, 131.

11. Oral communication from Bayard Rustin to the author.

12. "Summary of Concerns," 10 July 1979, discussed in Rael Jean Isaac, "The Seduction of the Quakers," *Midstream*, Nov. 1979, p. 28.

13. The communication, signed by executive secretary Asia Bennett and chairperson Stephen Cary, is dated 20 Nov. 1981 and was attached to Chuck Fager's *Friendly Letter* of 21 Dec. 1981.

14. The 1985 figure was supplied by Warren A. Witte, associate executive secretary for information and interpretation; the 1962 figure is given in the AFSC fact sheet in the *Friendly Letter* of 21 Dec. 1981.

15. Zahn, "The Bondage of Liberation: A Pacifist Reflection," *Fellowship*, June 1977, pp. 3-7. The article had first appeared in the March 1977 issue of *Worldview*.

16. Edward J. Holland, response to Gordon Zahn, *Fellowship*, June 1977, p. 9.

17. Goodman, letter to the editor, *Fellowship*, Sept. 1979, p. 30.

18. Undated communication sent to Dorothy Hutchinson, Kay Camp, et al., SCPC, DG 86, Temp. Box 5, Randall et al.

19. Dorothy Detzer to Mercedes Randall, 1 Feb. 1971 and 27 Sept. 1974, SCPC, DG 110, Box 1, Correspondence Dorothy Detzer.

20. Dorothy Hutchinson to Mercedes Randall, 5 Dec. 1975, *ibid.*, Dorothy Hutchinson.

21. Johanne Gjermoe to Mercedes Randall, 4 Jan. 1974, *ibid.*, International Correspondence.

22. Nelly Weiss to Mercedes Randall, 5 Apr. 1975, *ibid.*

23. Charles Bloomstein to WRL executive committee, 6 Oct. 1967, copy made available by Bloomstein.

24. Muste, cited by Milton Mayer, "The Christer," *Fellowship*, Jan. 1952, p. 1.

Notes to Chapter 12

1. Halstead, *Out Now! A Participant's Account of the American Movement against the Vietnam War* (New York, 1978), p. 80.

2. Hassler, "60 Years," *Fellowship*, Dec. 1975, p. 17.

3. Pickard, *Peacemaker's Dilemma: Plea for a Modus Vivendi in the Peace Movement* (Wallingford, Pa., 1942), p. 36.

4. Cadoux, *Christian Pacifism Re-examined* (Oxford, 1940), p. 141.

5. Trueblood, *The People Called Quakers* (New York, 1966), p. 206.

6. Weigel, *Tranquillitas Ordinis: The Present Failure and Future Promise of American Catholic Thought on War and Peace* (New York, 1987), p. 247.

7. Niebuhr, "The Christian Faith and the World Crisis," *Christianity and Crisis,* 10 Feb. 1941, p. 4, reprinted in *Reinhold Niebuhr on Politics,* ed. Harry R. Davis and Robert C. Good (New York, 1960), p. 151.

8. Niebuhr, *Christianity and Power Politics* (New York, 1969), pp. x, 28.

9. Walter W. van Kirk, *Religion Renounces War* (Chicago, 1934), pp. 6-7.

10. Thomas in a symposium on a publication of the American Friends Service Committee, *Speak Truth to Power: A Quaker Search for an Alternative to Violence,* in *The Progressive,* Oct. 1955, p. 12.

11. Thatcher, quoted in the *New York Times,* 21 Feb. 1985.

12. Von Clausewitz, *On War,* ed. and trans. by Michael Howard and Peter Paret (Princeton, N.J., 1976), p. 370.

13. Chamberlain, cited by Donald Kagan, "World War I, World War II, World War III," *Commentary,* Mar. 1987, p. 30.

14. Statement added by Sidney Hook to his entry in *Who's Who in America* (Chicago, 1984), p. 1545.

15. Camus, *Neither Victims nor Executioners,* trans. Dwight McDonald (New York, 1980), p. 39.

16. Niebuhr, *Christianity and Power Politics,* pp. 25, 175.

17. Hartill, "The Philosophy of Christian Pacifism," in *The Church, the Gospel and War,* ed. Rufus M. Jones (New York, 1971), p. 53.

BIBLIOGRAPHICAL NOTE

Much of the literature on American pacifism, the peace movement generally, and the antiwar movement of the 1960s is authored by participants. This has a clear advantage: these writers have an intimate, personal acquaintance with the events they are describing. It also means, however, that many of these works lack a critical perspective essential for a detached and judicious assessment of these social movements.

The early history of American pacifism is told in Merle Curti's *Peace or War: The American Struggle, 1636-1936* (New York, 1936), and Charles Chatfield's *For Peace and Justice: Pacifism in America, 1914-1941* (Knoxville, 1971). Taking a somewhat broader approach is Lawrence S. Wittner's *Rebels against War: The American Peace Movement, 1933-1983* (Philadelphia, 1984). The best — if somewhat brief — account can be found in Peter Brock's *Twentieth Century Pacifism* (New York, 1970). A scholarly journal specializing in the history of the peace movement is *Peace and Change*.

There exist no comprehensive scholarly studies of the major American pacifist organizations. The work by Gertrude Bussey and Margaret Tims — *Women's International League for Peace and Freedom, 1915-1965: A Record of Fifty Years' Work* (London, 1965) — provides relatively little information on the American section of the WILPF, and, on account of its time frame, does not include the crucial new developments of the last twenty years. For this period, then, readers will have to turn to more primary sources: the journals sponsored by these groups — such as *Fellowship, Liberation, WIN, WRL News, The Nonviolent Activist, Four Lights, Peace and Freedom,* and *Peacework* — as well as the writings of their major figures. Most of these writings consist of articles; A. J. Muste and Dave Dellinger have also written books. Valuable insights into the thinking of some of these men can be gained from the interviews that James Finn conducted and subsequently wrote about in *Protest: Pacifism and Politics* (New York, 1967). The more recent history of the peace movement in this country is summarized by David Thomas in "Apocalypse Now: The American Peace Movement in the 1980s," in *European Peace Movements and the Future of the Western Alli-*

ance, edited by Walter Laqueur and Robert Hunter (New Brunswick, N.J., 1985).

A comprehensive scholarly history of the movement against the Vietnam war, in which pacifists played a major role, still remains to be written. Meanwhile, readers will find much interesting information in Fred Halstead's *Out Now! A Participant's Account of the American Movement against the Vietnam War* (New York, 1978), and in the book by Nancy Zaroulis and Gerald Sullivan, *Who Spoke Up? American Protest against the War in Vietnam 1963-1975* (Garden City, N.Y., 1984). Two former leaders of Students for a Democratic Society (SDS) have also published accounts: James Miller authored *"Democracy Is in the Streets": From Port Huron to the Siege of Chicago* (New York, 1987), and Todd Gitlin wrote *The Sixties: Years of Hope, Days of Rage* (New York, 1987).

Indispensable sources for the history of American pacifism are the papers of the pacifist groups and the correspondence of many of their leaders deposited in the Swarthmore College Peace Collection. The *Guide to the Swarthmore College Peace Collection* (2nd ed., Swarthmore, Pa., 1981) is itself a capsule history of this social movement. The papers of the American Friends Service Committee are housed at the national headquarters of the organization in Philadelphia and, except for those papers from the most recent years, are also accessible to qualified researchers. Some useful materials can be found in the Sophia Smith Collection of Smith College. A brief guide to archival materials on the peace movement generally is *Peace Archives: A Guide to Library Collections of the Papers of American Peace Organizations and of Leaders in the Public Effort for Peace,* edited by Marguerite Green and published by the World Without War Council in Berkeley, California, in 1986.

INDEX

Abortion, 181, 227
Abrams, Floyd, 145
Abzug, Bella, 115
Addams, Jane, 16, 234
Afghanistan, Soviet invasion of. *See* Soviet Union
African National Congress (ANC), 178, 230
AFSC. *See* American Friends Service Committee
Allen, Devere, 4, 6, 18
Alloy, Evelyn, 210-11
American Forum for Socialist Education, 20
American Friends Service Committee (AFSC): and anti-communism, 220-21; and antiwar movement, 31-33, 40-44; and Cambodia, 141-43, 210; and campaign against aid to Saigon, 50-54; and Central America, 157-62, 164-68, 221; and civil disobedience, 179-81, 192-96; and coalition policies, 18-19, 182; and Cuba, 146-47, 149-50; and disarmament, 188, 191; early history of, 17-19; governance of, 30, 41, 221, 227, 231; and Grenada, 152-55; and human rights, 117, 200-202; and Middle East, 175-77; and nuclear freeze movement, 189; and revolutionary violence, 46-47, 173-74; and Socialist Republic of Vietnam, 114-15, 123-28, 133; and South Africa, 228-30; and Soviet threat, 183-85; and Vietnamese Buddhists, 53; and withdrawal from Vietnam, 28-30, 44-47
American League Against War and Fascism, 6-8, 10, 16, 210
American Peace Mobilization, 10

American People's Mobilization, 10
American Student Union, 10
American Workers party, 5, 183
American Youth Congress, 10
Americas Watch, 150
Amnesty International, 119-20, 132, 135, 142, 144-45, 150
Anatomy of Anti-Communism (1969), 220
Andropov, Yuri, 198
Angola, civil war in, 148, 200, 226
Antal, Jim, 151-52
Anti-anti-communism, 14, 24, 57, 78, 90, 183, 220-22
Anti-communism, 23-24, 57, 59, 137, 142, 183, 217-18, 220-21
Antiwar movement, 31-44, 56-69, 80-85, 89-104, 110, 209, 238-39
Appeal for Reconciliation (AFSC), 115-16
Appeal to the Government of Vietnam (Neuhaus-Forest appeal), 115-23, 126-27
Arms race, 244

Baez, Joan, 138-39
Baldwin, Roger, 6
Ballantyne, Edith, 213
Barron, John, 142, 192
Batovrin, Sergei, 196
Becker, Norma, 110, 123
Bernal, J. D., 12
Berrigan, Daniel, 38, 74-75, 118, 138
Berrigan, Philip, 38, 74-75, 138
Berryman, Phillip, 157, 160-61
Bishop, Maurice, 153-54. *See also* Grenada
Black Panthers, 37
Black power, 96
Bloomstein, Charles, 44, 57, 92, 95-99, 117, 137, 235, 239
Boat people, 135, 137